UNIVERSITY OF ST. THOMAS LIBRARIES

BE THE INNOVATORS

How to accelerate team creativity

START HERE

PETER LING

DEDICATION

To my dear wife, Alicia, who encouraged me to write this book.
To the late Mr Lee Kuan Yew, who achieved his vision of transforming our birthplace, Singapore, from Third World to First and thus enabled us to be global citizens.

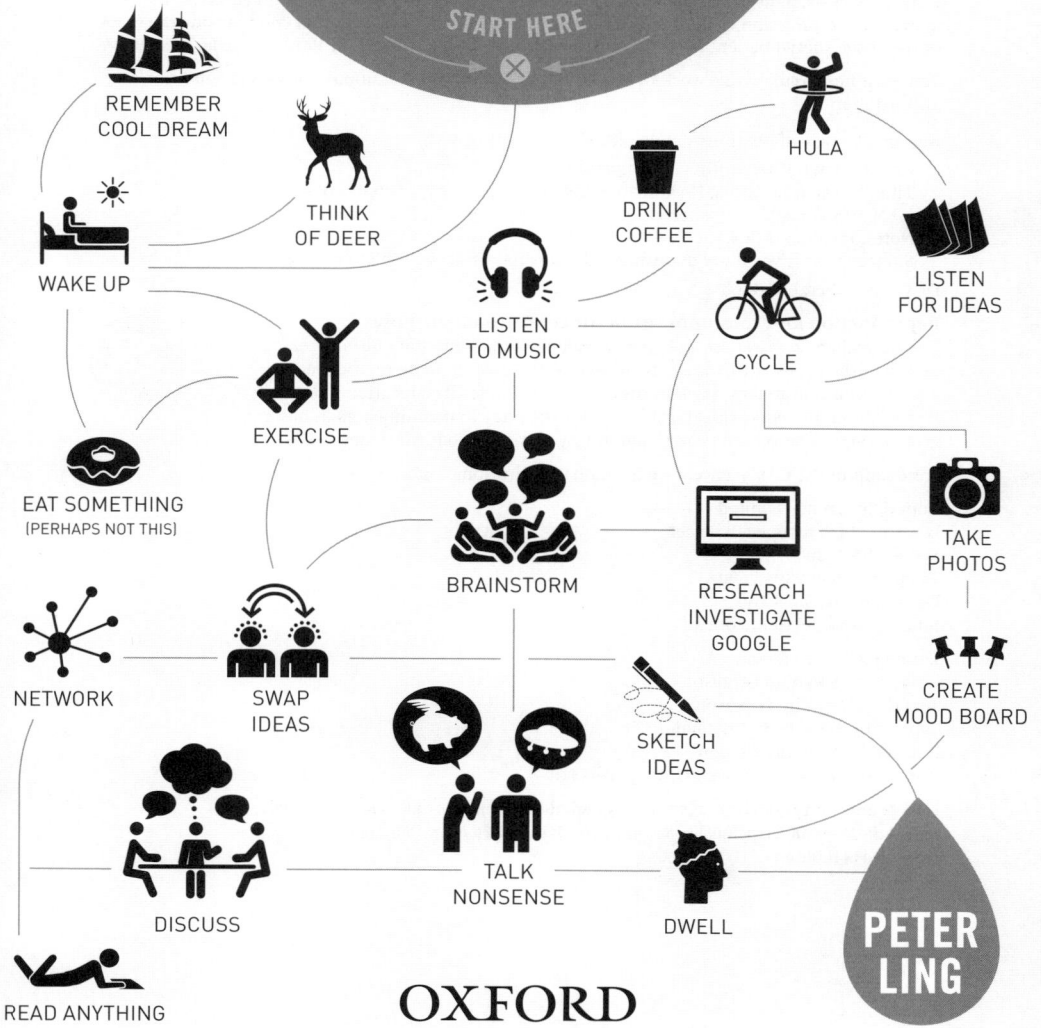

OXFORD
UNIVERSITY PRESS

Oxford University Press is a department of the University of Oxford. It furthers the University's objective of excellence in research, scholarship, and education by publishing worldwide. Oxford is a registered trademark of Oxford University Press in the UK and in certain other countries.

Published in Australia by Oxford University Press
253 Normanby Road, South Melbourne, Victoria 3205, Australia

© Peter Ling 2016

The moral rights of the author have been asserted.

All rights reserved. No part of this publication may be reproduced, stored in a retrieval system, or transmitted, in any form or by any means, without the prior permission in writing of Oxford University Press, or as expressly permitted by law, by licence, or under terms agreed with the appropriate reprographics rights organisation. Enquiries concerning reproduction outside the scope of the above should be sent to the Rights Department, Oxford University Press, at the address above.

You must not circulate this work in any other form and you must impose this same condition on any acquirer.

National Library of Australia Cataloguing-in-Publication data

    Creator: Ling, Peter, author.
    Title: Be the innovators: How to accelerate team creativity / Peter Ling.
    ISBN: 9780195590173 (paperback)
    Notes: Includes index.
    Subjects: Creative ability in business. Success in business. Problem solving.

Dewey Number: 658.4063

Reproduction and communication for educational purposes
The Australian *Copyright Act 1968* (the Act) allows a maximum of one chapter or 10% of the pages of this work, whichever is the greater, to be reproduced and/or communicated by any educational institution for its educational purposes provided that the educational institution (or the body that administers it) has given a remuneration notice to Copyright Agency Limited (CAL) under the Act.

For details of the CAL licence for educational institutions contact:

Copyright Agency Limited
Level 15, 233 Castlereagh Street
Sydney NSW 2000
Telephone: (02) 9394 7600
Facsimile: (02) 9394 7601
Email: info@copyright.com.au

Edited by Kirsten Rawlings
Cover design by Kim Ferguson
Text design by Kim Ferguson
Typeset by diacriTech, Chennai, India
Indexed by Frances Paterson
Printed by Sheck Wah Tong Printing Press Ltd.

Links to third party websites are provided by Oxford in good faith and for information only. Oxford disclaims any responsibility for the materials contained in any third party website referenced in this work.

CONTENTS

Tables and Figures vi
Preface viii
About the Author x
Acknowledgements xi

CHAPTER 1	Innovation and Team Creativity Catalysts	1
CHAPTER 2	Mastery Modelling: Benchmarking Innovation	7
CHAPTER 3	Intensive Immersion: Empowered Exploration	21
CHAPTER 4	Group Germination: Collective Growth	36
CHAPTER 5	Mind Netting: Brainstorming	60
CHAPTER 6	Mind Netting: Creative Problem Solving Process	75
CHAPTER 7	Mind Netting: Synectics Innovative Problem Solving	83
CHAPTER 8	Mind Netting: Lateral and Multidimensional Thinking	105
CHAPTER 9	Mind Netting: TRIZ Inventive Problem Solving	115
CHAPTER 10	Mind Netting: Attribute Listing and Morphological Synthesis	125
CHAPTER 11	Conclusion: Accelerating Team Creativity and Innovation	138

APPENDICES
A. Research on adult team creativity 149
B. Other authors modelling genius 157
C. News media modelling mastery 159
D. Modelling innovative companies 163
E. Modelling innovative countries 167
F. Synectics-based DREAM training 174

NOTES 177
INDEX 204

TABLES AND FIGURES

Tables

1.1	Typology of creativity catalysts and related dimensions	4
4.1	Corporate accelerators versus incubators	56
6.1	CPS stages and steps (2006)	78
6.2	CPS working with the police	78
6.3	The CIA framework	80
7.1	Listening out-in	91
9.1	TRIZ principles frequently used in management	119
9.2	TRIZ principles to resolve contradictions	120
9.3	TRIZ principles and SCAMPER	121
10.1	Attribute listing—toffee-apple sticks	126
10.2	Morphological synthesis of sandwich favourites and companions	127
10.3	Morphological synthesis of favourite sandwiches, food companions and bread types	128
10.4	Morphological synthesis for children's educational toys	128
10.5	Morphological box to create a new lamp	129
10.6	Morphological synthesis of a candy bar	129
10.7	Morphological synthesis on cereals	130
10.8	Morphological synthesis on Vegemite variants	130
10.9	Morphological synthesis for Home and Away	131
10.10	Creating the Creative Services major	131
10.11	Morphological synthesis of multiple intelligences for book ideas	132
10.12	Analysis of three MasterCard commercials	133
10.13	Morphological box for creative thinking tools and techniques	134
A.1	Interconnected contemporary creativity theories	151
A.2	Interconnected creativity theories	153
C.1	Vanity Fair New Establishment entrepreneurs and visionaries	161

D.1	2014's most innovative companies, synthesised from seven sources	166
E.1	Bloomberg Innovation Quotient 2012–14 rankings	168
E.2	Global Competitiveness Index	169
E.3	Global Competitiveness Index: Innovation top ten	169
E.4	Global Innovation Index 2008–14	171
E.5	IMD World Competitiveness Ranking	172
E.6	Most innovative countries, synthesised from five sources	173

Figures

4.1	The Tasmanian light shipbuilding cluster	40
4.2	The Savannah Way cluster	40
4.3	P&G's open innovation model of leveraging its networks	45
7.1	Task analysis example	95
7.2	Synectics steps and Disney's thinking modes	99
7.3	Synectics steps and DREAM process	100
8.1	How to mind map	110
8.2	Multidimensional mind mapping around 'love'	112
8.3	Multidimensional mind mapping around 'strip'	113
8.4	Mind mapping 'sources of ideas'	113
A.1	Mind map of creativity catalysts	155

PREFACE

Innovations have changed people's lives. Electricity, clean tap water, sewage disposal, aeroplanes, ATMs, laptops, the internet, mobile phones and non-invasive surgery have made things better for people around the world.

We used to read about individual inventors such as da Vinci, Edison, Bell, Tesla and the Wright brothers; we now read about the individual creativity of technology entrepreneurs such as Jobs, Gates, Brin, Page and Zuckerberg. As organisations grow in a complex technology-driven environment, chief executives have expressed the need for more creative employees to steer innovation.

However, only a small percentage of organisations are world-class innovators or innovation leaders. The desire to be more innovative and the ability to actually realise a vision have been hampered by an absence of visionary leadership, passion for excellence, cross-pollination of ideas and risk-taking.

Be the Innovators provides readers with ideas for benchmarking best practices in innovation, empowering creative excellence, leveraging collective growth and connecting a spectrum of individual and team ideas. The team creativity catalysts I present in this book emerged from my industry practice, from my training of groups, from facilitating team creativity sessions and from empirical research.

Whether you are striving to innovate or just beginning to think about innovating in your organisation, this book will help you learn how to:

- model geniuses, innovators, innovative companies and innovative countries
- immerse empowered employees in your corporate mission, values, vision, innovation time and research
- grow collectively through competitive collaboration, cluster collaboration, outsourcing, open innovation, crowdsourcing, crowdfunding, incubators and accelerators
- net the spectrum of ideas of individuals and teams through a diversity of interconnected creative thinking tools that have an underpinning philosophy of Challenge-Ideas-Action (CIA), such as brainstorming, Creative Problem Solving process, Synectics innovative problem solving, lateral thinking, Six Thinking Hats, mind mapping, multidimensional thinking, TRIZ inventive problem solving, attribute listing and morphological synthesis.

Specifically, you will learn about the thinking patterns of geniuses; the similar benchmarking practices of the late Steve Jobs and Lee Kuan Yew as well as Apple and Singapore; the use of innovation time by world-class innovators such as Apple, Google, 3M, Amazon, Procter & Gamble, Microsoft, Facebook and IBM; the collective growth strategies of innovative organisations through geographic clusters, lead users, outside-in open innovation, academic and industry partnerships, supplier collaboration and crowd wisdom; the crowdsourcing strategy of Procter & Gamble to supplement its research and development staff; the creative contests Unilever runs to tap the global creative playground; and the creative methods of innovative organisations such as IDEO design firm, Apple, Unilever, Samsung, Procter & Gamble, 3M, Pixar and the Virgin Group.

Thoroughly researched and referenced, with appendices for readers who want to know more about the background behind key ideas in chapters, *Be the Innovators* will trigger new creative connections in your mind to help you accelerate innovation through team creativity in your organisation.

This practical book is structured around the team creativity catalysts framework.

The introductory chapter provides a summary of innovation, innovation barriers and the creativity catalysts framework of Mastery Modelling, Intensive Immersion, Group Germination and Mind Netting.

Chapter 2, on Mastery Modelling, helps readers to benchmark their creativity and innovation goals against individual and corporate masters in innovation.

Chapter 3, on Intensive Immersion, advocates a Nike 'Just Do It' culture of employee-empowered exploration and practised perfection in achieving accelerated team creativity and innovation.

Chapter 4, on Group Germination, highlights the importance of leveraging group resources within and outside the company.

The six chapters exploring Mind Netting (Chapters 5 to 10) present popular creative thinking tools that will help you net or capture the diverse experiences and thoughts of team creativity colleagues.

The concluding chapter synthesises the team creativity catalysts and explores how you can accelerate team creativity and innovation in your organisation. If your learning style is to read the conclusion before the beginning chapters, you will come first to the comprehensive Q&A format in this last chapter, which provides a detailed picture of how the team creativity catalysts accelerate innovation!

My wish is that the knowledge in *Be the Innovators* will accelerate your personal, team and group creativity processes to help your corporation innovate in many ways.

Peter Ling

ABOUT THE AUTHOR

Dr Peter Ling has had a varied career in journalism, public relations, retail advertising, advertising agency management, marketing communication consultancy, team creativity consulting and academia. He has worked in Singapore, Taipei, Perth and Melbourne, including training attachments with Young & Rubicam Advertising in New York, and Lintas Advertising in Sydney.

Peter has written hundreds of industry articles and cases for various publishers. He is lead author of *Consumer Behaviour in Action*, published by Oxford University Press. His doctorate at the University of Western Australia was on 'Accelerated adult team creativity: A Synectics-based DREAM case study'. Trained in the Synectics team creativity process in the USA and UK as well as in other creative thinking tools such as the Creative Problem Solving process, lateral thinking, Six Thinking Hats, mind mapping and TRIZ inventive problem solving, Peter created a creative thinking course, the Creative Services major and the Bachelor of Marketing and Creative Services at Edith Cowan University (ECU) in Perth, Australia. Peter taught creative thinking, advertising, consumer behaviour and marketing communication between 2004 and 2010 at ECU, where he was also line manager overseeing the coordinators of majors in advertising, broadcasting, journalism, mass communication, media studies, public relations and scriptwriting.

He joined RMIT University in Melbourne, Australia, in 2011 and has been Associate/Deputy Dean in the School of Media and Communication, supervising program directors in advertising, communication, communication design, creative writing, editing and publishing, photography, professional communication and public relations. He has also been the School's Deputy Dean International.

He has won awards in many areas, including industry leadership, industry engagement, teaching, best paper, and for supervising a team that became the Asia-Pacific winners in the Google Online Marketing Challenge in 2010.

ACKNOWLEDGEMENTS

This book has been made possible by generous knowledge sharing from the following Synectics alumni:

- Rick Harriman, who as President of Synectics Inc in the 1980s freely shared the company's knowledge resources.
- The late George Prince, co-founder of Synectics Inc in Cambridge, Massachusetts, USA, who shared his knowledge, skills and resources.
- The late Vincent Nolan, who provided his Synectics UK experiences and resources.
- Roger Neill, Sandy Dunlop and Ned Preble, who had invited me to co-facilitate team creativity workshops in Asia-Pacific.
- My wife, Dr Alicia Quek, who spent a year training in Synectics offices in the UK and USA and shared her knowledge through co-facilitation and co-authoring of *Dream to Innovate*.

Thanks also go to the following organisations:

- Singapore Institute of Management for publishing *Dream to Innovate* (2001), which eventually motivated me to start my doctoral journey.
- The University of Western Australia for enabling me to complete my doctorate on accelerated adult team creativity and for awarding me the Fogarty Prize for Best Doctoral Thesis in 2005.
- Edith Cowan University for allowing me to create the Creative Thinking course and to teach hundreds of undergraduate and postgraduate students who provided feedback that the course had enhanced their creative ability and confidence.
- Oxford University Press, particularly Karen Hildebrandt, for believing in my book *Be the Innovators* and for facilitating invaluable peer review feedback.
- RMIT University, particularly Professor Martyn Hook, the Dean of the School of Media and Communication, for research leave to write this book.

INNOVATION AND TEAM CREATIVITY CATALYSTS

CHAPTER 1

When respondents in a Hewlett-Packard (HP) global survey were asked for innovations that their organisations had implemented, the answers were diverse: an imaging system; creation of social/e-commerce channels; efficient automation of the source-to-pay process; immuno-oncology treatment; a conference room booking system; improved process/software; introduction of collaboration platforms; new processes to drive IT; an online application system; patient-specific technologies; insurance for voluntary non-profits; and using design thinking. The recent innovations were delivered through internal, collaborative and partnership sources for the benefit of business, teams, industry and society.[1]

INTRODUCTION

Innovation exists in various forms in different organisations. Over ninety per cent of respondents in the HP survey indicated that innovation is vital to an organisation's competitiveness, success and survival. Yet a majority of respondents felt their organisations had achieved only some innovation and needed to work harder at it. What seems to be obstructing innovation? Is it due to lack of creativity within organisations? What facilitates innovation? This introductory chapter will briefly explore creativity and innovation and how my concept of team creativity catalysts can help facilitate innovation capability.

CREATIVITY AND INNOVATION

The words *creativity* and *innovation* have been bandied around but do they mean the same thing? There are numerous definitions of each (see Appendix A for my in-depth review of creativity literature as part of empirical research) but the simplest distinction is that creativity is about producing novel and useful ideas while innovation is the successful implementation of these ideas.[2] This does not mean that creativity is absent during the implementation stage, as creativity is required during concept development as well as implementation.[3]

More than 1500 chief executive officers from sixty countries across thirty-three industries also stated that creativity is the most crucial factor for future success, even more important than vision, integrity, management discipline and rigour.[4]

BARRIERS TO INNOVATION

So why are few companies world-class or even high achievers at innovation? The HP study indicated that only six per cent of organisations are world-class innovators while another study reported that only seven per cent are innovation leaders.[5]

An analysis of four recent reports reveals that the core barriers to innovation are resources (funding, talent, knowledge, inaccurate measures, company size), leadership (strategy, priority, communication, investment) and culture (risk averse, silos, innovation time, bureaucracy, traditions, not listening).

Respondents in the HP study cited the following barriers to innovation: lack of internal resources, higher priority issues, unwillingness to take risk, bureaucracy, lack of funding, absence of leadership to drive innovation and lack of talent.[6]

A report by the IESE Business School in Spain revealed these barriers to innovation: the absence of a well-communicated innovation strategy as well as insufficient understanding of the external environment.[7]

An IBM report indicated that barriers to innovation include inaccurate measures on innovation's return on investment, lack of funding, risk avoidance, 'siloing' and time commitments.[8]

A Fast Company innovation event surfaced ten innovation barriers: closed-mindedness, traditions that hamper vision, jealousy or 'not invented here' syndrome, lack of money, generational gap among workers, poor communication to present great ideas, company size, no refresher education or training, lack of thought leadership and resources.[9]

What are the solutions to overcoming barriers to innovation? The reports suggested having an innovation culture, such as at the leadership level, and having a clear view of world-class best practices; having innovation as a corporate value; being open to other ideas internally and externally; and having a spectrum of ideas for breakthrough innovations.

TEAM CREATIVITY CATALYSTS

These solutions to achieve more innovation success resonate with my theory of team creativity catalysts. I developed this theory through training working adults in Synectics team creativity techniques (see Chapter 7 on Synectics), facilitating innovation workshops, participant feedback and empirical research.

My team creativity catalysts cover four integrated dimensions, all aligned with industry solutions to overcome barriers to innovation: Mastery Modelling, Intensive Immersion, Group Germination and Mind Netting. Mastery Modelling is having a view of world-class best practices; Intensive Immersion is like having an empowered innovation culture; Group Germination is akin to openness to internal and external ideas; and Mind Netting is similar to having a spectrum of ideas.

Mastery Modelling

This is where participants learn benchmarks, models or visions of mastery. The benchmarks are identified, demonstrated, visually displayed and discussed, so they become 'anchored' in the minds of participants from the very beginning, during group sessions, and during sharing of learning after training or workshops.

Intensive Immersion

This is where participants are empowered and motivated to fully immerse themselves in the team creativity process to find creative solutions for their tasks. This immersion enables participants to openly and proactively facilitate training or workshop sessions, to explore, experiment, review and learn. Intensive Immersion leads to practised perfection where participants experientially change their mindsets, creative confidence and creative competence.

Group Germination

This is where team members help one another to germinate their thinking and learning, with faster 'germinated' or 'nourished' experienced learners helping to 'germinate' or 'nourish' others through roles of facilitator, task owner or idea contributor. Creative solutions also germinate faster through constant camaraderie and playful productivity in the group.

Mind Netting

This is where teams 'net' or harvest the diverse experiences, thoughts and ideas through 'baits' such as personal metaphors, learning metaphors, listening for connections, multidimensional mind mapping, different creative thinking techniques, seemingly unconnected wacky playful activities and unrelated creative connections.

MIGN

I refer to the team creativity catalysts as MIGN (pronounced *mine*): Modelling, Immersion, Germination and Netting. The MIGN creativity catalysts fit into physical, self-actualising, emotional and mental dimensions. The physical dimension of observing and benchmarking best practices is related to Mastery Modelling. The self-actualising dimension is about empowered exploration to achieve one's personal best. The emotional dimension of individual self-concept and group dynamics is akin to Group Germination. The mental dimension is a natural connection to Mind Netting. See Table 1.1.

TABLE 1.1 Typology of creativity catalysts and related dimensions

Physical dimension Mastery Modelling	Emotional dimension Group Germination
Self-actualising dimension Intensive Immersion	Mental dimension Mind Netting

The four dimensions are interconnected. Mastery Modelling is setting the benchmark or vision for the team. Intensive Immersion is mission-driven empowerment of the team to work towards the mastery benchmark and reflect on different perspectives to improve along the vision journey. Group Germination is strategic collaboration with diverse internal and external resources to accelerate achievement. Mind Netting is harvesting creative ideas from diverse groups through different creative 'baits'. Since diverse people have different perspectives, the netted harvest of these various thoughts often leads to amazement, paradigm shifts, more self-confidence and accelerated innovation.

The MIGN catalysts also align with the popular 4Ps of creativity—product, place, person and process. Mastery Modelling is like the 'product' of novel and feasible solutions. Intensive Immersion aligns with the 'place' of an innovation environment. Group Germination ties in with the 'person' element. Mind Netting is similar to the 'process' of creative thinking.

The MIGN creativity catalysts could be applied singly, collectively or in a different order. We now look at examples of situations they can be used in: individual applications, team bonding, team creativity or innovative problem-solving sessions, and organisational outcomes.

Individual applications

Individuals could use the Mind Netting catalyst in the following situations:

- describing each person as a metaphor
- using a wacky activity as a meeting ice-breaker for example, personify a chair with feelings
- using metaphoric drawing as a game with the family
- using an unrelated metaphor to find creative solutions at home, study or work
- using multidimensional mind mapping to help children think of diverse perspectives around a keyword or image. This was a favourite idea of participants who wanted their children to think of diverse possibilities.

Team bonding

The MIGN framework could be adapted to team bonding:

- Mastery Modelling: The facilitator models a visual emblem to introduce himself or herself, with elements such as 'my happiest time', 'words that I would like in my obituary', 'my vision', 'my special skills and interests'.
- Intensive Immersion: Team members individually immerse themselves in illustrating their emblems using the facilitator's model as an example.
- Group Germination: Each team member tells a story about his or her emblem. Usually, there would be laughter and surprise at each story sharing.
- Mind Netting: The team could draw up a composite metaphor to represent the team's emblem of values, vision, skills, etc.

Team creativity framework

Facilitators or consultants could plan a team innovative problem-solving session using the MIGN catalysts:

- Mastery Modelling: Model upfront whichever process you would like to use for your team creativity session.
- Intensive Immersion: Immerse everyone in the chosen process by motivating team members to participate fully—to experience the process, to discover, to reflect and to learn while finding solutions for a relevant task.
- Group Germination: Divide diverse participants in mini-groups of three or four. For example, a group could have a mix of participants from marketing, engineering and psychology disciplines. The group mission is to optimise the input of every member and to have equal airtime.
- Mind Netting: Use various creative thinking tools to net the ideas of diverse participants. An engineer could look at a problem through paradoxes while a psychologist could turn the problem into personal metaphors.

Organisational outcomes
An organisation could use the MIGN catalysts in the following way:

- Mastery Modelling: Ask teams the question: 'Which person, sports team, organisation, country, animal or nature would you like our company to be benchmarked against?'
- Intensive Immersion: Immerse every participant by asking them to speak or write down their thoughts on sticky notes, then ask each team to select from its central list of preferred benchmarks.
- Group Germination: Assign to each group one benchmark to explore further; for example, one group could consider how your company could be like the Manchester United soccer team, while another group could extract innovation lessons from Singapore Airlines.
- Mind Netting: Net the thoughts from different groups as well as subsequent thoughts that emerge after each sharing and at the end of the session.

SUMMARY

This chapter reviewed the distinction between creativity and innovation, barriers to innovation and my theory of team creativity catalysts that aligns with industry innovation solutions.

The four creativity catalysts can be applied flexibly in different situations, and the following chapters expand on the applications to help accelerate team creativity and innovation in organisations. Chapter 2 discusses how Mastery Modelling could be used to benchmark innovation. Chapter 3 examines how Intensive Immersion could motivate empowered exploration. Chapter 4 illustrates how Group Germination could lead to collective growth for organisations. Chapters 5 to 10 highlight how tools of creative thinking used in Mind Netting could lead to a spectrum of ideas for innovation. Chapter 11 synthesises all the chapters illustrating the team creativity catalysts.

My wish is that the team creativity catalysts and broad applications in this book will help your corporation innovate and grow, rather than be a laggard or wither.[10]

MASTERY MODELLING: BENCHMARKING INNOVATION

CHAPTER 2

The late martial arts master Bruce Lee Jun Fan learnt the Wing Chun style of 'gung fu' at the age of thirteen from Master Yip Man in Hong Kong. While Bruce also became a boxing and cha-cha dance champion as a teenager in Hong Kong, he moved to Seattle to work and study, and to start his Jun Fan Gung Fu Institute. Bruce immersed himself in the philosophy and techniques of martial arts, equating yin and yang to hard and soft physical movements. He taught celebrities such as Steve McQueen, James Coburn and James Garner his art of Jeet Kune Do, or 'the way of the intercepting fist.'[11]

INTRODUCTION

Learning from the masters exists in every sector. An apprentice learns from a kung fu master, a master craftsperson or a master chef. Hence, the creativity catalyst of Mastery Modelling is about modelling the mastery of the experts to provide benchmarks for accelerating team creativity and innovation. This chapter highlights modelling practices: modelling through neurolinguistic programming; modelling geniuses and innovative people; modelling innovative companies; and modelling innovative countries.

NEUROLINGUISTIC PROGRAMMING

Neurolinguistic programming involves modelling the cognitive, language and behavioural patterns of exceptional individuals for other people to emulate. Neurolinguistic programming founders Richard Bandler and John Grinder, who had modelled the skill patterns of exceptional therapists such as Virginia Satir and Milton Erickson in the 1970s, believed that human behaviour could be transformed if people emulated special skills. The desired skills would then be 'anchored' or imprinted as a learning process.[12]

GENUISES

Robert Dilts, a neurolinguistic programming practitioner who runs an NLP University website, analysed the thinking and behavioural processes of Aristotle, Sir Arthur Conan Doyle, Walt Disney, Wolfgang Amadeus Mozart,[13] Albert Einstein,[14] Sigmund Freud, Nikola Tesla, Leonardo da Vinci,[15] Charles Darwin and Jesus of Nazareth.[16]

Dilts concluded that geniuses had ten patterns of thinking.[17]

1. Visual ability: Geniuses visualised as part of their creative process. Freud visualised even small details in his dreams.
2. Sensory links: Geniuses synthesised their sensory dimensions. Mozart saw, felt and tasted his music.
3. Multiple perspectives: Geniuses searched for different, new or non-traditional perspectives. Da Vinci looked at different perspectives in a situation.
4. Perceptual switching: Geniuses took different viewpoints—theirs and others. Disney identified with his characters and audiences while da Vinci used a mirror to change his perceptual state.
5. Back-and-forth thinking: Geniuses move between the big picture and the details. Da Vinci shifted between macro and micro thinking. Even when they were paying attention to detail, geniuses did not lose sight of the bigger vision.
6. Abstract and concrete thinking: Geniuses moved between abstract thinking and concrete reality, using reflection to refine each thinking process. Tesla built machines exactly as he had imagined them.
7. Cognitive balance: Geniuses were dreamers, realists and critics—Disney thought this way, and these functions are analogous to Freud's id, ego and superego. Da Vinci was able to dream, draw and evaluate his work.
8. Asking basic questions: Geniuses keep asking questions to help make imagination a reality. Aristotle asked questions to understand principles in nature.
9. Using metaphors and analogies: Einstein used metaphors to explain theories, da Vinci understood water movement through a flowing and curling hair analogy, Freud used symbols, Tesla compared robots with his nervous system and Mozart used the analogy of creating a dish out of morsels for music composition.
10. Mission beyond individual identity: Geniuses seek something larger, such as da Vinci wishing to work miracles, Einstein aspiring to know how God thinks and Freud probing into unconscious thinking.

If we synthesise Dilts' ten patterns of thinking processes, we can see that geniuses have a bold mission and a 'whole brain, whole person' perspective. Geniuses draw on metaphors, analogies, multiple perspectives, sensory synthesis, perceptual switching, abstract–concrete thinking, back-and-forth thinking, big picture–details thinking, and imagination–reality thinking, such as dreamer-realist-critic. In a separate article analysing the words and actions of Jesus Christ, Dilts concluded that people could model around a belief system of self-worth, mission, belonging, hope, capability, responsibility and parables.[18]

Just as Dilts had done, Murray, Buzan, Keene, Gelb and Caldicott (see Appendix B) had identified da Vinci as the model master because of his multiple talents and diverse perspectives. Da Vinci had a vision of something larger; he used analogies to make new creative connections; he was a macro–micro thinker; he embraced curiosity, ambiguity and experiential learning; and he was a dreamer and critic as well.

Inspired by geniuses

Geniuses have inspired famous people (see Appendix C on news media modelling creative and innovative people). For example, Leonardo da Vinci's constant quest for knowledge, advanced understanding of science and futuristic ideas inspired Microsoft's Bill Gates—in 1994 Gates paid US$30.8 million for a 500-year-old manuscript by da Vinci, which he displays in his office to draw inspiration for his own inventions, such as a nuclear reactor to burn depleted uranium and a thermos system to keep vaccines potent for fifty days.[19]

Serbian inventor Nikola Tesla was the inspiration for the name of Martin Eberhard and Marc Tarpenning's company, Tesla Motors. Inventor Tesla had more than 700 patents and had created the induction motor.[20]

Charles Dickens inspired Amazon founder Jeff Bezos. Dickens' way of publishing his novels in newspapers before books encouraged Bezos to develop a process to deliver Kindle Serials—weekly digital ebook instalments.[21]

Steve Jobs

Steve Jobs inspired Marc Benioff, founder of Salesforce.com, the global customer relationship management (CRM) enterprise. The cloud-computing pioneer was ranked by *Forbes Magazine* as the world's most innovative company for the fourth consecutive year in 2014.[22] Marc said that Jobs was a guru, inspiration and mentor behind many things created at Salesforce.com.[23]

When Jobs passed away in 2011, Facebook founder and fellow college dropout Mark Zuckerberg called him a mentor who inspired him about changing the world;[24] Google founders Larry Page and Sergey Brin wrote about how Jobs had inspired them with his passion for excellence, vision, user focus and leadership advice;[25] Disney CEO Bob Iger praised Jobs as an original who inspired people, changed lives and defined a creative culture;[26] and Microsoft's Bill Gates said that it was an 'insanely great honour' to have worked with Jobs as colleagues and competitors and that his impact would be felt for generations.[27]

US broadcaster CNBC voted Jobs the number one person to have an impact on business since its first live broadcast in 1989, ahead of Bill Gates and the Google founders. But who inspired Steve Jobs? Who has been described as 'our generation's Edison and Ford and Disney and Elvis, all rolled into one'[28]?

Jobs' technology journey started at age fourteen when he immersed himself in computers, joining an Explorers Club on Hewlett-Packard's campus and asking Bill Hewlett for electronic components for a project. Keen on Shakespeare and technology, Jobs was already an enabler of genius in his teenage years when he collaborated with Stephen Wozniak to assemble battery-powered machines that could facilitate free international calls. Jobs later worked as a technician at video game company Atari, sought Asian spiritualism in India, joined the hobbyist knowledge-sharing Homebrew Computer Club, where he and Wozniak sold microcomputer circuit boards to members, and then partnered with Wozniak to form Apple in 1976. The friendly and approachable Apple brand name was modelled on Sony, which had changed its name from Tokyo Telecommunications Engineering Corporation. Jobs positioned Apple as a nimble David against the uninspiring Goliath of bigger technology companies. He gained inspiration from visiting department stores to help him develop a personal computer that was more like a home appliance than an industrial machine, and he networked energetically to secure 'angel' investment for the company.

Intel's CEO Andy Grove, who also had wide-ranging interests, inspired Jobs with his expansive pragmatism; Regis McKenna, a business and marketing strategist, was Jobs' early mentor on corporate storytelling; Jobs' team at Pixar, particularly CEO Ed Catmull and animation guru John Lasseter, inspired him with creative leadership, such as how to motivate and manage creative talents and how to have the balanced skill of a child's curiosity combined with attention to detail; and Xerox Corporation's Palo Alto Research Center provided benchmarks for Apple's interactive personal computer, which Jobs metaphorically described as a 'bicycle for the mind'.[29]

Jobs modelled his career on that of Edwin Land, inventor of instant photography at Polaroid. Also a college dropout, and forced out of his own company, Land was a master at dramatic scientific demonstrations, obsessive about product design and a firm believer in startling inventions that were not based on market research.[30]

Jobs is an example of an entrepreneur who had failed as part of his journey to success. After he had failed with the Lisa and Macintosh computers and was ousted from Apple in 1985, he started NeXT computer company, bought Pixar (the Computer Graphics Division of film director George Lucas), returned to Apple in 1997 and turned the unprofitable company around with innovative products such as Power Macintosh, iMac, iPod, iTunes, MacBook Pro, iPhone, MacBook Air and iPad.[31]

In 2008 Jobs started an internal Apple training program, often referred to as Apple University, to orientate employees to its innovation culture as well as to learn from the mistakes and successes of companies and innovators. In the program, employees learn how Picasso's great art without the details has influenced the simple design of Apple products; how designers of New York's Central Park, who had turned the rocky swamp into a natural space for urban residents, had influenced Jobs' philosophy of making complex computer technology natural and understandable; how Apple looked at Google's TV remote control with seventy-eight buttons and designed the Apple TV remote control with three buttons; and how Apple eventually made the iPod and iTunes software compatible with Microsoft's Windows system.[32] Some employees commented that they had learnt about the rise and fall of supermarket chain A&P and about Swiss watchmaking from the 1500s to the twentieth century.[33]

Jobs spoke highly of Nike advertising, which he said honoured great athletes. In an internal meeting in 1997, Jobs introduced Apple's 'Think Different' campaign created by advertising agency Chiat\Day to honour geniuses such as Albert Einstein, Alfred Hitchcock, Amelia Earhart, Bob Dylan, Buckminster Fuller, Frank Lloyd Wright, Jim Henson (with Kermit the Frog), John Lennon (with Yoko Ono), Mahatma Gandhi, Maria Callas, Martha Graham, Martin Luther King Jr, Muhammad Ali, Pablo Picasso, Richard Branson, Ted Turner and Thomas Edison. The television script characterised geniuses as people who perceive differently, are unusual and unconventional, break rules, ignore the status quo, are distinctive, push people forward and change the world. Print advertisements and promotional posters also featured selected geniuses.[34]

Jobs' innovation principles cover passion, bold vision, connecting vast experiences, simplicity, customer service and enriching lives:[35]

- 'Do what you love': Jobs was passionate about optimising people's potential through tools that integrate technology and arts.
- 'Put a dent in the universe': The bold vision of Apple founders Jobs and Wozniak was to have a personal computer in everyone's hands. This vision inspired Jobs' team to create an impact on the universe.

- 'Creativity is connecting things': Jobs connected his experiences, especially those from outside his chosen field, to the projects he was working on.
- 'Say no to 1000 things': Jobs believed in making things simpler and uncluttered, rather than having too many products or features.
- 'Create "insanely great" experiences for customers': Jobs used the Ritz-Carlton Hotel as a model for the Apple Store to provide the best customer service.
- 'Sell dreams, not products': Jobs spoke about helping people to achieve dreams and enrich their lives, not just about buying computers. He was adept at convincing people to act on his ideas.

In Steve Jobs' 2005 Stanford address, which has had over twenty-two million views on YouTube, he shared three ideas with the graduating students. First, as Jobs said, connect the dots. Jobs dropped out of normal classes that he had to take and dropped in on interesting courses. The calligraphy classes that he had attended influenced his choice of typography for Macintosh computers. Jobs' advice was to connect the past with the present. Second, he advised to love what you do. He loved to be an entrepreneur and started Apple with Steve Wozniak in a garage. He faced public failure head on, built up Pixar with his team, and sold it to Disney. Third, he said to use death to drive your life. If today were the last day of your life, what would you do? Don't live someone else's life. Follow your heart and intuition. Stay hungry, stay foolish.[36]

Jobs was an inspiration for many people but he also learned from experiences and benchmarked best practices from a variety of sources: Sony, Intel's Andy Grove, strategist Regis McKenna, Pixar, Xerox, Microsoft, Google, Nike, the Ritz-Carlton Hotel, New York's Central Park, Swiss watchmaking, calligraphy, department stores, inventor Edwin Land, Picasso and many geniuses.

Who could you model your life and work on—Jobs, Land, da Vinci, Tesla, Dickens or other geniuses who have inspired famous people over the years?

INNOVATIVE COMPANIES: GOOGLE

Various sources publish lists of innovative companies based on criteria such as perceptions of senior executives, research and development spending, innovation management principles, innovation strides and invention patents (see Appendix D on modelling innovative companies).

A synthesis of these listings shows that the higher-ranked companies are Apple, Google and Amazon, followed by Samsung, Tesla, Salesforce.com, 3M, Dropbox, Microsoft and IBM.

The last section focused on innovative people and highlighted the mastery of Steve Jobs, Apple's innovation champion. This section focuses on Google's eight pillars of innovation, ten innovation commandments and championing of innovation for a better world for many people.

Pillars of innovation

Google's eight pillars of innovation cover mission, the big–small thinking paradox, continual innovation, sourcing ideas, sharing knowledge, imagination–data dynamics, open technologies and taking risks.[37]

1. 'Have a mission that matters': Google's mission, 'organise the world's information and make it universally accessible and useful', guides, empowers, motivates and connects Googlers (Google employees). Gmail symbolises the company's mission.
2. 'Think big but start small': Google Books started with a scanner and now millions of books are accessible online, while AdSense started with advertisements in Gmail but now is the largest internet advertising network.
3. 'Strive for continual innovation, not constant perfection': AdWords was not popular in 1999 but improved through iterations, quality experiments and early feedback from users.
4. 'Look for ideas everywhere': Google seeks ideas from Googlers, advertisers, partners and everyone else. Some ideas originate in the hallways at Google or in micro-kitchens, on ideas boards and during random break times. Visit a Google office and you will see snacks everywhere!
5. 'Share everything': Google management shares board decisions with employees quarterly to trigger discussion in small teams working in cubicles. The Google Talk instant messaging service emerged from such 'cube-mate' chats.
6. 'Spark with imagination, fuel with data': Googlers believe in making the impossible a reality, such as the driverless car. Googlers combine intuition with insight to focus on pursuing their pet projects.
7. 'Be a platform': Google believes in open technologies that other people can add to, such as Google Earth for people to learn about their world through diverse perspectives, and the Google Android mobile platform, for which half a million independent developers have created 200,000 apps.
8. 'Never fail to fail': Google takes risks, fails many times and learns from failures to improve a service or use the knowledge elsewhere. Google Answers, where experts answer user questions online, failed after four years but AdSense became a success.

Innovation commandments

What are Google's ten innovation commandments? Focus on the user and all else will follow; it's best to do one thing really, really well; fast is better than slow; democracy on the web works; you don't have to be at your desk to need an answer; you can make money without doing evil; there's always more information out there; the need for information crosses all borders; you can be serious without a suit; and great just isn't good enough.[38]

Championing innovation

Google is committed to championing innovation to create a better world. It donates over US$100,000,000 in grants and prizes yearly for various projects.

Google's Global Impact Awards is for entrepreneurial projects such as sourcing clean water, safeguarding endangered species through DNA barcodes and securing land rights for the poor through mobile messaging systems.

The Google Impact Challenge supports the non-profit sector to innovate using technology; the public then votes for high-impact projects. It has helped fund initiatives around the world in places such as Australia, Brazil, India, Japan, the United Kingdom and the United States. Winning projects include 'Engineers without borders Australia' and 'Bring me a book'.

Community Impact is to help non-profits make schools and communities better. Initiatives have included disaster relief, Googlers Giving Back and community grants for park rehabilitation and robotics training.[39]

Google Ideas brings engineers, experts and users together to 'think-do' through summits and working groups, hence accelerating technology-driven projects with public or private partners to address social issues such as human trafficking, violent extremism, illicit networks and online digital attacks.[40]

Google Online Marketing Challenge is for tertiary students. Since 2008 more than 80,000 tertiary students from different regions have participated in real-world AdWords advertising. Student teams find a small business client, obtain a marketing brief, prepare a strategy paper for the client to approve, create and run the online campaign over three weeks with US$250 Google-sponsored money, analyse the live analytics provided by Google, improve the campaign and then write a post-campaign report. Global and regional winners receive free trips to Google offices and computers.[41]

Google Ad Grants provides non-profit charity organisations with approximately US$10,000 of AdWords monthly advertising to promote social causes. Some successful grants include protecting the kiwi's natural habitat in New Zealand, empowering orphaned and street children in India, improving Indigenous health in Australia and benefiting disadvantaged children in Ireland.[42]

Google's 'intrapreneurs', with 'Googliness' qualities of passion and drive, have created products and services that have benefited communities. These innovations include Google's Person Finder, a database of missing persons that went live after the 2011 Japan earthquake and received thirty-six million page views within forty-eight hours; Random Hacks of Kindness, which enables participants to create software solutions to respond to disasters; Speak2Tweet, which enabled Egyptians to use their telephones to tweet messages in the midst of their government's blackout of the internet and communication channels in 2011; and Health Speaks, which translates health information into Swahili, Arabic and Hindi.[43]

Google and Apple have something in common: they learn from diverse sources, learn from mistakes and innovate for society's gain. Thinking about the Google and Apple models, or those of any of the highly ranked innovative companies mentioned in this chapter, do you see opportunities in your organisation for your own innovation principles, commandments, processes, community projects and risk-taking to produce 'intrapreneurs' and innovation leaders?

INNOVATIVE COUNTRIES

While we tend to benchmark against people and companies, what about modelling on the most innovative countries?

Based on frequency of mentions of innovative countries from various sources, the most innovative countries are Switzerland, Singapore, the USA, Sweden, Finland, South Korea, Hong Kong, Japan and Germany (see Appendix E on modelling innovative countries).

The following section profiles Switzerland and Singapore to see how they are most innovative, which could provide innovation benchmarks for your organisation.

Switzerland

Switzerland is a small country with eight million people, yet it is known for many things: caviar; cheese; bread; the Swiss army knife; Velcro fasteners; tennis stars such as Roger Federer and Martina Hingis; chocolate brands such as Suchard, Lindt and Tobler; and companies such as Nestlé, Rolex, Omega, Swatch and Credit Suisse.

With limited natural resources, Switzerland optimises its people's brainpower through its decentralised education system covering primary, secondary, tertiary and adult education. After years of compulsory education, students choose between a vocational education and training pathway and an academic option. Two-thirds choose the former; they attend school and are apprenticed in a company to learn theory and practice. This dual-track pathway produces an innovative workforce.

Switzerland prides itself as a research nation, with the majority of research funded by the chemical, electronic, metal and pharmaceutical industries—the country's research spending is about three per cent of its GDP. It has a long tradition of public–private partnerships; two examples are research and development of a solar-powered aircraft and a hydrogen-powered street sweeper vehicle. The Swiss National Science Foundation, founded in 1952, funds research projects and nurtures scientific talent. The Commission for Innovation and Technology facilitates knowledge transfer between universities and businesses. Switzerland has won seven Nobel Prizes for research in physics, chemistry and medicine.[44]

Switzerland was a late starter in watchmaking, following England, France, Germany, Italy and the Netherlands, but grew to be associated with timekeeping design, technological innovation, precision and quality. Switzerland exports ninety-five per cent of its watch production, and is home to brands such as Rolex, Omega, Patek Philippe, Piaget, Jaeger-LeCoultre, Vacheron Constantin and Swatch, a fashion accessory that helped Switzerland regain its watchmaking leadership in the 1980s. The country showcases its watchmaking quality through two annual exhibitions: Baselworld, whose 2000 exhibitors attract 100,000 visitors; and the International Salon for Prestige Watchmaking, which exhibits limited watch editions to invited guests.[45]

Switzerland is a leading chocolate manufacturer but its introduction to chocolate was through Brussels in 1697 and Italy in 1750. Leveraging its rich water supply, import of raw materials and entrepreneurship, Swiss chocolate manufacturers invented the sugar-cocoa-powder mixer, the tempering process and specialty filled hazelnut and milk chocolate. Switzerland has eighteen chocolate manufacturers exporting over sixty per cent of their production, including well-known brands such as Suchard, Lindt and Nestlé.[46]

Research and luck contributed to the Swiss production of caviar. Engineers working on a railway link project noticed the high temperature of the mountain water and brainstormed how to leverage thermal energy while protecting the ecosystem. The idea that emerged was to build a hothouse for fish that could survive in such a climate.

This was where the country's research culture came in. The Innovation Promotion Agency, Bern University's Centre for Fish and Wildlife Health, the World Sturgeon Conservation Society and the new hothouse company identified that the nearly extinct Siberian sturgeon fish would survive in the hothouse.

A project started in 2005 with 1200 sturgeon and grew to 60,000 in 2014. The commercial hothouse now markets caviar under the brand name Oona, which means 'the one' in Gaelic.[47]

Singapore

The International Monetary Fund World Economic Outlook Database 2015 ranked Singapore as the richest city in Asia with a per capita GDP of US$85,198, third in the world behind Qatar (GDP per capita US$143,532) and Luxembourg (GDP per capita US$93,174). Singapore was ahead of Brunei, Kuwait, Norway, United Arab Emirates, San Marino, Switzerland and Hong Kong.[48]

How did Singapore turn from a poor country into Asia's richest city, especially after it suffered Japanese military brutality during the Second World War, communist-triggered riots, extremist Malay communalists, aggressive Indonesian confrontation, forced separation from Malaysia and untimely British withdrawal of troops from its naval base? Singapore's Cambridge-educated and longest-serving prime minister, Lee Kuan Yew, who passed away in March 2015, had contributed to the country's success by modelling on Western best practices and Confucius values.

Dutch economist Dr Albert Winsemius was part of a team from the United Nations Development Programme in 1960 who explored Singapore's industrialisation potential. Winsemius became Singapore's chief economic advisor for twenty-five years between 1961 and 1984. He advised the Singapore government to eliminate communism, seek more foreign investments, industrialise with high-technology industries, create public housing, and develop Singapore into financial, air and sea transport hubs.[49]

Singapore's Economic Development Board was set up in the 1960s when Singapore was a third-world country with a GDP per capita of US$320. Since then, the board has promoted Singapore as a global business centre for investors and companies. It now has global overseas offices in major regions to woo investors.

Singapore has values that attract investors and companies. It is known for integrity, reliability, stability, productivity, quality, competitiveness, foresight and the best intellectual property protection in Asia. The World Intellectual Property Office set up its first Asian office in Singapore in 2009. Global corporations that have set up operations in Singapore include Unilever, Roche, Dell, Siemens, Procter & Gamble, DHL, Lucasfilm, IBM, Rolls-Royce, Mitsui Chemicals and Tata. The Economic Development Board's International Advisory Council includes senior executives from Alibaba Group, General Electric, GlaxoSmithKline, MasterCard, McKinsey, Philips, Procter & Gamble and Shell.[50]

Building the economy would not have been possible without an education system that could provide a well-educated workforce to meet investors' needs. Singapore's education system went through three phases: survival driven, 1959–78; industry efficiency driven, 1979–96; and ability driven, 1997 to the present.[51]

Singapore's education system has produced students who excel globally, particularly in mathematics. Singapore has been ranked first in four out of the five surveys on the mathematics ability of Primary 4 and Secondary 2 students between 1995 and 2011.[52] The mathematics surveys are part of the four-yearly International Mathematics and Science Study conducted by the International Association for the Evaluation of Educational Achievement (IEA), based in Boston.[53]

Singapore also has a Continuing Education and Training (CET) scheme that enables companies to apply for training grants when sending employees to approved courses. Employees too can qualify for course fee funding when they enrol directly with the CET for courses that help to enhance Singapore's innovation and global competitiveness, such as in animation, engineering services, information and communication technology and service excellence.[54]

Whenever Lee Kuan Yew faced a problem, he would find out who else had had the same issue and how successfully they had solved the problem. In his memoirs, *The Singapore Story*[55] and *From Third World to First*,[56] Lee wrote about how Singapore had modelled other countries' best practices in diverse areas. One was its use of the British colonial government's central provident fund retirement savings scheme, which Singapore inherited and evolved to include funding for home ownership and medical services.

Singapore also modelled Israel, which provided benchmarks for military training and which leapfrogged its region to attract manufacturers in the developed world. It adapted the Vatican's papal electoral system—Lee arranged to have approved cadre members elect central executive committee members of the People's Action Party to safeguard from the left-wing infiltration that had happened in the past.

Australian plant experts and New Zealand soil experts helped Singapore become a green city. Japan provided benchmarks for productivity and advised Singapore to play the role of a regional knowledge and information centre to complement Tokyo. This role redoubled Singapore's emphasis on the teaching of computers, mathematics and science in all schools.

Singapore modelled Hong Kong's entrepreneurial spirit, attracting entrepreneurs in garments, furniture, jade and ivory carving, jewellery, plastics and textiles; and offering Approval-in-Principle permanent residence to a few thousand Hong Kong families. The recruitment and promotion system of 'helicopter quality' used by the Anglo-Dutch company Shell, a combination of looking at the broad picture as well as the details, inspired Lee's political party and government to recruit people with traits of analysis, imagination and a sense of reality.

Singapore had benchmarked Switzerland in 1984 when the government envisioned a Swiss standard of living by 1999.[57] These days it is not surprising to read about other countries learning from Singapore's success in different areas.

China, where Singapore has invested over S$7 billion, has sent numerous delegations to Singapore to learn about attracting foreign investments and tourists, city planning, home ownership for the majority of its population, and its green–clean environment. Singapore has collaborated with China on several industrial parks, such as the Suzhou Industrial Park and the Sino-Singapore Tianjin Eco-City. Singapore's transformation into a global city has also been a model for Vietnam, which has four Vietnam Singapore Industrial Parks in north and south Vietnam.[58]

Countries such as the USA, Australia and South Africa are learning from Singapore's educational achievements in mathematics at Year 4 and Year 8 levels.[59] In June 2015, US President Barack Obama told young Southeast Asian leaders that Singapore was a model for other countries, especially in managing its economy and race relations.[60]

As Singapore continues its innovation journey, its vision is to be Silicon Valley for Southeast Asia with a pledge of S$16 billion for scientific research and development.[61] There are already 42,000 start-ups employing more than 300,000 in the small country, attracted by low taxes, venture funding schemes, multiple incubators and an educated workforce.[62]

How could you benchmark Singapore and Switzerland? Both these small countries with limited natural resources have optimised brainpower through education and training, have a research culture, have public–private partnerships, and have learnt from other people to be the most innovative nations.

SUMMARY

This chapter on Mastery Modelling has examined the mastery of geniuses, innovative people, innovative companies and innovative countries that you could use as benchmarks for team creativity and innovation. Geniuses such as Leonardo da Vinci have multiple perspectives of thinking, principles and competencies that you could emulate. Innovative people such as Steve Jobs have innovation principles and practices that you could benchmark against to help you accelerate your team creativity and innovation—such as passion to change something, a vision that drives the innovation journey, an attitude of using failure as an opportunity for success, and learning from the successes and mistakes of other people and organisations.

Innovative companies such as Google empower their intrapreneurs to research, innovate and engage with industries, universities and communities. Innovative countries such as Switzerland and Singapore have friendly innovation policies, procedures and infrastructure as well as the ability to develop brainpower and tap foreign talents to facilitate further growth. Singapore and Apple, as well as Lee Kuan Yew and Steve Jobs, are model examples of how to benchmark against others to be a world-class innovator. The next chapter looks at how you can immerse yourself intensively in team creativity and innovation.

INTENSIVE IMMERSION: EMPOWERED EXPLORATION

CHAPTER 3

Janssen, the pharmaceutical division of Johnson & Johnson, has an innovative program called Immersion, which started when the company found that a majority of employees working with emerging markets had never spent any time in those markets. The Immersion program enables Janssen teams from silo departments across regions to intensively gain in-country experience and explore diversity of thinking when finding solutions to global health problems. For one Immersion project, which aims to treat 80,000 Romanians with hepatitis C by 2020, the Janssen teams worked with the Romanian Ministry of Health and various other stakeholders. Janssen's Immersion program is a discovery-driven process that gives teams the freedom to explore ideas for projects that may yield long-term success.[63]

INTRODUCTION

The general concept of intensive immersion has been applied in various fields, such as learning a foreign language in its country of origin and observing a cultural group through ethnographic research. Likewise, my creativity catalyst of Intensive Immersion is about intensively immersing empowered staff to explore and innovate. Empowered exploration in an intensive immersion environment can be a reality in a company that has a clear mission and explicit values and vision to guide the team creativity and innovation journey.

This chapter explores innovative company missions, values, vision, innovation time, research and development investment, and learning from failures.

MISSION

A company's mission is its reason for existence. The mission guides the never-ending journey of a corporation and motivates employees to be purpose-driven. A mission is distinct from a corporate vision, which is an aspiration for what things will look like at certain periods of the mission journey. The vision could involve modelling against a benchmark, such as Lee Kuan Yew's vision of transforming Singapore from third- to first-world standards. Both the vision and mission of a corporation facilitate the flow of innovation.

While company founders live passionately by their mission, new employees may be neither highly aware of, nor motivated by, the corporate mission. Sometimes this is because companies or departments change their mission; for example, Pixar's development department changed its mission from generating ideas for movies to a mission of assembling incubation teams to help film directors refine their ideas and convince senior filmmakers about how great their films would be.[64] Induction sessions and constant reminders can help to immerse and empower employees to be mission-driven.

Innovative companies have clear mission statements. Amazon's mission is 'to be Earth's most customer-centric company, where customers can find and discover anything they might want to buy online, and endeavors to offer its customers the lowest possible prices'.[65]

Samsung's mission is to 'inspire the world with innovative technologies, products and designs that enrich people's lives and contribute to a socially responsible, sustainable future'.[66]

Tesla Motors' mission is 'to accelerate the advent of sustainable transport by bringing compelling mass market electric cars to market as soon as possible'.[67]

3M's mission is to 'improve every life through innovative giving in education, community and the environment'.[68]

Microsoft's 'mission is to be the world's #1 provider of innovative technology solutions that help realise the full potential of its diverse customers and partners around the world'.[69]

IBM's mission is 'dedication to every client's success; innovation that matters; and trust and personal responsibility in all relationships'.[70]

Starwood Hotels and Resorts' mission is 'to consistently exceed our guests' expectations in terms of the products and services we provide to our business and leisure travelers'.[71]

Salesforce.com's mission is to be a 'customer company'[72] while Dropbox's mission is to 'simplify life for people around the world'.[73]

Apple's mission is to bring 'the best personal computing experience to students, educators, creative professionals and consumers around the world through its hardware, software and Internet offerings'.[74] Apple's mission is best illustrated by CEO Tim Cook, who took over from Jobs:

> We want ideas coming from all of our 80,000 people, not five or three ... You want people to explore ... It's people who care enough to keep thinking about something

until they find the simplest way to do it ... It's caring enough to call the person who works over in this other area, because you think the two of you can do something fantastic that hasn't been thought of before. It's providing an environment where that feeds off each other and grows.[75]

The above examples indicate that what these companies have in common is being consumer-driven; their missions are expressed differently to align with the passion and competencies of the founders. You may wish to review your corporate mission statement to see whether it succinctly conveys the purpose and continuing journey of your organisation. Magazines such as *Entrepreneur* (www.entrepreneur.com) and *Inc* (www.inc.com) have published articles about how to write clear mission statements.

VALUES

Mission statements often have embedded in them corporate values, beliefs or principles. A 2012 IBM Global Survey of 1700 CEOs revealed that values empower employees and serve as innovation enablers.[76]

IBM uses corporate values to underpin its mission. While mission statements do not change as often as vision statements, IBM reviewed its hundred-year-old corporate values in 2003 under new CEO Sam Palmisano. He proposed to his 300 top managers four concepts: respect, customer, excellence and innovation; tested these concepts through focus groups and surveys across 1000 employees, who preferred the values of customer, excellence and innovation; and discussed the proposed values through the IBM intranet over a seventy-two-hour 'Values-Jam' online forum.

About 50,000 IBM employees followed the discussion and posted 10,000 comments, with three emerging themes of 'commitment to the customer, excellence through innovation and integrity that earns trust'. Through further analysis, Palmisano and his team refined the values which now appear on the company's website.[77]

Other innovative companies highlight their corporate values differently. General Electric says, 'Our team is mission-based: We build, move, power and cure the world ... we are a "We Company"'.[78]

Salesforce's 'vision to reinvent CRM in the cloud' has been made possible with values such as volunteering, where employees get six days off to spend on their pet volunteer project, and the company matches up to $5000 when employees donate to non-profit organisations.[79]

Canon's values centre on *kyosei*, which is about people working harmoniously and happily.[80] Canon's culture also revolves around the *San-ji* spirit, which is about the 'three selfs' of self-motivation, self-management and self-awareness.[81]

VISION

While a mission statement describes a company's reason for existence, a vision statement sets a direction for the future and intrinsically empowers employees to work in that direction.

Often a vision statement includes a time period; for example, Samsung's Vision 2020, which aims to 'inspire the world, create the future', with corporate values of change, excellence, integrity and co-prosperity.[82] BMW Group's 2020 vision is to be 'the world's leading provider of premium products and premium services for individual mobility'.[83]

Some vision statements do not include a milestone period, such as Tesla's vision to 'Create the most compelling car company of the 21st century by driving the world's transition to electric vehicles'[84] and Microsoft's vision 'To be led by a globally diverse workforce that consistently delivers outstanding business results, understands the various cultural demands of a global marketplace, is passionate about technology and the promise it holds to tap human potential, and thrives in a corporate culture where inclusive behaviors are valued'.[85]

Many corporate websites do not feature vision, mission and core values on one page, so it is refreshing to come across examples such as that of Coca-Cola Company, PepsiCo, Singapore's Economic Development Board and Ministry of Education, and Pixar.

Coca-Cola Company[86]

- Mission: 'To refresh the world; to inspire moments of optimism and happiness; to create value and make a difference'.
- Values: Leadership, collaboration, integrity, accountability, passion, diversity and quality.
- Vision: Its 2020 vision is 'to continue achieving sustainable, quality growth' covering people, portfolio, partners, planet, profit and productivity.

PepsiCo[87]

- Mission: 'The world's premier consumer products company focused on convenient foods and beverages'.

- Values: 'Sustained growth through empowered people acting responsibly and building trust.'
- Vision: 'Making PepsiCo a truly sustainable company'.

Singapore's Economic Development Board[88]

- Mission: 'We create for Singapore, sustainable economic growth with vibrant business and good job opportunities'.
- Values: Care, integrity, team, imagination, courage, excellence and nation.
- Vision: A global leader.

Singapore Ministry of Education[89]

- Mission: 'The mission of the Education Service is to mould the future of the nation, by moulding the people who will determine the future of the nation'.
- Values: Self-reliant with teamwork, individually competitive with social conscience.
- Vision: 'Thinking schools, learning nation'.

Pixar's employees are driven by its filmmaker-led mission, its values of collective creativity among talented people, the freedom of cross-department communication, the magical combination of technology and art, searching for ideas like an 'archaeological dig', taking risks and engaging with academic as well as industry communities, and by its vision of producing breakthrough computer-animated movies.[90]

Intensively immersing new employees in your company's mission, values and vision can help them fully understand your corporate purpose, culture and direction, hence empowering them in the innovation journey. You could intensively immerse new (as well as current) employees through induction, work planning and evaluation, 'compliance' education, professional development training programs, project work with senior staff, corporate retreats, and sharing of strategic goals, successes and failures.

ALLOWING TIME FOR INNOVATION

Since a corporation's mission, values and vision can intrinsically empower employees, time given to pursue a passion or favourite project can be an explicit form of self-motivation and self-management. Universities often give their academics twenty per cent or more of their week to pursue their research interests, but 3M is the benchmark in the area of granting passion time. This section discusses the passion time given to 3M employees and also explores how innovative companies such as Apple, Google, Amazon and Procter & Gamble have adapted passion time for employees to help accelerate team creativity and innovation.

3M

The Minnesota Mining and Manufacturing Company, now known as 3M, started in 1902 and has been known for innovative products such as waterproof sandpaper, masking tape and Scotchgard Fabric Protector.[91]

Since 1948, 3M has empowered employees to use company resources and fifteen per cent of their work time to freely pursue creative projects, allowing mistakes along the way. 3M calls this passion time 'Dream Day' or 'Time to Think', and it has led to innovative projects—including Post-it Notes. Senior scientist Dr Spencer Silver had developed an adjustable adhesive paper in 1968 but did not see its value until 1974 when his scientist colleague Art Fry was looking for a removable adhesive bookmark for his church hymnal. Now there are 4000 variants of the product, for indexing, filing, messaging, reminders and so on. Another product to come out of 3M's passion time is 3M Display Film, which reflects and shapes light plus enhances colour, hence brightening and colour-enhancing LCD displays as well as protecting mobile and tablet devices.[92]

3M also provides Genesis Grants of about US$30,000 to US$75,000 twice yearly to fund research for six to eight ideas that emerge from 'Time to Think' projects. In addition, 3M recognises its innovators through the Circle of Technical Excellence & Innovation and the prestigious Carlton Society, which has inducted 160 scientists.[93]

3M scientists network with each other at the yearly Technical Forum, which since 1951 has enabled peers to stay abreast of what colleagues are doing, to advise each other or to team up on projects. 3M's top twenty overachievers also get awarded four days with their partners at a corporate retreat.[94]

Apple

Steve Jobs had the vision to make computers simple household items and the aim of creating Apple Stores that would enrich consumer lives. Hence, Jobs hired people with passion rather than proficiency; for example, the project team on the Macintosh comprised artists, historians, musicians, poets and zoologists who were also top computer scientists, while the Apple Store model empowers employees to spend time to ensure customer satisfaction even if there is no sale outcome.[95]

Apple has always empowered its artists, designers, dreamers, engineers and scientists to think diversely, do their best and make a difference in the world.[96]

Besides a cohesive cross-disciplinary holistic vision, Jobs also empowered his staff to engage in transparent debate and creative conflict during idea formation, rather than passive aggressiveness behind the scenes, to ensure a high-performance innovation culture.[97]

Driven by Apple's 'Think Different' culture, employees have the flexibility and freedom to dress as they like and have their own office hours as long as they excel in their jobs.[98] Apple's creative employees in its restricted-access Industrial Design Group work with background music like employees at a small design firm and engage directly with top executives.[99]

During the reign of Steve Jobs, Apple teams focused intensively on top-down projects to create world-changing products. However, CEO Tim Cook seems to be giving more leeway to select employees with a blue-sky perk that enables them to work on a favourite engineering project for a few weeks.[100]

Google

Google believes in empowering its employees to meaningfully and passionately shape its working environment. Hence, it provides numerous channels for its employees to be immersed in innovation, such as Google Cafes and Google+ Conversations for casual discussions; weekly TGIF meetings for employees to ask Google leaders about any corporate issue; Google Moderator, a tool that that enables employees at meetings to vote on topics, questions and ideas; Google Universal Ticketing System to file and review issues; Googlegeist feedback on issues, resulting in the creation of volunteer teams to find solutions to challenges or problems; internal innovation reviews for presentations of ideas to top executives; regular surveys to identify the best managers (to be role models) and non-performing managers (to receive support and personal development); and twenty per cent of employees' time can be spent on personal projects.[101]

The twenty per cent time for personal projects was described in a 2004 founders' IPO letter signed by Google founders Larry Page and Sergey Brin:

> We encourage our employees, in addition to their regular projects, to spend 20% of their time working on what they think will most benefit Google. This empowers them to be more creative and innovative. Many of our significant advances have happened in this manner. For example, AdSense for content and Google News were both prototyped in '20% time.' Most risky projects fizzle, often teaching us something. Others succeed and become attractive businesses.[102]

There have been reports that have raised doubts about whether Google's twenty per cent time is actually practised. Former Google spokesperson Marissa Mayer, who joined Yahoo as CEO, said that the twenty per cent project time is not an alternative to, but is in addition to, one's regular job and that it's really 120 per cent time for those who wish to work on special projects.[103] According to Google HR boss Laszlo Bock, the twenty per cent idea still exists but only ten per cent of Googlers devote two to five per cent of their time on projects outside their regular job.[104]

Amazon

Jeff Bezos was with an investment group when he saw an opportunity to sell books online in 1995. He empowers his 'S Team' or senior executives to meet every Tuesday for four hours and twice yearly for two days to explore ideas and strategic issues. Bezos is prepared to wait for the seeds of ideas to turn into trees as long as they achieve his vision of universally uplifting customer-centricity. Facilitating this customer-centricity, Bezos' philosophy is to be afraid of customers rather than of competitors. New employees must work in fulfilment centres and participate in two days of customer service activity every two years.[105]

Bezos prefers to keep his project teams to five to seven people, small enough to feed with two pizzas. He also believes in doubling experiments to double inventiveness, and accepts failure as part of the process. Hence, Bezos recruits inventors, pioneers and explorers.[106]

Procter & Gamble Clay Street Project

A five-storey nineteenth-century brewery in Clay Street, Cincinnati, USA, is the creativity retreat centre for global Procter & Gamble multidisciplinary teams seeking ideas for business projects. It started in 2004 with ten employees in the baby-care business spending three months away from work. The Clay Street Project, as it is known, has since hosted about twenty sessions and 200 teams to create new product categories, deliver product innovations and revitalise brands.

With a core principle of unleashing human potential, the Clay Street Project operates on a tri-factor of innovation forces: work based on human insight, diverse purpose-driven teams and internal systems that nurture innovation. Facilitators help project participants see and think differently by drawing on brainstorming, metaphorical excursions, mythology, neuroscience, theatre, Zen Buddhism exercises and experiences of multidimensional teams from consumer research, design, finance, marketing and sales.

Projects could take a day to ten weeks depending on the objective; for example, imagining possibilities could take up to four days, building cohesive solution teams could take up to four weeks and big projects could be over eight to ten weeks.

The Clay Street Project has been described as a hybrid team approach, with immersion teams working in an innovation lab. In the hybrid team approach, talented people from an organisation work like 'ingenious guerrillas' or 'pop-up teams' on secret projects.[107]

Other immersion programs

Intensive thinking events have been practised and described in various ways. This section explores hackathons, skunk works, innovation labs and immersion programs.

Hackathons

A hackathon is not an effort to gain unauthorised access to a computer but an intensive, collaborative computer programming event lasting several days.[108] There can be internal hackathons for employees, corporate hackathons to involve outside developers and community hackathons to work with general programmers on any project.[109]

Hackathons can be staged to find solutions for various subjects and issues, such as autism, clean energy, education, grocery shopping, photo filters, text messaging services and water pollution. Hackathons often go through several stages: propose an idea; form a team with diverse disciplines; create a functional software or prototype; demo the product to a panel; and receive a gift, funding or start-up accelerator.

Companies such as AT&T, Facebook, LinkedIn, Microsoft, Nokia, Unilever and Foursquare have hosted hackathons. Foursquare, for example, staged a global hackathon simultaneously in New York, Paris, San Francisco and Tokyo and attracted 500 program developers.[110]

Professional networking company LinkedIn had a 'hackday' each month for employees to work on their passion projects. Realising that one day a month was limiting, several 'hackday masters' conceived the idea of a quarterly incubator where any employee could propose an idea, organise a team, pitch the project to senior executives and get three months to develop the project with a senior executive as advisor. Successful projects to come out of this include a 'go/book' meeting-room booking system through a user interface.[111]

Microsoft's version of the hackathon is the Garage, set up in Redmond, Washington, as a twenty-four-hour idea factory. Here, Microsoft inventors and tinkerers work on their passion projects, whether unrelated to work (such as a metal volcano) or relevant to work (such as the 'Forgotten Attachment Detector', 'Mouse without borders', 'Bing keyword distribution graph' and 'Bus Alarm').

A notable Garage case is 'CodeFlow', a software code reviewing process. The idea started over beers, progressed to a prototype with forty Garage members involved, caught the interest of a Microsoft veteran who championed for wider usage simplicity, attracted 40,000 Microsoft engineers to use the process, won a Microsoft Engineering Excellence Award and became a mainstream investment.

The Garage enables colleagues to be fully immersed in projects that they love to be involved in or find collaborators who have presenting and technical skills. More than 3000 Microsoft employees have participated in 10,000 projects since 2009. There are now eighteen chapters of the Garage worldwide, with workshops, hackathons, science fairs and monthly series of 'Stay Late' nights.[112]

Evolving from an internal-only idea factory, the Garage has expanded and made its side-project and leisure-productivity apps available to the public through its website, with the hope of seeking consumer feedback.[113]

Facebook started a Hackathon website in 2004 to enable its employees to explore ideas collaboratively in a fun environment.[114] At Facebook, hackathons take place every six weeks and run overnight, starting with Chinese takeout food and ending with a dawn pancake or doughnut breakfast. During the intensive all-night hackathons, engineers often work on dream prototypes, with outcomes such as Facebook Chat, the friend suggester and the type-ahead search feature. There is often no compensation for top ideas except free Facebook T-shirts.[115]

Leading up to each Facebook hackathon, an internal wiki is used by participants to brainstorm, promote their ideas and seek team members interested in unfamiliar technology or a project unconnected to their day job. In one hackathon, 500 Facebook employees together worked on apps for new internal tools and non-profit apps. A prototype forum follows each hackathon, in which the project developer has a week to refine the idea and then present it to the company in two minutes.

The Facebook hackathon group might include engineers, sales personnel and interns. Other employee groups at Facebook, such as business development, human resources and legal, also run hackathons to rethink their jobs or ideas. Pedram Keyani, a hackathon champion at Facebook, has suggested that hackathons could be transformed into 'think week' rather than overnight sessions, with the free time used for employees to explore amazing ideas.[116]

Facebook has extended all-night hackathons as competitions to campuses of Harvard, University of Michigan, and University of California, Los Angeles, among others. Winners from each college fly to Facebook HQ to competitively present final prototypes.[117]

There are also public hackathon competitions, such as the AngelHack Global Hackathon Competition. AngelHack is a developer relations agency and has staged the global competition since 2011. Its sponsors include Amazon, Facebook, Google, Intel and PayPal.[118] PayPal also finds hackathon competitions good sources for recruiting tech talent.[119]

Skunk works and labs

A skunk work is a small, independent experimental laboratory. The term came from a secret project at Lockheed Aircraft Corporation in 1943 whose goal was to build a jet fighter, which the project team managed in 143 days. The project engineers worked in a rented circus tent next to an odour-emitting manufacturing plant. One engineer referred to the secret space as 'Skonk Works', which later became 'Skunk Works'.

Lockheed's team leader Kelly Johnson proposed rules and practices for skunk works operations, such as complete control by the project manager, limiting participation to a small group of people, funding for the project, a monthly cost review, and rewarding good performance.[120]

IBM has used skunk works to develop risky start-ups such as its billion-dollar wireless mobile computing venture, and more than twenty emerging business opportunities.[121] At an Intel skunk works in Ireland, the team spent sixty days to produce a fully working low-cost chipset and board.[122] NASA's skunk works team has designed a smaller, newer satellite CubeSat.[123]

Apple had a skunk works team working on the highly secretive iPhone project, code named Purple. Only a select few staff worked on the Purple project, and the access approval process included staff signing legal documents.[124]

However, one innovation commentator associates skunk works with twentieth-century, not twenty-first century, innovation. The former is characterised by disruption (for example, the IBM personal computer), process innovation to incrementally improve product materials or introduce line extensions, and innovation by exception that operates like a start-up with its own sales channel. According to the commentator, the twenty-first century requires innovation by design and continuous innovation to improve existing products while inventing new ones.[125]

Hence, there is a variation of skunk works: corporate labs where engineers and thinkers are empowered to develop projects. A *Business Insider* article highlighted the existence of some 'mysterious corporate labs' across various vehicle, technology and retail sectors.[126]

Corporate labs in the vehicle sector include Raytheon's Bike Shop, modelled after the Wright brothers' bicycle shop, where the defence contractor works on rapid innovations; Ford's Special Vehicle Team and Silicon Valley Lab, which work on performance vehicles and user experience; and Audi's Quattro GmbH, which designed and developed the Audi R8 sports car.

Corporate labs in the technology sector include HP Labs, where researchers work with universities to improve current products as well as look into the future; Xerox PARC, with research in futuristic communications and flexible electronics; IBM's Thomas J. Watson Research Center, which built the PC in a year and has created more patents than other American companies; and Samsung Advanced Institute of Technology, with projects on next-generation digital technologies.

Corporate labs in the retail sector include Nike's Innovation Kitchen and Sports Research Lab, with projects on weaving and clothing technologies; Walmart Labs, with projects on understanding consumers better, e-commerce and speedy delivery; Staples Velocity Lab, with blue-sky thinking and the aim to be an innovative online retailer; and Nordstrom Innovation Lab, with a goal of achieving high impact rapidly through its Lean Startup Thinking, even if it only expects a twenty per cent success rate for start-ups.

Other retailers with innovation labs include Zappos, an online clothing and shoe store, which launched 'Ask Zappos', where Zappos would find a consumer product based on a photo sent by email, Instagram or text message; Lowe's Home Improvement, which has launched Holoroom to create home improvement virtual replicas and robots to help customers locate products; Westfield Group, which enables brands to lease incubation space and test tech-driven ideas for digital and store shopping; and Target, which has projects on digital activations, connected devices, robotics and virtual reality.[127]

Commonwealth Bank in Sydney has an Innovation Lab that serves as an idea incubator and accelerator on innovative services and solutions in collaboration with start-ups and customers. Commonwealth Bank also has an Unleashing Innovation program, where employees present their ideas to senior executives with the hope of having the ideas accepted for incubation in the Innovation Lab.[128] Commonwealth Bank has consistently been a top innovative Australian company in the BRW most innovative companies ranking—number two in 2012 and 2013.[129]

Further examples

There are some other interesting examples of immersion programs or centres. Starwood Hotels & Resorts has its Design Lab and Brand Immersion Center in its global headquarters in Stamford, Connecticut. Its 'idea lab' enables customers, developers, owners and partners across Starwood brands (Aloft, Four Points, Element, Le Méridien, Sheraton, Westin) to immerse themselves in brand programming, event activation, food initiatives, guest-facing technology and model guest rooms.[130]

VMware, a software company, has a Take 3 (T3) program that empowers technical employees to take up to three months to move from their usual role to another team working on research, service learning or sales.[131]

If you wish to immerse your employees in innovation labs before investing in costly set-ups, you may wish to consider the 'Pop Up Innovation Lab' concept. A company, 650 Labs, specialises in hosting immersion residency of two to eight weeks in Silicon Valley, the benchmark for innovators. During the residency, your team would be involved in Silicon Valley culture, idea generation, project creation and business relationship building with investment bankers, serial entrepreneurs, start-up companies and venture capitalists.[132]

An alternative idea is the Silicon Valley Immersion Program offered by the University of San Francisco School of Management, which runs over a week or two with groups of fifteen to twenty participants. The immersion program includes workshops, projects, company visits, coaching sessions and networking events. So far, more than 1500 participants from fifteen countries have attended the program, which covers innovation in health care, technology, tourism and wine. Participants have included tertiary institutions, consulting firms, investment network companies, government agencies, incubators and accelerators.[133]

Ultimately, you could model your organisation's innovation or passion time based on the best practices of one or several innovative companies highlighted in this section: 3M's fifteen per cent of work time; Apple's project time of a few weeks; Google's twenty per cent time for personal projects; Amazon's weekly and twice-yearly exploration time for senior executives; Procter & Gamble's Clay Street Project time from four days to ten weeks; Salesforce.com allowing employees six days to work on passion volunteer projects; LinkedIn's project development time of three months; VMware's allowance of three months for inter-department immersion; overnight, weekly or monthly hackathons; secret-location skunk works; multipurpose innovation labs; and internal or external immersion programs. Research the one that best suits your purposes.

FUNDING INTENSIVE IMMERSION

There is an obvious need to fund research and development (R&D) projects that take place in hackathons, skunk works, innovation labs and immersion centres.

Booz & Company, now known as Strategy&, has been analysing R&D spending of innovative companies since 2005 and reported that the biggest R&D spenders are in auto, computing, electronics and health care. Companies in the Global Innovation 1000 Survey (2014) spent US$647 billion on R&D in 2014, with the top ten being Volkswagen, Samsung, Intel, Microsoft, Roche, Novartis, Toyota, Johnson & Johnson, Google and Merck & Co. The top twenty, which included Amazon and IBM, spent an average of eight per cent of sales on R&D. The following companies had the highest R&D spend as a percentage of sales: Intel (20.1 per cent), Roche (19.8 per cent), Novartis (17 per cent), Merck & Co. (17 per cent) and GlaxoSmithKline (14.8 per cent).

The survey also revealed that while thirty-two per cent of companies are 'much better' innovators and forty-four per cent are 'better' innovators, there was no equation between R&D spending and return on investment except for companies that were able to capture consumer insights and gain operating income three times over peers.[134]

Steve Jobs aptly commented in 1998: 'Innovation has nothing to do with how many R&D dollars you have. When Apple came up with the Mac, IBM was spending at least a hundred times more on R&D. It's not about money. It's about the people you have, how you're led, and how much you get it.'[135]

The Strategy& survey revealed that successful innovators sync innovation portfolios with consumer needs; develop and retain tech-knowledgeable people; align business and innovation leaders to a corporate mission, values and vision; and adopt one of three innovation models—need seekers, who involve customers with the goal of being the first to introduce new products, processes or services; market readers, who cautiously monitor the market before implementing value-added changes; or technology drivers, who leverage their technological competencies, R&D investment and insights on unexpressed consumer needs to launch incremental change as well as breakthrough innovation. Apple, Procter & Gamble and Tesla Motors are need seekers; Samsung and Caterpillar are market readers; and Google and Siemens are technology drivers. Which innovation model does your organisation fall under and which innovative company do you aspire to benchmark against?

Hence, R&D investments enable innovation scientists, innovation leaders, innovation champions and innovation project leaders to strive for innovation excellence.

LEARNING FROM FAILURES

It is worth noting that learning from failures is part of the empowered and intensive innovation journey. Edison, Jobs, Google, Amazon and 3M used failures as opportunities for success. As intrapreneurs and entrepreneurs explore uncharted territories and experiment with ideas, mistakes are bound to happen.

Entrepreneur Richard Branson has written about embracing failure.[136] A study of 2.8 million small retailers in Texas over a twenty-two-year period concluded that entrepreneurs are 'made' through practice, practice and practice.[137] A researcher at Babson College in the USA revealed that entrepreneurs need to experiment, iterate and learn from multiple experiences.[138] UK research of 576 entrepreneurs surmised differently that serial or sequential entrepreneurs who fail are more likely to be over-optimistic and fail again, while portfolio entrepreneurs who run businesses simultaneously are more likely to learn from failure.[139]

SUMMARY

This chapter has focused on empowering employees to immerse themselves intensively in the innovation journey through corporate mission, values, vision, innovation time, research and development investment, and learning from failures. Corporate values as part of a company's mission or purpose do empower employees, especially when there is a bigger vision to influence a global community. Passion time for empowered employees to innovate has been practised differently, such as 3M's fifteen per cent of time for 'Time to Think', VMware's three-month inter-department immersion, hackathons, skunk works, innovation labs and immersion programs. While investments in research and development are needed to fund innovation activities and centres, it is not how much you spend but how you use it and how you empower passionate employees to learn from failures and accelerate team creativity and innovation. It is also how you leverage internal and external resources, the topic for the next chapter.

CHAPTER 4
GROUP GERMINATION: COLLECTIVE GROWTH

The ancient Olympic Games started in 776 BCE, were suspended in 392 ACE and resumed in 1896. The modern Olympic Games have grown to be the world's greatest sporting event with host cities including Rio de Janeiro, London, Sydney and Beijing, plus worldwide partners such as Atos, Bridgestone, Coca-Cola, Dow, GE, McDonald's, Omega, Panasonic, Procter & Gamble, Samsung and Visa. Each Olympics event is successful also because of the vast numbers of volunteers covering the production of innovative ceremonies, customer services, health services, operational support, press and communication, protocol and languages, technology and transport as well as sports support during training, warm-up sessions and competitions.[140]

INTRODUCTION

The creativity catalyst of Group Germination sees diverse internal and external groups facilitating team creativity and innovation and, thus, corporate growth. This concept of Group Germination aligns with previous research on the need for managing various sources of innovation;[141] an industry survey where eighty-eight per cent of respondents affirmed that partnerships drive innovation;[142] as well as the innovation practices of 'need seekers' and 'market readers', mentioned in the previous chapter, who seek input from consumers, suppliers, other industries and competitors. This chapter explores different forms of Group Germination; namely competitive collaboration, cluster collaboration, outsourcing, open innovation, crowdsourcing, crowdfunding, and corporate incubators and accelerators.

COMPETITIVE COLLABORATION

Competitors can collaborate across various areas, such as information sharing, research and development, innovation, purchasing, production, market expansion, marketing, distribution and sales.[143]

There have been numerous examples of competitive collaboration throughout the years but following are some examples of collaboration for innovation and social good between competitors and across industry categories.

Ford and General Motors have engineering teams collaborating on truck speed automatic transmissions.[144] Airbus, Boeing and Embraer signed a memorandum of understanding to collaborate on sustainable new jet-fuel sources, including lobbying various stakeholders.[145]

Coca-Cola, PepsiCo and the Dr Pepper Snapple Group collaborated to reduce sugary drink calories by twenty per cent by 2025 through no-calorie or low-calorie drinks, smaller packaging plus educational campaigns, in an effort to help fight associated issues such as obesity, diabetes and heart disease.[146] And Coca-Cola, PepsiCo, Nestlé, Unilever and Walmart have collaborated to combat waste in Chile through a new recycling network.[147]

PepsiCo, Coca-Cola, Unilever and Procter & Gamble formed a Refrigerants Naturally partnership to promote refrigerants free of fluorinated gases that damage the ozone layer.[148] The Bioplastic Feedstock Alliance was formed by Nestlé, Procter & Gamble, Unilever, Heinz, Danone, Coca-Cola, Nike, Ford and the World Worldlife Fund to guide the making of plastics from agricultural materials and to promote bioplastics sustainability.[149]

The Strauss Group, whose core business is coffee, collaborates with Danone on know-how exchange, manufacturing and marketing of Danone products in Israel; with PepsiCo in the dips and spreads category for markets in North America, Australia and Mexico; and with Richard Branson's Virgin Group to market Virgin Pure products.[150]

Unilever, Coca-Cola, Marks & Spencer, BT Group and Carlsberg formed a non-profit platform, Collectively.org, to accelerate sustainable living. The Collectively.org website features stories of inspiration and change such as 3D-printed solar-powered architecture, printing your own house and actor Emma Watson lobbying for gender equality.[151]

Which of your competitors could you collaborate with to benefit the industry and community? One caution about competitive collaboration is not to breach any country's law. The European Commission fined Procter & Gamble and Unilever £280 million in 2011 for 'breaching competition law in the laundry detergent market in eight countries'. The two companies had agreed on simultaneous launch marketing and pricing to switch consumers from big-box laundry detergents to cold-water concentrated detergent with the goal of reducing the impact on the environment.[152]

CLUSTER COLLABORATION

Another form of Group Germination is industry cluster collaboration, where similar industries and like-minded corporations in a region, such as Hollywood or Silicon Valley, collaborate for competitive advantage and industry growth. This section introduces the cluster concept of scholars Michael Porter and Stuart Rosenfeld, as well as Australian examples of industry clusters.

Porter

In 1998, Michael Porter defined clusters thus:

> Clusters are geographic concentrations of interconnected companies and institutions in a particular field. Clusters encompass an array of linked industries and other entities important to competition. They include, for example, suppliers of specialized inputs such as components, machinery, and services, and providers of specialized infrastructure.[153]

Porter elaborated that cluster collaboration is competitive cooperation that enhances productivity, innovation and business expansion. It allows companies better access to employees, suppliers, specialised information, government and public institutions, cost comparisons, and complementary services such as transportation, shopping outlets, restaurants and accommodation. Companies will have a better picture of customer needs, trends, technology and availability of various resources. These inter-related companies can experiment creatively and economically. Companies can quickly identify opportunities in products or services and access readily available human or financial assets.

Cluster formation has to address four issues. First, location. Locations with low costs in wages, utility and taxes may not be the best solution if they lack efficient infrastructure for productivity, innovation and growth. Second, engage locally. There must be ongoing engagement with local human assets, suppliers and government as well as educational and research institutions. Third, upgrade the cluster. The cluster needs constant development, such as addressing manufacturing gaps, labour force training and youth scholarships. Fourth, work collectively. The cluster could function as a trade association, with collective action on productivity and innovation, idea exchange, information collection, trade events, research facilities, training programs, marketing, and effectively working with the government to promote cluster growth.

Porter illustrated his cluster concept with examples of the California wine, Italian leather, Boston Life Sciences and Australian tourism clusters.

The Californian wine cluster is a collaboration of independent wine-grape growers; commercial wineries; suppliers of grape stock, fertilisers, herbicides, pesticides, irrigation technology, harvesting equipment, barrels, bottles, corks, labels and communication services; and academic and research institutions.

The collaborative Italian leather fashion cluster includes tanneries, footwear machinery, leather-working machinery, plastic-working equipment, woodworking equipment, injection-moulding machinery, design service and producers of different types of footwear, belts, clothing, handbags and gloves.

The interconnected companies and associated institutions of Boston Life Sciences include suppliers of health and beauty products, surgical instruments, medical equipment, dental instruments, ophthalmic goods and diagnostic substances: specialised business services, risk capital networks, research service providers, teaching and specialised hospitals, research organisations and educational institutions.

The Cairns tourism cluster in Queensland includes tour operators, travel agents, restaurants, hotels, airlines, cruise ships, theme parks, casinos, sports, local retail and health services, souvenirs and duty free shops, banks and foreign exchange, local transportation, food suppliers, property services, public relations and market research services, government agencies, educational institutions and industry groups such as the Queensland Tourism Industry Council.[154]

Rosenfeld

Another cluster expert, Stuart Rosenfeld, distinguished clusters from membership-based associations and networks by focusing on the geographical nature of clusters:[155] 'Clusters are simply geographic concentrations of interrelated companies and institutions of sufficient scale to generate external economies.'

Rosenfeld also further distinguished networks as collaborative, associations as cooperative, and clusters as cooperative, *plus* competitive ecosystems that access labour markets, suppliers and services in a location to leverage external economies for cluster benefits—such as 'Socks City' in Datang, China, which has a population of 200,000 but produces over a billion pairs of socks each year.[156] According to Rosenfeld, entrepreneurial businesses or 'clusterpreneurs' often form clusters but government investments accelerate growth and cluster competitiveness.

Australian examples

You may find the following Australian cluster examples useful. The Tasmanian light shipbuilding cluster produces fast ferries for the world market.[157] Figure 4.1 illustrates the diverse disciplines within the light shipbuilding cluster.

FIGURE 4.1 The Tasmanian light shipbuilding cluster

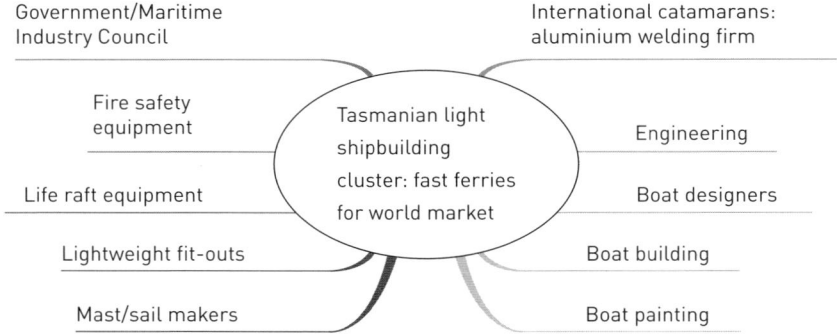

The Savannah Way cluster brings together tourism services to enhance visitor experiences along the adventure drive between Broome in Western Australia, Darwin in the Northern Territory and Cairns in Queensland. Savannah Way Limited, a non-profit company, works with communities, tourism and service businesses, tourism organisations and government agencies. Work includes research, training, tourism promotion, brochure and merchandise distribution, and road signage.[158] Figure 4.2 shows the interconnected businesses in the Savannah Way cluster.

FIGURE 4.2 The Savannah Way cluster

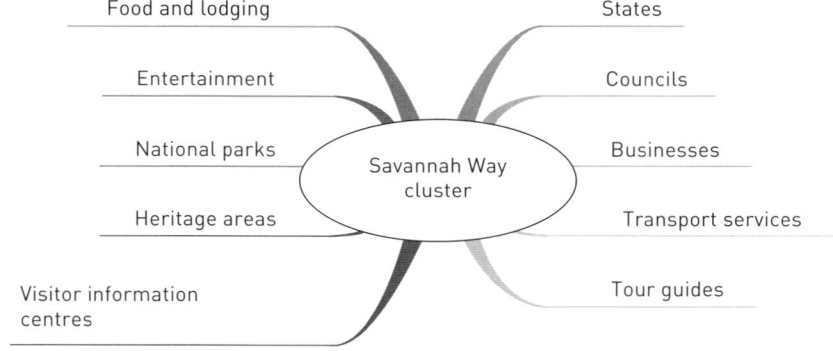

Based on the industry cluster collaboration concepts presented—Porter's, Rosenfeld's and these two Australian examples—do you see a way that your company could take the initiative to form or upgrade your industry cluster in a specific location with various stakeholders to achieve productivity, innovation and business expansion? You can learn more about clusters through the Harvard Business School's Institute for Strategy & Competitiveness (www.isc.hbs.edu/competitiveness-economic-development/frameworks-and-key-concepts/Pages/clusters.aspx).

OUTSOURCING

Outsourcing is about contractually obtaining goods or services from an external supplier.[159] The term outsourcing is used in different ways, such as selective outsourcing, excessive outsourcing, wholesale or total outsourcing, and internal outsourcing to different sites of a company.[160] There is also 'reshoring', where companies move their offshore manufacturing back to their homeland.[161]

There is outsourcing offshore, offshoring business services overseas to save on costs; for example, many Queensland businesses outsource services such as bookkeeping, graphic design and IT functions to the Philippines.[162] Other Australian enterprises outsource engineering and technical design, game development, mobile app development, human resources, payroll, recruiting, blog writing and translation services.[163]

Well-known companies provide strategic outsourcing services, such as IBM offering improved IT services at reduced costs through its global reach and technology expertise.[164] This is not surprising, as the IT industry pioneered outsourcing in the 1980s.[165]

Some companies outsource research and development but the Centre for European Economic Research revealed that this could affect the managing of the innovation process, despite cost saving from outsourcing, unless companies set up research and development centres in key consumer markets, such as Eastman Chemical with its research centres in China, England, Germany, Netherlands and Singapore.[166]

A survey of 250 executives on business process outsourcing highlighted eight strategic practices between partners that are critical:[167]

1. An end-to-end approach, which manages holistic inter-related processes in both the client and supplier organisations.
2. Collaborative business process outsourcing governance, where senior leaders take time to understand the objectives and strategies of both parties, resolve conflicts together and adapt to changing conditions.
3. Prioritising change management, even when there is resistance to change.
4. Value more than cost, where service is more important than cost reduction.

5   Focus on business outcomes, with financial incentives and penalties to drive specific performance indicators.
6   Domain expertise and analytics, where industry and process knowledge could be used to improve business outcomes.
7   Transformation of the retained organisation, especially in organisational structures, operating models, skill enhancement and interaction between client and outsourced employees.
8   Technology as a business enabler, with differentiated technology used to improve the partnership.

If you wish to know more about outsourcing, the International Association of Outsourcing Professionals could be a good source for information. It has 120,000 members and affiliates worldwide, thirty geographical chapters and thirteen topical or industry chapters covering cloud computing, financial services, legal, customer, call centre, human capital, tools and technology innovation, data security and privacy, governance, sales and marketing, healthcare industry, domestic sourcing and transboundary sourcing.[168]

OPEN INNOVATION

Professor Henry Chesbrough introduced the term 'open innovation' in his book *Open Innovation: The new imperative for creating and profiting from technology* (2003). Open innovation is a two-way process in which companies use external resources and allow other companies to access unused internal resources.

Chesbrough distinguished between 'outside-in' and 'inside-out' open innovation.[169] The outside-in model, widely researched and practised, means that companies open their innovation processes to invite external contributions. The inside-out model, less adopted in research and practice, sees companies offering their under-utilised or unused ideas to external parties.

The traditional, closed vertical innovation model is internally driven and usually consists of research and development, product development and sales distribution. The open innovation model leverages both internal and external ideas, expertise, resources and intermediaries to accelerate innovation and market expansion of innovative outputs.[170] For example, Philips Research optimises both outside-in and inside-out models of open innovation, drawing on inputs of individuals, companies and entrepreneurial start-ups to access new technologies and insights as well as making its skills and resources available to outside parties through contract research.[171]

Chesbrough cited some examples of open innovation in practice: Apple leverages external innovation through developers, partners, suppliers and users because the company spends only two per cent of sales on research and development; Facebook started after Friendster and MySpace but performs better by sharing its interface with gaming companies and enhancing customer experience; and companies such as Amazon, IBM, Zara and Xerox are now thought of as open innovation services and not simply as product companies.[172]

Some of the leading innovative companies that operate under the outside-in model are General Electric, Samsung, Johnson & Johnson, Unilever and Procter & Gamble.

General Electric
General Electric has an Open Innovation Manifesto: 'We believe openness leads to inventiveness and usefulness. We also believe that it's impossible for any organization to have all the best ideas, and we strive to collaborate with experts and entrepreneurs everywhere who share our passion to solve some of the world's most pressing issues'.[173]

Samsung
Samsung is associated with cooperation between industry and academia, participation in global consortiums, synergy with equipment and materials vendors and operation of overseas research centres.[174]

Johnson & Johnson
On Johnson & Johnson's website under the 'Team' tab, the company says: 'We employ experts around the globe. Because a great idea can come from anywhere'. The company seeks ideas for pharmaceuticals, medical devices and diagnostics, consumer, cross-sector platforms and other practice areas.[175] Johnson & Johnson has an 'idea portal' for people with a patent filing to upload ideas.[176] People who submit ideas need to indicate whether they are seeking distribution of commercial product, equity investment, incubator access, a licence, mergers and acquisition, new co-creation, research and development collaboration, or sponsored research.

Unilever
Unilever's open innovation is associated with its vision: 'We have a vision of a better future for our world and our business—and we want partners to share it'.[177] The company believes that 'the world is full of brilliant people, with brilliant ideas—and we are constantly looking for new ways to work with potential partners'.

Interested Unilever collaborators are directed to a third-party-website submission portal (https://oiportal.yet2.com), an open innovation service provider who screens submissions before submitting them to Unilever. Potential collaborators provide contact information, state whether they are representing themselves or a business, agree to legal terms, provide a solution overview with title, description, key benefits and competitive technological differentiation, and highlight whether they desire a licence, sale or other outcome. There is no reward for a technical submission but, if successful, there could be a mutually agreed contract for licence, patent acquisition, technology acquisition or joint venture.

Procter & Gamble

Procter & Gamble's Connect + Develop website describes open innovation as co-creation and crowdsourcing and highlights the fact that its open innovation strategy has resulted in more than 2000 agreements with innovation partners globally. Procter & Gamble (P&G) invites partners to submit ideas for key business areas through its innovation submission process.[178]

A *Harvard Business Review* article highlighted P&G's innovation success across three commercial areas, its innovation model and its global collaboration success.[179]

Commercial areas

Since P&G's vision is to have fifty per cent of innovations from outside the corporation, it sources ideas under three areas:

1. Consumer needs: Each P&G business generates a top ten list of consumer needs that would drive brand growth. The consumer needs then become science problems and technology briefs for P&G's global network.
2. Adjacencies: P&G identifies concepts or products adjacent to existing brands; for example, Crest toothpaste has expanded to include dental floss, a power toothbrush and whitening strips.
3. Technology game boards: This is like a chess game in which questions are asked about technologies that can be strengthened, acquired, sold, licensed or further co-developed.

Innovation model

P&G believes that there are 200 equally good engineers and scientists externally for each of its 7500 researchers and support staff, making a potential pool of 1.5 million talents for the company to tap into. Hence, P&G launched its

Connect + Develop innovation model a decade ago to collaborate with a variety of people and organisations, shown in Figure 4.3.

FIGURE 4.3 P&G's open innovation model of leveraging its networks

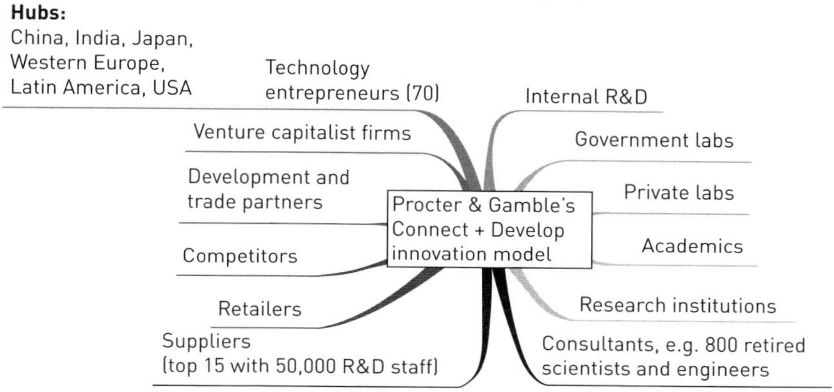

Hubs:
China, India, Japan, Western Europe, Latin America, USA

Spokes around Procter & Gamble's Connect + Develop innovation model:
- Technology entrepreneurs (70)
- Internal R&D
- Venture capitalist firms
- Government labs
- Development and trade partners
- Private labs
- Competitors
- Academics
- Retailers
- Research institutions
- Suppliers (top 15 with 50,000 R&D staff)
- Consultants, e.g. 800 retired scientists and engineers

Collaboration success

One global P&G innovation collaboration is the Mr Clean Magic Eraser household cleaning product. In 2001 a technology entrepreneur in Osaka, Japan, came across a popular household stain-removing sponge branded as Cleenpro in a market and sent product samples to P&G Cincinnati for evaluation. P&G researchers were enthusiastic about the product. P&G found out that German chemical company BASF was the manufacturer of the melanin resin foam called Basotect, an insulation and soundproofing product for automotive and construction usage but marketed by a Tokyo-based consumer goods company as a household cleaning sponge. P&G bought Basotect from BASF and launched it as Mr Clean Magic Eraser in 2003 in Japan and later in Europe. BASF and P&G then co-created Magic Eraser Duo and Magic Eraser Wheel & Tire for the US market in 2004.

P&G's Pringles brand is also a story about cross-industry collaboration. A P&G team brainstormed in 2002 about how to make its Pringles potato crisp more fun and how it could stand out from its competitors. One great idea they had was to print an image from pop culture on each crisp. The concern was how to print edible dyes of consistently sharp colours onto the crisps. The team circulated a technology brief to its networks and found an Italian bakery whose owner-cum-professor had created equipment for printing images onto cakes and cookies.

The first collaboration was to adapt the bakery equipment for Pringles Prints. The second collaboration was in 2004 with Hasbro, a leader in leisure entertainment products: Pringles Prints featured 2400 fun trivia questions and answers from Hasbro's Trivial Pursuit Junior game.[180] In 2012 P&G sold Pringles to Kellogg's for $2.7 billion.[181]

If your organisation has not implemented 'open innovation' before, consider the outside-in or inside-out option and align it with your corporate mission, values and vision. Are there lessons you could adapt from how Johnson & Johnson, Unilever and P&G seek ideas from potential partners and global networks?

Academic–industry partnerships

A common theme in open innovation is partnerships with academia and industry. Some examples of success in this area come from Apple, Procter & Gamble, IBM, Google and the Australian Government.

Apple

The Apple Distinguished Educators program is a global community that recognises education leaders for their innovative use of Apple technology. There are more than 2000 ADEs globally, and an ADE Online Community that is accessible to members only.[182]

Procter & Gamble

P&G has twenty research projects with the University of Leeds. Its P&G Simulation Centre on the Leeds campus recruits final-year PhD students for twenty hours a week over six months.[183] P&G has also forged academic partnerships with the University of Cincinnati, the state universities of Michigan and Ohio, Durham University in the UK, and Indiana University, where researchers developed Crest toothpaste. P&G also collaborates with Fraunhofer, the largest application-oriented research company in Europe, and the Council of Scientific & Industrial Research in India.[184]

IBM

IBM has an Open Research Program as well as several academic awards. The IBM PhD Fellowship Awards Program honours exemplary doctoral students in the fields of computer science and engineering, electrical and mechanical engineering, physical sciences, mathematical sciences, and public sector and business sciences. The IBM Faculty Awards allows an IBM employee to nominate an outstanding professor in a PhD or MBA program where research or curriculum innovation align with IBM's strategy. The successful recipient could get up to US$40,000 a year.

The IBM Shared University Research equipment award program is for corporate research technology projects that benefit universities, IBM, the community and the world. The IBM Students for a Smarter Planet Award enables teams to use technology on study-related projects that also benefit communities.[185]

Google
Google has several academic and external research support programs. The Google Faculty Research Awards fund technical research in computer science, engineering and related fields. The Google Focused Research Awards fund two or three years of research in specific areas, including artificial intelligence, algorithms and mathematical optimisation, economics and market algorithms, cloud computing, energy efficiency in computing, social computing, culturomics and software-hardware systems infrastructure. The Visiting Faculty Program invites Google-sponsored top academics to work with research and engineering teams, explore projects and experience Google culture.[186] Google also has a Director of Education and University Relations and publishes hundreds of research papers annually. See more details at http://research.google.com/index.html

Australian Government
The Australian Government's business.gov.au website also encourages businesses to collaborate with different industries and with local or international researchers. The website highlights benefits from industry-research partnerships such as access to networks, skilled researchers, research funding schemes and technology. The website shows the support available to facilitate innovation, such as Connecting Australian–European Science and Innovation Excellence; the Research & Development Tax Incentive; Small and Medium Enterprise Engagement Centre; National Research Flagships; Linkage Projects; Industrial Transformation Research Program; and National Measurement Institute.[187]

Does your organisation engage with academia and industries through research projects, academic awards and visiting faculty programs? Such collective partnerships could enhance your personnel resources and know-how for faster innovation growth.

Supplier collaboration
According to AT Kearney, a global management consultancy corporation, suppliers can provide expertise that is unavailable internally, contribute ideas, increase product or service differentiation, reduce development costs, reduce the time-to-market launch, facilitate price premium and improve profit. The best innovators have a structured supplier collaboration process.[188]

A report by the Boston Consulting Group revealed that seventy-seven per cent of procurement executives look for cost savings from suppliers, forty-six per cent look for innovation, thirty-four per cent for higher quality and thirty-three per cent for increased efficiency.

Some examples in the report included Chrysler, which has a program called Supplier Cost Reduction Effort (SCORE) that has saved the company billions of dollars since it started in 1989. In that year, Chrysler was facing a financial crisis and asked its twenty-five biggest suppliers for help to reduce costs. Two other examples are the collaboration between Boeing and its aerospace parts supplier Nordam over eighteen months to develop a window frame for the 787 Dreamliner; and Toyota's sharing of long-term plans to enable suppliers to improve designs, systems and quality.[189]

Some companies also have supplier innovation awards. BMW's program recognises outstanding suppliers for their innovation achievements. Its 2014 winners included Bridgestone Corporation for efficient driving dynamics; Corning Incorporated for its lightweight glass partition; and Pirelli for its vulcanisation technology to create quality tyres.[190] Johnson & Johnson's Supplier Enabled Innovation Awards recognises suppliers for best product, best process and best business model.[191] The National Australia Bank (NAB) has delivered supplier awards since 2010 to recognise suppliers who have demonstrated performance and value in innovation, product or service excellence, and environmental sustainability.[192]

Are you sufficiently leveraging your supplier expertise and ideas through a structured supplier collaboration process? Perhaps you could begin by following the example of supermarket chain Tesco, which recently launched an online supplier network to provide a forum for its 5000 global members to share ideas and discuss issues such as innovation and food waste.[193]

CROWDSOURCING

While Procter & Gamble explicitly equates crowdsourcing with open innovation, different authors and practitioners have other perspectives. One source mentioned that crowdsourcing started in the eighteenth and nineteenth centuries: the British government sought public ideas on computing longitude in 1714; King Louis IV of France sought ideas for making sea salt alkali; and the Oxford English Dictionary catalogued words in 1884 with the help of its readers.[194] This section examines modern crowdsourcing concepts of lead users and crowd wisdom, and the eYeka crowdsourcing provider.

Lead users

In 1986, Eric von Hippel from the Massachusetts Institute of Technology wrote about using leading-edge innovators who are trend spotters as lead users for 'need-forecasting' and high-technology product development.[195] His concept:

> Lead users face needs that will be general in a market place—but face them months or years before the bulk of that marketplace encounters them, and lead users are positioned to benefit significantly by obtaining a solution to those needs.

An example of this approach comes from 3M, which was in need of a breakthrough product for its expensive surgical drapes—adhesive plastic films that protect a surgical patient's incision area from infection.[196] After field trips to hospitals in different countries, the team decided to broaden its search for cheap and effective solutions that prevent the start or spread of infections. The team found leading-edge lead users in surprising places: vets who had to keep costs down while keeping infection rates low and Hollywood makeup artists who were experts at applying non-irritating and easy-to-remove materials to the skin.

Lead users took part in a workshop to find an infection control that was revolutionary and low cost. Among the concepts generated were a line of 'skin doctor' handheld devices that could apply anti-microbial substances and suck up blood or liquids during an operation; an 'armour' line to coat anti-microbial protection on catheters and tubes, which would open up a new $2 billion market catering to the control of blood-borne, respiratory and urinary tract infections; and pre-surgery treatment of patients at high-infection risk from diabetes or malnutrition.

3M set up a discovery centre to diffuse the new infection-control strategy and has since implemented the lead-user method in various product divisions to achieve breakthrough thinking.

Crowd wisdom

Modern-day authors started writing about crowdsourcing from the early 2000s. In his book, *The Wisdom of Crowds* (2004), James Surowiecki highlights the 'collective intelligence' of crowds during cognition, coordination and collaboration. 'Wise crowds' have diverse opinions, are independent and decentralised.[197]

In 2006, journalist Jeff Howe wrote about the 'rise of crowdsourcing', a process in which companies use the internet to leverage the 'spare processing power of millions of human brains' who could be anywhere in the world. Howe refers to this internet-driven sourcing of 'latent talent' as crowdsourcing rather than outsourcing. He also highlighted several significant examples of crowdsourcing: iStockphoto, which is a free image-sharing exchange where amateur photographers contribute their pictures; pharmaceutical maker Eli Lilly's use of Innocentive, a crowdsourcing network, to engage with external experts to develop drugs and who found among the problem solvers an undergrad and a patent lawyer; and Procter & Gamble who, faced with rising research costs, used the crowdsourcing networks Innocentive, YourEncore and NineSigma. This crowdsourcing strategy enabled Procter & Gamble to supplement its research and development staff with 1.5 million researchers externally.[198]

Innocentive, mentioned several times in Howe's article, has about 400,000 registered solvers across 200 countries. It has received nearly 2000 external challenges and more than 40,000 submissions for business, policy, scientific, social and technical challenges.[199]

Howe also published a book in 2008: *Crowdsourcing: Why the power of the crowd is driving the future of business*. Affirming that the crowd is not only wise but creative and productive, he highlights the deep expertise of individuals who can access information and collaborate innovatively with companies through open software platforms.[200]

Carl Esposti, founder and CEO of crowdsourcing research firm Massolution, continued his company's focus by establishing Crowdsourcing.org in 2010 as a community-based platform. The website mentions that crowdsourcing is sometimes associated with collective wisdom, community production, connected intelligence, constituent-driven innovation, human networks, intelligent networks, mass collaboration, mass solutions and open innovation.

Crowdsourcing.org defines crowdsourcing as follows:[201]

> Crowdsourcing is the act of outsourcing tasks, traditionally performed by an employee or contractor, to a large group of people or community (a crowd) through an open invite (call). Crowdsourcing is typically enabled through online communities consisting of members with common skills or interests and is applied as a model that enables individuals and groups to innovate, create, produce, report, predict, collaborate, fund and to engage customers.

In 2011, Massolution surveyed thirty-two crowdsourcing service providers who represented categories such as expertise-based tasks, software services, micro-tasks, freelance services and ideation-based tasks. These were some of the findings about the growing market: North America and Europe hosted ninety per cent of crowdsourcing clients, who are mostly small enterprises and start-ups; about seventy per cent of market revenues are from internet services, media and entertainment, and technology; seventy-seven per cent of crowd workers have a primary job, with the majority aged eighteen to forty years, male, well educated and living in developed countries; about fifty-seven per cent of crowdsourcing workers participate daily while seventy per cent take part weekly; average crowdsourcing monthly earnings vary from US$500 for micro-tasks to US$8000 for expertise-based tasks and software services; crowdsourcing workers were from North America (forty-one per cent), Asia Pacific (thirty-five per cent), Europe (eighteen per cent) and South America (six per cent).[202]

Crowdsourcing.org's website features directories of crowd creativity, crowdfunding and open innovation. Some of the links are interesting:

- Amazon Studios, which develops feature films based on global audience feedback.
- My Starbucks Idea, where customers contribute ideas and videos.
- MySears Community, where online community members share ideas, opinions and stories to improve the Sears company.
- NASA Tournament Lab, established by NASA, Harvard Business School and TopCoder to competitively create innovative solutions for NASA researchers.
- The TED Open Translation Project, started by the Technology, Entertainment and Design non-profit organisation, has translators worldwide to bring TED Talks to non-English-speaking audiences.
- Yahoo Answers, an online community where people ask or answer questions, with participants gaining points for answering, including the 'Best Answer'.
- GE Ecomagination Challenge, where students, innovators, entrepreneurs and businesses submit ideas for renewable energy, grid efficiency and eco-homes or eco-buildings, with the hope of getting funding from GE.
- Invent with Nokia, where the company seeks inventions for new mobile solutions, and Nokia Beta Labs, where loyal customers access new products and provide feedback or improvement ideas.
- Lego Design by Me, where fans use the Lego Digital Designer software for their own Lego creations, and Lego Mindstorms, where the company awards the best ideas for interactive toys.
- Pepsi Refresh Project, where the online community submit funding ideas for cultural, education, environmental and health initiatives.

Crowdsourcing as an industry practice has gained more awareness, with the word added in 2013 to the Oxford English Dictionary[203] and with books such as *Crowdsourcing for Dummies* being published.[204] A crowdsourcing service provider wrote that 2014 was the year that crowdsourcing solidified as an approach, with PepsiCo increasing its use of the strategy by over 325 per cent for the year.[205] It's predicted that by 2017, crowdsourced solutions will account for seventy-five per cent of research and development capabilities and consumer innovation in over fifty per cent of consumer goods manufacturers.[206]

Australia is reputed to be a global crowdsourcing hub. Crowdsourcing in Australia dates back to 1901 when a global Federal Flag design contest attracted 30,000 designs.[207] You may find this top ten list of Australian crowdsourcing networks useful: www.businessreviewaustralia.com/top10/1172/Top-10-movers-shakers-in-Australian-crowdsourcing.

As a result of the growing popularity of crowdsourcing, there have been numerous open innovation challenges on the internet, including the following:

- Innocentive Challenges: www.innocentive.com/ar/challenge/browse
- Nature.com Open Innovation Pavilion: www.nature.com/openinnovation/index.html
- Scientific American Open Innovation Pavilion: www.scientificamerican.com/openinnovation
- Open IDEO, with 'big challenges for social good': https://openideo.com
- Philips Open Innovation Challenge: www.experience.philips.com/events/open-innovation-challenges/about
- The Bill & Melinda Gates Foundation Grand Challenges website: http://grandchallenges.org
- The American Heart Association Open Innovation Challenge: http://hizforum.medstartr.com
- World Series of Innovation, hosted by the Network for Teaching Entrepreneurship, for young people aged fourteen to twenty-four: www.gew.co/wsi
- Open Innovation success stories: www.ideaconnection.com/open-innovation-success

eYeka crowdsourcing provider

A major crowdsourcing service provider outside the USA is eYeka, which has offices in Paris and Singapore. Connecting brands and creative outputs through online challenges, eYeka positions itself as the largest creative playground in the world, with 300,000 creative individuals from 160 countries.

eYeka works with clients in the following ways: the client briefs eYeka on its problem or objective; eYeka turns the brief into a 'call for entries' creative contest, with selection criteria such as originality of submission, relevance to the brief, narration and quality of execution; eYeka also establishes rules for the contest, such as no illicit content and acquiring intellectual property rights; the client views the consumer responses through eYeka's online platform 'beYond'; eYeka helps choose and reward winners to secure intellectual property rights.

The creative contests fall into the categories of design (graphic design, illustration, label and packaging), writing (creative writing and scriptwriting) and multimedia (photography, video and animation).

eYeka has worked on more than 700 projects with 83,000 creative submissions for clients such as BMW, Coca-Cola, Duracell, Heineken, HP, Hyundai, Intel, Johnson & Johnson, Kellogg's, Microsoft, Nescafé, Samsung, 3M and Toyota. Consumer goods manufacturers Unilever, Procter & Gamble, Nestlé and PepsiCo are the biggest users of eYeka creative contests.[208]

Unilever has run nearly forty creative contests for brands such as Axe, Clear, Lifebuoy, Lux, Ponds, Rexona, Sunsilk, Closeup, Pepsodent, Comfort, Continental, Cornetto, Knorr Seasoning and Lipton Milk Tea. The Lux and Cornetto creative contests could stimulate some ideas for your brands.

Lux

- Creative challenge: 'Show us, through an inspirational and insightful video/animation or an exquisite poster, the ideal beauty moment for a LUX woman, when she fully expresses her beauty, which will trigger love and admiration around her'.
- Format: Video or animation in sixty seconds or photo/illustration/print with explanation.
- Criteria: Creative, exquisite, insightful and inspirational expression of beauty through charm, elegance or glamour.
- Prizes: €10,000, €6000 and €4000 for the first, second and third winners in the video category; €3000, €1500 and €500 for the first, second and third winners in the design category.
- Results: Six winners from seventy-eight contributors across thirty-one countries.

The Lux team was amazed by the contributions, commenting that these 'opened a broader Lux world for us'.[209]

Cornetto

- Creative challenge: 'Surprise us with an original video or print that brings the Cornetto motto "enjoy the ride, love the ending" to life in a refreshingly unusual way, to catch teens' attention and make them want to share your entry with their friends.'
- Format: Print, video/animation of sixty seconds.
- Criteria: Creative, engaging, surprising and unexpected.

- Prizes: €10,000, €5000 and €2500 for the first, second and third winners in the video category; €3000, €2000 and €1000 for the first, second and third winners in the design category.
- Results: Six winners from eighty-eight submissions across twenty-two countries.[210]

Overall, crowdsourcing has its benefits. You could utilise an elite group of lead users; the mass input of crowd wisdom as latent talent to supplement your innovation agenda; or the global creative playground facilitated by crowdsourcing providers. You may also wish to explore more to learn how Unilever, Procter & Gamble, Nestlé and PepsiCo use eYeka to leverage crowd wisdom.

CROWDFUNDING

While crowdsourcing leverages the crowd for ideas, crowdfunding taps donors, investors and sponsors for financial contribution to fund non-profit or for-profit projects. Crowdfunding could be seen as a variation of crowdsourcing but the concept of sourcing money from crowds goes back to the eighteenth century. Author Alexander Pope had 750 subscribers pledging two gold guineas to kick-start the Greek-to-English translation of Homer's *Iliad*, with subscribers' names acknowledged in an early edition of the book. Mozart listed 176 sponsors in concerto manuscripts for financially helping him to achieve his new piano concertos.[211]

When France donated the Statue of Liberty to America in 1885 and a pedestal was needed for the statue to stand in New York Harbour, *The World* newspaper publisher Joseph Pulitzer published articles on the project for five months. More than 160,000 people donated to the pedestal project, with *The World* chronicling each donation. That birth of political crowdfunding might have inspired Barack Obama's political funding campaign in 2008, which raised US$750 million from small donors to help Obama be the first African American president of the USA. Another crowdfunding campaign in 2012 raised US$631 million for Obama's successful race for re-election against Mitt Romney. Stories on hope, change and moving forward influenced Obama's crowdfunding campaigns.[212]

There are different types of crowdfunding: donation crowdfunding, where donors contribute to social, charitable or political campaigns; reward crowdfunding, where donors obtain a perk such as a product that is being crowdfunded; debt crowdfunding, where donors expect repayment with interest; royalty crowdfunding, where donors get a percentage of revenue from the implemented venture; and equity crowdfunding, where donors become shareholders.[213]

The crowdsourcing.org website has a directory of more than 500 crowdfunding consulting and service providers[214] and you can learn more about crowdfunding and the service providers through top-traffic-based crowdfunding sites. The providers of these sites charge clients a fee ranging from 4.75 to ten per cent.[215] Top reward-based crowdfunding websites include Indiegogo, which funds films and cause-related campaigns; Peerbackers, which funds entrepreneurs and innovators, including entrepreneurs aged thirteen to seventeen; and Kickstarter, the most well-known such website, which funds arts, design, gaming and technology.[216]

There are obvious issues in crowdfunding, such as not delivering what is promised to donors and breaching some countries' investment laws. Here are some resources that you may find useful for planning effective crowdfunding:

- Taypayers Australia, on small business capital-raising issues: www.taxpayer.com.au/News/28298/Crowdfunding_could_solve_small_business_capital_raising_issues__CAMAC_report
- US Securities and Exchange Commission, which had proposed rules on selling securities through crowdfunding: www.sec.gov/News/PressRelease/Detail/PressRelease/1370540017677#.VMq829y8aIw

Is crowdfunding appropriate for your organisation or the non-profit sector that you may be engaging with? Perhaps donation crowdfunding or reward crowdfunding align more with your corporate mission, values and vision?

CORPORATE INCUBATORS AND ACCELERATORS

The open innovation model helps big companies to facilitate start-ups, such as Cisco inviting early-stage entrepreneurs into its incubation program.[217] This section is related to equity crowdfunding and projects from hackathons, skunk works, innovation labs and immersion programs that evolve into start-up companies requiring incubator and accelerator support. Incubators and accelerators can be excellent resources for intrapreneurs and entrepreneurs.

One way to distinguish between incubators and accelerators is to use the analogy of a life cycle, from childhood, through adolescence to adulthood. The incubator provides the 'child' start-up business with shelter and guidance through office space, training and networks. The accelerator helps the 'adolescent' become an 'adult' in business through consulting services to improve operational, organisational and strategic issues during rapid growth.[218]

The Boston Consulting Group published a comprehensive comparison between incubator, accelerator, venture capitalist and strategic partner. Since venture capitalists often invest in existing companies and strategic partners also collaborate with existing companies, this section focuses on the corporate incubator and accelerator that support start-ups. Table 4.1 is adapted from the BCG report.[219]

TABLE 4.1 Corporate accelerators versus incubators

CRITERIA	CORPORATE INCUBATOR	CORPORATE ACCELERATOR
Start-up stage	Early stage without existing business	Technically ready to 'spread wings'
Immersion nature	Close cooperation between sponsor and start-up	Transfer of expertise and best practices
Industries	Competitive industries: automotive, chemical and some consumer goods	Fast-changing industries: media, technology, telecommunications
Time frame	Twelve to thirty-six months	Three months
Investment	Up to twenty-five per cent of equity	No equity or up to five per cent
Resources	Array of business support resources and services	Structured fixed curricula
Benefits to start-up	Business skills training; professional network; management support	Mentorship and coaching; start-up network; technical support
Benefits to sponsor	Outsourced research and development function; enhanced employee recruitment	'First pick' in start-up

Idealab and Techstars

An example of an incubator is Idealab, while Techstars is a top accelerator.

Idealab is a member of the National Business Incubation Association, the global leader in advancing corporate incubation with more than 2000 members across sixty nations,[220] and is also a network partner of the Business Incubator Magazine together with the Chinese Business Incubation Association, the Dutch Incubator Association, the European Business & Innovation Centre Network and the UK Business Incubation.[221]

The mission of Idealab is to 'create and operate pioneering companies'; hence the incubator has prototyped hundreds of ideas and created more than 125 companies since 1996.[222] Some Idealab companies include Answers.com—launched in 1996 and acquired by NetShepard Inc in 1998; eToys—online retailer of children's products launched in 1997 to initial success but bankrupt in 2001 (the popular brand still exists after acquisition by KB Toys and subsequent ownership changes); Cooking.com—launched in 1998 and acquired by Target Corporation in 2013; HomesDirect.com—online auction site launched in 2000 and bought by eBay in 2001; and Shopping.com—launched in 1997 and bought by Compaq Computer Corp in 1999.[223]

Techstars is a member of the Global Accelerator Network, which has fifty accelerators on six continents.[224] The Techstars website highlights its seed funding of US$118,000 for seven to ten per cent equity, intensive mentorship and nearly 400 active companies. Applications to Techstars need to specify company uniqueness against competition; number of engineers, developers and employees; customer segments; cash invested to date; shareholders and equity; revenue history; and include a one-minute video about the founders and another one-minute video product demo.[225]

The Techstars network includes interesting brands such as Disney, Nike and Microsoft.

Disney Accelerator

This combines the mentorship model of Techstars with the Disney brand to offer entertainment and media technology start-ups US$120,000 investment funding to develop their dreams with mentorship from Disney executives.[226] Disney Accelerator companies in 2014 include ChoreMonster, which 'makes chores fun', and Smart Toy, where toys get smarter with downloadable content over time.[227]

Nike+ Accelerator

In this program, activity-related companies immerse themselves for three months in Portland, Oregon, USA, to develop products or services for everyday athletes and pitch ideas to 'angel' investors and venture capitalists. Companies selected include FitDeck, producers of exercise playing cards, and CoachBase, a digital coaching platform.[228]

Microsoft Accelerator
Start-ups are immersed intensely over three months to six months in locations including Bangalore, Beijing, Berlin, London, Paris, Seattle and Tel Aviv, with US$20,000 funding, office space and mentorship from Microsoft, investors and entrepreneurs.[229]

Samsung and Coca-Cola
While many companies target new entrepreneurs, two accelerators focus on experienced entrepreneurs. Samsung launched its Samsung Accelerator in 2013 to target entrepreneurs who have led teams, built products and have unique ideas about how to use cameras, home appliances, mobile phones, TVs and workplace solutions. The Samsung Accelerator does not have a fixed funding amount or program duration but provides entrepreneurs with access to Samsung resources.[230]

Coca-Cola has a Co-Founder Network where handpicked experienced entrepreneurs are invited to access Coca-Cola's resources, including an advisor. This Co-Founder Network is Coke's way of continuing the tradition of empowering entrepreneurs as bottlers to open up new markets.[231]

Virgin Group
The Virgin Group has two programs to help new entrepreneurs learn from existing entrepreneurs. Virgin StartUp is a new service in which members have access to start-up advice, events, competitions and exclusive content. Virgin Unite is the group's entrepreneurial foundation with a mission to create a better world through entrepreneurs, inspirational leaders, philanthropists and Virgin's community of customers, social media followers and global staff. In his blog, Richard Branson wrote:

> Every business within the Virgin Group began by sharing ideas. It is for this reason that I enjoy hearing from our team members and the public about how we can improve our products and services and what unchartered territory we should enter next. I've recently got into the habit of scrolling through new social media site, Ideapod—an online hub for people to share ideas and collaborate on bringing them to life ... Sometimes all an idea needs to become a reality, and make an impact, is for it to be shared. Many people don't share their ideas, because they fear they will be dismissed. The good, the bad and the ugly—any idea has the potential to become a great idea if supported by people with a shared passion.[232]

Since there are many examples of corporate incubators (for new start-up businesses) and accelerators (for more mature businesses), you may wish to learn more from Idealab, Techstars, the National Business Incubation Association, the Global Accelerator Network or any innovative company mentioned in this section.

SUMMARY

This chapter explored Group Germination or growth through diverse internal and external groups, such as competitive collaboration, cluster collaboration, outsourcing, open innovation, crowdsourcing, crowdfunding and funding from incubators and accelerators.

There are many examples of competitors collaborating responsibly in research and development, innovation, marketing and community development. Similar industries and like-minded businesses in a region collaborate through clusters for the benefit of the industry as well as for individual companies. Companies also outsource goods and services, including research and development and innovation. Open innovation is a two-way process enabling companies to use external resources for innovation and allowing external companies to use internal resources. Crowdsourcing taps into the wisdom, creativity and productivity of the crowd, while crowdfunding leverages the crowd to fund donations, projects, debt settlement and equity investment. Incubators provide funding when the company is at the 'child' stage while accelerators help the 'adolescent' company to be an 'adult'.

Hence, diverse Group Germination sources help to facilitate team creativity and innovation, thereby spurring corporate growth. The next few chapters explore how you could net a spectrum of ideas from germinating groups.

CHAPTER 5
MIND NETTING: BRAINSTORMING

Undergraduate student Alex Tew in the UK did not wish to still be paying for his studies fifteen to twenty years after graduation. He also needed money for accommodation, his social life and to pay for his hard-working parents to have time off from work. Around midnight in 2005 with a notepad on his bed, Alex brainstormed for ideas to make money. He jotted down random ideas. One idea emerged from his subconscious—sell a million pixels for US$1 each through a website. Alex launched the Million Dollar Homepage, sold 100-pixel blocks of 10 by 10 pixels for $100 and earned $1 million. He promised his advertisers that he would maintain the webpage for at least five years, till 2010, but it is still running![233]

INTRODUCTION

Many participants during our team creativity sessions use diverse creative thinking 'baits' to net creative ideas, such as brainstorming, the Creative Problem Solving process, Synectics innovative problem solving, lateral thinking, Six Thinking Hats, mind mapping, multidimensional thinking, TRIZ inventive problem solving, attribute listing and morphological synthesis. Depending on learning styles and their mix of multiple intelligences, some participants liked a more structured process such as Six Thinking Hats while other adults prefer the free flow of mind mapping.

Most, if not all, the creative thinking tools seem to have an underpinning philosophy of first finding out what the challenge is and then ideating divergently before acting on the ideas outcome. I call this the Challenge-Ideas-Action or CIA process.

One of the most frequently cited creative thinking tools is brainstorming. Hence, this chapter explores the origins of brainstorming, research, variations and industry examples.

ORIGIN

Alex Osborn from the New York advertising firm Batten, Barton, Durstine and Osborn (BBDO) introduced the brainstorming concept in 1939. He advocated divergent and convergent stages for brainstorming.[234]

Divergent thinking is generating idea options against an objective or challenge. Osborn's guidelines include going for quantity, deferring judgment, combining or building on ideas and seeking wild ideas.

Convergent thinking is evaluating idea options and developing the better ideas further. This stage focuses on the quality or novelty of ideas so that a raw or abstract idea becomes more concrete and feasible.

Osborn provided evidence that group brainstorming was forty-four per cent more productive of worthwhile ideas than was individual ideation. His guidelines for running a brainstorming session are as follows[235]: there should be a facilitator to lead the session, including having a warm-up exercise and setting ground rules for the session; there should be a recorder of ideas to support the facilitator; the task for the session should determine the five to ten participants, who should have diverse experiences with the task but should not be of different seniority levels; the brainstorming session should last thirty to forty-five minutes, but Osborn did encourage individual ideation before and after the group session, as his thinking was modelled on the Wallas process of preparation, incubation, illumination and verification.[236]

RESEARCH ON BRAINSTORMING

Contradicting Osborn's findings, research studies (based largely on students as the sample population) have concluded that group brainstorming is an ineffective idea-generation process compared to individual ideation. It's possible that these student-based studies are not relevant to the organisational context, where brainstorming is likely to be a more formal process. Osborn invented group brainstorming in an advertising agency, which involved factors such as group leadership and facilitation, preparation for brainstorming, carefully selected tasks and evaluation of outcomes.[237]

One researcher concluded that brainstorming groups were not effective for three reasons. First, 'production blocking', which occurs when there is more listening to what others say than thinking about your own ideas. Production blocking is also caused by 'topic fixation', when too much time is spent on few topic categories. Second, social inhibition—some participants fear what others might say about their ideas, especially in the presence of an authority figure.

Third, social loafing—since there is group responsibility in the outcome, some participants relax and do not put in the necessary effort.[238]

Other researchers reported that group brainstorming could be affected by the presence of the group's boss, conversation overload, less time for idea contribution, building on ideas that represent group norms rather than suggesting wacky ideas, and individual self-censorship during the team process.[239] Conforming to other people's ideas has been described as 'collaborative fixation', which affects original thinking.[240]

VARIATIONS

There have been variations of Osborn's brainstorming technique to improve the process. These models include SCAMPER, reverse brainstorming, electronic brainstorming, round-robin brainstorming, brainswarming, brainwriting, brainsketching, rolestorming, hybrid brainstorming, brainsteering and brainstorming boxes.

SCAMPER

SCAMPER evolved from Osborn's Idea Spurring Checklist to provide a brainstorming structure for developing new products and services. It stands for:

- substitute
- combine
- adapt
- magnify, minify or modify
- put to other uses
- eliminate
- reverse or rearrange.[241]

For example, if you were to use SCAMPER to think about what to do with a pair of old jeans, the process could be:

- substitute the buttons
- combine with scarf
- adapt with holes and colours
- minify as shorts
- put to other uses, such as rag, pyjamas or letter holder
- eliminate some parts of the jean
- reverse/rearrange by turning the jean inside out.

One writer suggested the following ideas for writing an article on 'Five easy steps to greening your home':[242]

- Substitute by focusing on an apartment rather than a house or on professional rather than do-it-yourself services.
- Combine with value-added features such as greening and lifestyle or greening and home investment value.
- Adapt by greening a commercial building or a small business.
- Magnify to twenty green ways or greening your neighbourhood.
- Put to other uses by writing about the financial value of greening, such as reducing energy consumption and utility bills.
- Eliminate some words in the title: 'Five ways to be green'.
- Reverse through an ironic news angle such as 'Five ways to throw away household energy'.

Reverse brainstorming

Following the 'reverse' in SCAMPER, it can be helpful to look at issues in another way to provide another perspective, either individually or in a group. Instead of solving a problem, look at causing the problem.[243] For example, instead of reducing teen pregnancy, focus on increasing teen pregnancy and then use the ideas as catalysts for solutions. Some of my students had fun while brainstorming to increase pregnancy, with ideas such as condoms with holes, condoms that do not fit, banning condoms, making condoms expensive, Glad Wrap as contraception, incentives to get pregnant, making teen pregnancy cool and school excursions to brothels. This fun reverse brainstorming approach also overcomes inhibitions to contribute ideas!

While reverse brainstorming could be used as an icebreaker, it can also provide fresh insights, by thinking the worst about a situation. If your group members are participating in a debate, you could have the two groups tackle the issue differently. For example, one group could brainstorm on 'how to have irate customers' while another group could focus on 'how to have happy customers'. Or one group can generate ideas on how to decrease tourism in Australia while a second group finds ideas to increase tourism in Australia.

Electronic brainstorming

While face-to-face brainstorming has the advantage of synergistic interplay between participants, individuals may not voice anything in large talkative groups for fear of idea relevance and evaluation. Hence, electronic brainstorming has been used to overcome some of these fears.

Technology enables groups to generate ideas via networked computers and brainstorming software—participants can be in the same room or building or in various locations worldwide in different time zones. An electronic brainstorming session could run with a facilitator and several computer software tools. Here are some guidelines:

1. Choose a facilitator with expertise in computer hardware, brainstorming software and knowledge of diverse creativity techniques.
2. Facilitator explains electronic brainstorming and software functions.
3. Facilitator types in the question to focus participants on the problem or challenge.
4. Participants freely type in initial ideas simultaneously without waiting or interrupting, as would happen in a traditional brainstorming session.
5. Participants type in other ideas triggered by what they see on their screen.
6. Participants may type feedback, such as: 'That's a good idea!' or 'Who thought of that one?' since no one would know who contributes each idea.
7. During the review phase, the 'idea organiser' software tool sorts ideas by keywords provided by participants. Participants then generate idea categories by deleting or combining similar ideas.
8. Participants can use an 'alternative evaluation' software tool to rate each idea category on feasibility and benefits of implementation on a ten-point scale. The software displays all the ratings. A 'rank order voting' software feature prioritises ideas for implementation.
9. Participants use a 'topic commenter' tool to type in implementation comments, concerns, action steps, completion dates and responsibilities.
10. A summary of the electronic brainstorming output could be circulated for subsequent meetings with other staff or the data could easily be used to kick-start another brainstorming session.

Some studies have found that electronic brainstorming is more productive than traditional brainstorming in larger groups, with twelve-person groups generating 200 per cent more ideas. Groups in Australia, New Zealand, Europe and North America have found electronic brainstorming more satisfying than traditional brainstorming because the parallel-cum-anonymous nature of inputting ideas empowers 'equalised power' and facilitates surprising and novel ideas. With the requisite brainstorming software, any participant could generate ideas or comments anytime without keeping to a schedule.

Some participants see drawbacks in electronic brainstorming, such as the absence of social interactions, the loss of power control and the extra effort to edit-select-evaluate when there is idea overload.[244] Hence, while electronic brainstorming is a popular variation, it will not replace traditional brainstorming because there are many people who believe that face-to-face interactions are good for building relationships, teamwork, mentoring and personal growth.[245]

You may wish to investigate electronic brainstorming software such as XMind, Coggle, Freemind, Mindmeister or Think Tank. Companies that have used Think Tank include Procter & Gamble, IBM, Boeing and NASA.[246]

Round-robin brainstorming

This form of brainstorming enables participants to contribute ideas without being influenced by a dominant person. Each person writes an idea on a card, passes the card to the nearest person who then writes a build-on idea on a new card. The swap process goes on and the facilitator finally collects all idea cards to discuss further as a group.[247]

Brainswarming

The brainswarming process also avoids extrovert dominance and inefficient verbal sharing of one idea at a time in a group session. Using the analogy of successful food-hunting ants leaving trails for other ants to swarm towards, the brainswarming process provides a top-down thinking signal such as goals and a bottom-up thinking trigger such as resources to guide participants to swarm towards the task.

An example from the originator of brainswarming is the task of removing ice from power lines. Top-down thinkers start with refining goals, such as shaking lines and preventing ice from forming. Bottom-up thinkers indicate how some resources could be used to address the refined goals, with suggestions such as sonic gun, ladder, fan and helicopter to shake the lines, and de-icer to prevent ice from forming. Solutions emerge when top-down and bottom-up ideas interact or swarm together. The solution to the icy power line is to have a helicopter make a strong wind to shake the lines and loosen the ice.

During brainswarming, participants do not talk but write ideas on Post-it Notes that they pin on the wall—flowing down from goals or up from resources. The swarm of ideas from top-down and bottom-up thinking can provide as much as 115 ideas in fifteen minutes, compared to traditional brainstorming of 100 ideas in sixty minutes.[248]

Brainwriting

German marketing consultant Bernd Rohrbach developed the brainwriting technique in 1969 because he felt that German participants had issues with traditional brainstorming, namely the imprecise writing of ideas, unskilled moderators and insufficient time for personal ideas.[249] Horst Geschka wrote about various West German brainwriting techniques in 1983; we'll look at Method 635, the brainwriting pool and the card circulating technique.[250]

Method 635

Members of a six-person group each receive a sheet of paper with the names of the six participants and space for each person to write three ideas each in five minutes to solve a problem, such as improving the standard of English. When each person has completed three ideas on their sheet of paper, they pass it to the next person, who builds on what is written or varies the idea. The passing around means that each person writes three ideas on each of the six sheets, resulting in eighteen ideas per person and 108 ideas in total. When reviewing the written ideas as a group, participants are able to identify who has written which idea and which ideas are connected. You may wish to watch this video for a visual demonstration of the method: www.youtube.com/watch?v=TR1i1PPd8ZU.

Brainwriting pool

In this method, each participant of a brainstorming group writes four ideas for a task on a blank sheet of paper, places the completed sheet on a table and then continues to write more ideas on another empty sheet of paper. This process leads to a pool of papers with written ideas. Any participant who is stuck for ideas can take a sheet from the pool of papers, read it and then write additional ideas on that sheet of paper.

Card circulating technique

Like the round-robin brainstorming technique, each participant writes an idea on a card and passes the completed card to a nearby member who then uses the card to write an associated idea on a new card. The resulting pile of cards could then be clustered under themes for evaluation.

A professor from the Kellogg School of Management used the following brainwriting technique to give everyone the chance to voice ideas without being censored, and to energise the shy participants:[251]

1 Write one idea per card (do not write your name).
2 Write as many ideas as possible in ten minutes.
3 Post each idea card on the wall.
4 Review the ideas and vote on them.

I have also used the brainwriting technique in multicultural groups, where some participants write English better than they speak it or prefer to write ideas in their own native language. During the review process, the ideas in a foreign language get translated on the card. Participants also use cards or large Post-it Notes to write down further ideas triggered by the wall of ideas.

Brainsketching
A variation of brainwriting is brainsketching, where individuals sketch rather than write their ideas. Working in pairs, each participant sketches a solution to a problem and passes the sketch to their partner who modifies or comments on the sketch. When all partners have modified or commented on sketches, the group reviews the sketches to select one idea or synthesise connected sketches.[252]

Rolestorming
Consultant Rick Griggs, who used various thinking tools when working with Semiconductor and Intel, developed the technique of rolestorming, a combination of role playing and brainstorming. He observed that some participants in brainstorming slowed down in idea contribution or offered no idea for fear of ridicule and criticism. Hence, his technique is to ask participants to look at an issue from the perspectives of different people—for example, saint, sinner and winner, Steve Jobs, Napoleon, Mother Teresa, Lady Gaga, Barack Obama, Bill and Hillary Clinton and Martha Stewart. Offering ideas through a different role provides a form of protective climate that stimulates the brain to make neural connections from stored images of that person.[253]

Hybrid brainstorming
A variation of brainstorming is a hybrid process where individuals brainstorm alone with specific instructions on idea quantity within a set time and then work with a group. Some researchers found that the hybrid process produced more and better ideas when compared with traditional group brainstorming.[254] A hybrid process called metaphorming focuses on associative thinking through analogies, devices, figures of speech, puns, stories, symbols and visualisation.[255]

Consulting firm Jump Associates in the USA has another variation of hybrid brainstorming. The company uses collaborative comic storytelling, analysis of video footage, reverse brainstorming, and shopping for products that would be metaphors for the proposed solutions.[256] The company's employees are 'hybrid people' with chemistry degrees plus experience as skilled artists, anthropologists, design researchers and electrical engineers. These hybrid thinkers are part humanist, part technologist and part capitalist and straddle business, culture and design.[257]

Brainsteering

Two former McKinsey consultants who have been involved in hundreds of projects with companies from diverse industries, have a variation of brainstorming called brainsteering.[258] This question-based approach involves seven steps covering criteria, questions, participant mix, subgroups, expectations, wrapping up and following up.

First, know your organisation's criteria for evaluating possible solutions. What would be acceptable and restricted zones for ideas; for example, would your company encourage ideas on corporate policies, an IT agenda or a quick return on investment? If management does not wish to discuss the IT agenda at this stage, steer the group away from this.

Second, ask the right questions. Use fifteen to twenty questions for subgroups of participants to provide unfamiliar or new perspectives.

Third, choose the right people. Participants should be in a position to answer the questions prepared for the brainstorming session.

Fourth, divide and conquer. Assign a question to each subgroup of three to five people to discuss for thirty minutes. Have a subgroup of 'idea crushers' such as content experts, bosses and 'big mouths' who monopolise air time. This subgroup of 'idea crushers' may be best equipped to discuss a specific question.

Then, get set and go. Set expectations and explain the process before breaking into subgroups. Before each session begins to address a new set of questions, share stories from a previous session on how the question-based approach has contributed to good ideas.

Finally, wrap it up. Each subgroup shares its leading ideas with other subgroups. Do not encourage the plenary group to choose ideas from the list generated, as this would be done at executive level based on criteria and priorities. Wrap up the workshop by explaining how the winning ideas are going to be chosen and announced.

Remember to follow up quickly. The executive team should meet to sort the ideas, research further, implement immediately or plan to do so at another time, or reject ideas outright. Communicate decisions quickly so that staff are informed and motivated.

Brothers Kevin and Shawn Coyne, the authors of *Brainsteering: A better approach to breakthrough ideas* (2011), think that breakthrough ideas rarely happen during the unfocused brainstorming method. Rather than think wildly outside the box, the authors advocate thinking specifically inside the box with real time, money or other constraints known upfront. To find the right questions to ask in brainsteering groups, the authors suggest using 'logic trees' to explore sub-questions of sub-questions to uncover potential questions. Hence, the authors believe that better ideas emerge from brainsteering's complementary use of analysis and creativity.

For example, asking the question: 'What's the biggest hassle our customers face when buying stamps?' led to the successful launch by the United States Postal Service of the 'Forever Stamp', which saves customers from making unnecessary trips to a US Postal Service outlet when the postage rate increases.

So if you wish to have your staff produce better ideas constantly, you should have a system to build and rejuvenate an inventory of the *right* questions, even if it means 'stealing' questions competitors may have asked to produce their newest features.[259]

Brainstorming boxes

Authors Luc de Brabandere and Alan Iny, who work in consulting firm the Boston Consulting Group, also do not believe in the traditional brainstorming method of thinking outside the box, and they also advocate getting the questions right up front. Writing about thinking in 'new boxes', the authors suggest a method of framing the question, creating a favourable creativity environment, identifying brainstorming boxes and following up.[260]

Framing the question effectively is half the battle

Citing Albert Einstein spending fifty-nine minutes on getting the problem right and then finding a solution, the authors believe, as do the Coyne brothers, in asking the right question and specifying constraints and success criteria. Instead of asking: 'How can we improve our brand image in the Indian market?', the authors suggest asking: 'How can we get a 25-year-old woman in Mumbai to rave about us to her friends?'

Create conditions that foster creativity

The right environment is important for brainstorming. Some factors to consider: support the need for creativity, think outside the normal routine, have full participation, accept far-fetched ideas and have a diverse mix of participants.

Identify brainstorming boxes

Identify the 'boxes' of your company, such as vision, strategy, philosophies, organisational structures and mental frameworks. For example, BIC reframed its box of making plastic pens to a new box of producing plastic consumer goods. Also, bring some new boxes to the brainstorming session to trigger ideas, such as success scenarios, different perspectives and diverse analogies.

Remember to follow up

To ensure subsequent actions, vote on ideas, encourage evolving ideas and prioritise ideas to continue the innovation journey. This is also something that brainsteering specifies.

Choosing the right brainstorming method

Which brainstorming variation would you use? Your decision will depend on learning styles and whether there is self-blocking of ideas, social inhibition, social loafing and collaborative fixation in your group. SCAMPER is useful if you wish to follow a structure. If you wish to overcome fear of contributing ideas, you could use reverse brainstorming, electronic brainstorming, round-robin brainstorming, brainswarming, brainwriting, brainsketching, rolestorming and/or metaphorming. If you wish to focus on asking the right questions as a means of securing ideas, then the McKinsey approach of brainsteering or the Boston Consulting Group method of brainstorming boxes would be ideal. You could have a hybrid of brainstorming techniques combining some of the brainstorming variations that include the use of actual products as metaphors and associations with saints, sinners or winners.

Industry examples

IDEO

Design firm IDEO treats brainstorming as a religion and 'idea engine' while it works with famous clients such as 3M, GE, Ikea, Microsoft, PepsiCo, Procter & Gamble, Samsung, Toyota and Unilever. IDEO, which has consistently won Industrial Design Excellence Awards, has perfected brainstorming through practise and prototyping ideas, driven by a corporate slogan 'Fail often to succeed sooner' and a culture of sharing stories about best practices and show-and-tell sessions about projects.[261]

IDEO's general manager Tom Kelley shared secrets of brainstorming in his book *The Art of Innovation* (2001):

- Sharpen the focus: Describe a problem or topic in a broad open-ended manner that focuses on a specific consumer need.
- Have playful rules: The walls of IDEO meeting rooms have six-inch-high letters on brainstorming rules, such as 'One conversation at a time', 'Go for quantity', 'Defer judgment' and 'Encourage wild ideas'.
- Number the ideas: This helps participants keep track of where they are during brainstorming.

- Build and jump: Participants are encouraged to build on ideas or switch gears when the momentum tapers off.
- The space remembers: The flow of ideas needs to be visible to tap into spatial memory, hence IDEO uses giant Post-it Notes, markers and large charts on walls.
- Stretch your mental muscles: IDEO uses warm-up or mental-stretching exercises such as word games, show-and-tell items or content-related homework.
- Get physical: IDEO brainstorming sessions include actual products or elegant solutions from competitors and other fields, sketching, diagrams, mind mapping, stick figures, materials for building concept models, and 'bodystorming', a form of role playing of consumer behaviour as a catalyst to improve the user experience.

Kelley also cautioned about brainstorming 'killers':

- The boss gets to speak first: A dominating CEO with a limited agenda could restrict thinking.
- Everybody gets a turn: Going around the room, especially with many participants, to let each person speak first is pointless, painful and not a brainstorm.
- Experts only: Do not restrict the brainstorming session to discipline experts only, as cross-pollination from other disciplines could provide insights.
- Do it off-site: The buzz of creativity should be felt in your office just as regularly as the seaside breeze.
- No silly stuff: Allow silly ideas, fun and flights of fancy.
- Write down everything: Leave detailed note-taking to the scribe and focus participant attention on brainstorming. It is fine to doodle or note your thoughts while someone else is contributing an idea.

With IDEO as a brainstorming master, it is not surprising to see seventy-five to a hundred ideas at each brainstorming session. The facilitator acts like an auctioneer asking for more ideas. A better idea often emerges from the quantity of ideas. For example, IDEO created Fisher-Price's freestanding base Jumperoo for babies and toddlers from one of the easel-size Post-it Note sketches. The product now sells a million units yearly. A brainstorming evangelist, IDEO even prints brainstorming rules on business cards.[262]

Kaiser

Kaiser pharmaceuticals held brainstorming sessions with seventy-five nurses, doctors, patients and vendors in groups of seven at round tables, guided by trained facilitators. The goal was to reduce nurse interruptions that led to dispensing the wrong drug or dosage, causing deaths or sickness.

During the warm-up exercise, each team shared stories about their visits to a different industry to search for relevant practices and ideas. Participants wrote ideas on Post-it Notes, put them on the wall, reviewed them, shortlisted a couple of must-pursue ideas, built a prototype of their solution, and presented it to the plenary session.

The brainstorming event produced fifteen to twenty feasible ideas, with three ideas leading to the launch of its medical administration process called KP MedRite. This reduced nurse interruptions by fifty per cent and increased efficiency by fifteen per cent.[263]

Shell
Shell collaborated with CNBC, the business and financial news channel, on a series of brainstorming events in key cities around the world. For its London event, Shell had eighty stakeholders across eleven tables brainstorm on a 2035 vision of reducing emissions by twenty per cent. A representative from each table pitched the group's best idea for plenary voting. The winning idea was a seven-stage process combining energy data and smart technology.[264]

IBM
IBM staged an InnovationJam online brainstorming event in 2006 over two seventy-two-hour sessions in which 150,000 IBM stakeholders (employees, family members, universities, business partners and clients) from 104 countries and sixty-seven companies posted 46,000 ideas for research-led technologies and business possibilities. IBM invested US$100 million to explore ten business ideas that emerged from InnovationJam.[265]

Tesco
The UK grocery retailer ran a one-day TJam open innovation event with seventy customers in various groups focusing on the online shopping experience, grocery savings, convenient and quick shopping, inspiration for weekly shopping plus the use of mobile technology and social networking media. The groups generated 800 ideas, imagined how consumers would use some of the ideas, and finally voted on the best idea for further development.[266]

Procter & Gamble
P&G brought together two independent facilitators, twenty internal engineers and managers plus seven external experts to brainstorm over a two-day innovation tournament to develop renewable energy plans for its plants in the USA, Mexico and Malaysia. P&G teams briefed the experts on the plants via webinar, the external experts proposed 150 ideas, the internal and external experts voted

online to select forty-five promising ideas, and then all participants met to develop ideas further. Such an innovation tournament accelerated the idea generation and development processes over two days rather than over a year.[267]

Virgin Group

Virgin founder Richard Branson is a firm believer in brainstorming. He regularly socialises and brainstorms with his senior managers on his resort-home, Necker Island. There is also an innovation culture throughout the Virgin Group; for example, every Virgin America staff member from the CEO to the accountants attends a yearly Refresh training program for building team spirit, celebrating achievements and stimulating creativity through brainstorming sessions. Such an innovation culture has helped the airline to be highly ranked with excellent customer satisfaction scores.[268]

When Branson was asked in a Twitter Q&A for a 'twenty-second elevator pitch' to explain what grabs his attention in a business idea, he responded: 'An idea that stands out from the crowd. An idea that is original and will make a radical difference to people's lives.'[269]

In his book *Screw Business as Usual* (2011), Branson mentioned that a brainstorming group was discussing a name for a new approach to business where everyone has to be responsible for each other in the global village. The name 'Capitalism 24902' emerged when someone mentioned that the Earth's circumference is 24,902 miles.[270]

Branson has his own tips for brainstorming: be innovative every day rather than only during specific 'think out of the box' or 'blue-sky thinking' sessions; choose a creative environment outside the office to enjoy the scenery before brainstorming, and take refreshing breaks through playing games, exercising or listening to music; focus everyone on the problem, especially when someone strays from the purpose; invite people from different departments because they may have fresh ideas; encourage everyone to listen and contribute ideas instead of just listening to the vocal ones; write down all ideas for follow up; take the risk to turn the best ideas into reality; and take the lead to say yes to seemingly impossible ideas.[271]

SUMMARY

Alex Osborn originated the technique of brainstorming in a corporate context with a facilitator to guide divergent and convergent thinking. Since then, there have been contradicting research studies on the effectiveness of brainstorming, with some studies suggesting that individual brainstorming is much more effective at producing quantity and quality of ideas than group brainstorming, which is restricted by self-censorship in groups, social inhibition, social loafing and collaborative fixation.

There have been variations of Osborn's brainstorming technique, such as SCAMPER, reverse brainstorming, electronic brainstorming, round-robin brainstorming, brainswarming, brainwriting, brainsketching, rolestorming, hybrid brainstorming, brainsteering and brainstorming boxes. There are different practices on the use of brainstorming, such as the famous design firm IDEO using the process religiously for its diverse clients and Richard Branson having a brainstorming innovation culture within his organisation. Brainstorming practice also emphasises the need to focus on the task at hand, the use of questions, metaphors and associative thinking (with saint or sinner and role playing or 'bodystorming' as used in IDEO). The next chapter examines the Creative Problem Solving process, a creative thinking tool closely associated with brainstorming.

MIND NETTING: CREATIVE PROBLEM SOLVING PROCESS

CHAPTER 6

Alex Osborn was an advertising executive at BBDO and Sidney Parnes was an army veteran who had completed his doctorate in education at the University of Pittsburgh in 1954. They met at the first Creative Problem Solving Institute (CPSI) conference in 1954 and formed a dynamic partnership for creative education that lasted until Osborn died in 1966. The Osborn-Parnes Creative Problem Solving process integrated practice and theory. This deliberate structured creativity process recognises that everyone can learn creativity, which involves a balance of divergent and convergent thinking. The CPSI conference has run yearly for six decades with programs for practitioners, educators and students aged seven to seventeen years.[272]

INTRODUCTION

Alex Osborn founded the Creative Education Foundation, in 1954, which has been promoting creativity education over the last six decades, and he authored several books: *Your Creative Power; Wake Up Your Mind; How to Think Up; How to Become More Creative; Unlocking Your Creative Power;* and *Applied Imagination*.[273] This chapter examines Osborn's other legacy, the Creative Problem Solving (CPS) process, covering its origin and evolution, my CPS learning, and industry examples.

ORIGIN

Osborn developed a structured Creative Problem Solving process in his 1952 book, *Wake Up Your Mind*,[274] and 1953 book, *Applied Imagination*. Version 1.0 of his Creative Problem Solving process had seven steps integrating rational and irrational elements: orientation—pointing up the problem; preparation—gathering pertinent data; analysis—breaking down the relevant material; hypothesis—piling up alternatives by way of ideas; incubation—letting up to invite illumination; synthesis—putting the pieces together; verification—judging the resultant ideas.[275]

Covering facts, ideas and solutions, Osborn then collapsed his seven steps under three main stages in his Creative Problem Solving process Version 1.1: fact finding—problem definition and preparation; idea finding—idea production and idea development; and solution finding—evaluation and adoption.

EVOLUTION

Osborn collaborated with Sidney Parnes, who in turn worked with his colleagues to incorporate other creativity methods to develop the Creative Problem Solving process Version 2.0, known as the Osborn-Parnes CPS process. This five-stage process expanded on facts, ideas and solutions:[276]

1. Fact finding: discover relevant facts
2. Problem finding: determine the real problem
3. Idea finding: generate options
4. Solution finding: evaluate ideas against criteria
5. Acceptance finding: prepare to act on idea

Over fifty years, scholars have researched and refined the Creative Problem Solving process. Researchers from the Creative Problem Solving Group Inc and the Center for Creative Learning introduced CPS Version 6.1 in 2000 with the following framework: understanding the challenge—constructing opportunities, exploring data and framing problems; generating ideas; and preparing for action—developing solutions and building acceptance.[277]

Another creativity researcher and practitioner, Dr Min Basadur has an applied creativity variation on the Creative Problem Solving process, covering three stages and eight steps to focus on problem, solution and implementation:[278]

1. Problem formulation: problem finding, fact finding and problem definition
2. Solution formulation: idea finding, then evaluation and selection
3. Solution implementation: action planning, gaining acceptance and action taking

The Creative Education Foundation website in 2015 now describes the Creative Problem Solving process as the CPS Learner's Model. This covers four stages with six steps emphasising challenges, ideas and implementation:[279]

1. Clarify: explore the vision, gather data and formulate challenges
2. Ideate: explore ideas
3. Develop: formulate solutions
4. Implement: formulate a plan

Whatever the variations of the Creative Problem Solving process, the underpinning philosophy seems to focus on starting with a challenge, creating ideas and acting on them. Hence, I describe it as the Challenge-Ideas-Action or CIA framework. This article may be of interest if you wish to learn more about the evolution of CPS over five decades: www.cpsb.com/research/articles/creative-problem-solving/Celebrating-50-Years-of-Creative-Problem-Solving.html

MY LEARNING

I learnt the Creative Problem Solving process in the USA in 2006. The framework incorporated brainstorming divergent-convergent dimensions for each step to explore possibilities and then focus on the most important element.

1. Explore the challenge
    a. Objective finding: identify the goal or wish
    b. Fact finding: gather data about the situation
    c. Problem finding: clarify the problem
2. Generate ideas
    a. Idea finding: find possible innovative solutions
3. Prepare for action
    a. Solution finding: select and strengthen solutions
    b. Acceptance finding: plan for action

While the three stages and six steps of this 2006 version seem to be sequential, there is flexibility in using the process. It's cyclical, hence you may move back and forth during the process. See Table 6.1 for guidelines that I learnt during the training workshop.

TABLE 6.1 CPS stages and steps (2006)

STAGES AND STEPS	DIVERGE	CONVERGE
STAGE 1 EXPLORE THE CHALLENGE		
Objective finding	What do you wish would happen?	Which wish would you want to do something about?
Fact finding	What are the facts about the wish?	What opportunities and concerns emerge?
Problem finding	How else can you restate the wish?	Which restatement gets to the heart of the matter?
STAGE 2 GENERATE IDEAS		
Idea finding	Generate ideas using different triggers.	Select seemingly impossible intriguing ideas.
STAGE 3 PREPARE FOR ACTION		
Solution finding	List criteria to evaluate top ideas.	Evaluate ideas against criteria and improve 'hot' ideas.
Acceptance finding	What's needed to act on the idea/s?	Who does what and when?

As part of the training session, I worked with a small group to apply the Creative Problem Solving stages to a community task of working with the police. Table 6.2 presents an extract of the outcome.

TABLE 6.2 CPS working with the police

STAGES AND STEPS	DIVERGE	CONVERGE
STAGE 1 EXPLORE THE CHALLENGE		
Objective finding	I wish: • teens respect police • teens know police better • police shared skills • teens interact with police.	I wish teens would interact more with police.

STAGES AND STEPS	DIVERGE	CONVERGE
Fact finding	Facts were given on the who, what, why, where, when and how of the task.	The most important converged fact was that interactions with police were mostly negative.
Problem finding	• How to get more police involved • How to have more positive interactions with police • How to involve children of police • How to involve police with more teenage girls	Have win-win interactions between police and teenage girls
STAGE 2 GENERATE IDEAS		
Idea finding	1 Team sports 2 Team projects 3 Community projects 4 Female police as mentors 5 Attachment programs 6 Police as coaches	Combine ideas 3, 5 and 6: interactions between teenage girls and police through community projects, attachment programs and police as coaches
STAGE 3 PREPARE FOR ACTION		
Solution finding	Criteria for solution: • mass benefit • mutual benefit • easy to implement.	Evaluation matrix was used to evaluate the combined 3-5-6 ideas against the criteria
Acceptance finding	• Identify skills needed • Align with police skills database • Community and police meeting	Task owner to write proposal paper on police-community engagement

If you prefer a shorter Creative Problem Solving variation, try my Challenge-Ideas-Action (CIA) framework (Table 6.3). After I taught the full Creative Problem Solving process to students, I offered them my simplified CIA framework as an option for when they have less time for problem solving. Naturally, students found the CIA framework easier to follow and suggested teaching this version first before introducing the longer CPS version!

TABLE 6.3 The CIA framework

STAGES	DIMENSIONS	STEPS
Challenge	Diverge	Reframe task
	Converge	Choose clear task
Ideas	Diverge	Generate ideas
	Converge	Choose best idea/s
Action	Diverge	Plan actions
	Converge	Prioritise actions

I recently came across Apple's CreativeIQ framework, which seems to embody the Creative Problem Solving/Challenge-Ideas-Action philosophy of understanding the challenge, creating ideas and acting on the big ideas. The CreativeIQ framework has four elements:

1. Search: What do you wish to improve or create? What industries could provide clues and additional information? (The first question is like the challenge while the second question is akin to benchmarking the innovators, as described in Chapter 2 on Mastery Modelling.)
2. Prepare: Ensure a creative thinking environment, such as nurturing positive triggers and exercising the imagination. (This could be part of the challenge in the CIA framework.)
3. Create: Visualise, imagine, fantasise and mentally create an idea prototype. (This is like the ideas element in CIA.)
4. Innovate: Develop a working prototype, test it and action it to turn it into a reality. (This is like the action in CIA.)

Apple's CreativeIQ emerged in 2011 after a senior team benchmarked Pixar and Google; researched neuroscience, physiology and psychology; and modelled artists, inventors, musicians and scientists.[280] Kamran Loghman, a master trainer of creative performance at Apple and a serial entrepreneur, developed CreativeIQ.[281]

Industry examples

Numerous companies have successfully used the Creative Problem Solving process over the years. Procter & Gamble, DuPont, IBM, 3M, Exxon and Citigroup have used the CPS process for developing creative and innovative teams, product development, strategic change, climate intervention or CPS facilitation skills.[282]

The Frito Lay Corporation in Texas achieved its five-year goal of saving US$500 million one year earlier by training all staff in the Creative Problem Solving process to synergistically work on opportunities, challenges and solutions.[283] Alcan Limited reduced plant maintenance costs and Quaker Oats introduced an intermediate heat exchanger to eradicate syrup blockages during production.[284] Monsanto launched NutraSweet while Mead Fine Papers improved product features and quality.[285]

Xerox invented its GlossMarks technology to prevent counterfeiting by redefining its Creative Problem Solving objective—from removing print and photocopy gloss to creating innovative products.[286] Xerox has a variation of the Creative Problem Solving process covering six steps: identifying and selecting the problem; analysing the problem; generating potential solutions; selecting and planning solutions; implementing the solutions; and evaluating the solutions.[287]

The Creative Education Foundation has been successful in four areas relating to Creative Problem Solving. First, hosting the yearly Creative Problem Solving Institute (CPSI) international conference, which focuses on creativity, innovation and change. More information about CPSI can be found at www.cpsiconference.com. Second, teaching creativity as a skill since 1954 through the International Center for Studies in Creativity at Buffalo State. Third, publishing the *Journal of Creative Behavior* since 1967.

The foundation's fourth success was establishing the Sydney J. Parnes Global Fellowship in honour of Parnes, who died in 2013 after decades of contributions to creative education. Supported also by the Parnes family, the two-year fellowship enables fellows to learn from creativity experts, apply Creative Problem Solving to a community challenge, present and publish on the challenge and plan for solution funding.

There are also Creative Problem Solving activities for the young. CEF YouthWise enables young people to learn the Creative Problem Solving process and creative thinking skills during the CPSI conference each year.[288]

The Future Problem Solving Program International, founded in 1974 by Dr E. Paul Torrance (of the Torrance Tests of Creative Thinking fame), involves students annually in community and global problem solving in Australia, Canada, Hong Kong, Japan, Korea, India, Ireland, Israel, Malaysia, New Zealand, Portugal, Qatar, Russia, Singapore, South Africa, Switzerland, Thailand, Turkey, the United Kingdom and the USA. The Future Problem Solving process covers six steps:[289]

1 identify challenges
2 select an underlying problem
3 produce solution ideas
4 generate and select criteria

5   apply criteria
6   develop an action plan.

The 'Odyssey of the Mind' involves students from kindergarten to college in problem-solving competitions at local, state and world levels. Teams come from Argentina, Australia, Canada, China, Czech Republic, Germany, Greece, Hong Kong, Hungary, Japan, Kazakhstan, Lithuania, Mexico, Poland, Russia, Singapore, Slovakia, South Korea, the United Kingdom, Uzbekistan and the USA. The Odyssey of the Mind was founded in 1978 by Dr Samuel Micklus, a professor at Rowan University in New Jersey, who had challenged his students to invent wheelless vehicles and flotation devices.[290]

SUMMARY

Alex Osborn developed the Creative Problem Solving process as a structured mode to embed divergent and convergent thinking dimensions. Over the years, the process evolved through research and refinements. My abbreviated version is CIA, or Challenge-Ideas-Action. Apple has a CreativeIQ framework that seems to embody the challenge, ideation and action philosophy of Creative Problem Solving. Xerox also has a variation of the Creative Problem Solving over six steps.

The CPS process has had tremendous success, such as variations for children and students. The legacy of Osborn-Parnes can also be seen through the Creative Education Foundation, the yearly Creative Problem Solving Institute conference, the creativity studies program at Buffalo State, the *Journal of Creative Behavior* and the Sidney J. Parnes Global Fellowship.

The next chapter discusses Synectics innovative problem solving, which was developed during the same era as brainstorming and the Creative Problem Solving process.

MIND NETTING: SYNECTICS INNOVATIVE PROBLEM SOLVING

CHAPTER 7

While consulting on product development with a Synectics client in Japan, I spent a day with a Japanese homemaker having tea in her home, shopping with her in her regular supermarket and lunching with her in her favourite restaurant. Through an interpreter, I asked why she bought certain brands and probed her media habits. She told me she liked to read inspiring stories about people achieving their dreams and that her favourite music band was Dreams Come True. I found out that she had put on hold her wish of touring European art museums because of marriage and children. Reading and listening about achieving dreams was a way of keeping her dream alive! This discovery enabled the client to develop a new product portfolio.

INTRODUCTION

Creativity scholar Moe Stein once said that the Creative Problem Solving process and Synectics are 'the parents of most, if not all, existing creativity programs'.[291] This is because George Prince and William Gordon founded Synectics just after Osborn had introduced his Creative Problem Solving process. This chapter examines the work of Prince, Gordon, Vincent Nolan (a 'disciple' of Synectics in the United Kingdom) and Synectics consultants, and describes DREAM, my variation of the Synectics framework.

PRINCE

After serving as a navy officer during the Second World War, Prince joined an advertising company in Rochester, USA. Intrigued by the ideation process, Prince in 1958 joined the Invention Design Group of the Arthur D. Little Consulting Company (ADL) in Cambridge, Massachusetts. There he met William Gordon and the two left ADL with colleagues Dick Sperry and Carl Marden in 1960 to start Synectics.[292]

The uniqueness of Synectics (coined from Greek words that mean bringing diverse elements together) is its focus on a behavioural approach to the team innovation process. Prince and Gordon audiotaped and later videotaped thousands of problem-solving sessions to learn what had facilitated or hindered the team creativity process.

I am fortunate to have learned from Prince directly through training and indirectly through his books, articles and videos. After being exposed to Synectics during my training attachment at Young & Rubicam Advertising in New York, I received more comprehensive training in the US and UK offices of Synectics Inc. Some of the Synectics skills that I learnt were the nine-step framework, an abbreviated structure, process versus content, the discount-revenge dynamics, wishing, approximate thinking and excursions.

Synectics nine-step framework

The nine steps of the Synectics framework share the Creative Problem Solving/ Challenge-Ideas-Action philosophy of understanding the challenge before ideation and action:

1. task headline
2. task background
3. springboards of wishes
4. selection of wishes to develop
5. ways and means to develop selected wishes
6. emerging ideas
7. itemised response of pros, cons and ways to improve ideas
8. possible solutions
9. next steps.[293]

An abbreviated structure

Prince also taught me that the process could be achieved in six steps:

1. task headline
2. wishes (with excursion if required)
3. selection of intriguing wishes
4. develop wishes into ideas
5. pluses of and concerns about emerging ideas
6. action steps on possible solution.

Separate process from content

In a problem-solving meeting, there should be a facilitator whose sole role is to focus on the process. The content is the responsibility of the task owner and the idea contributors.

In his highly popular 1969 *Harvard Business Review* article 'How to be a better meeting chairman', Prince offered ten leadership principles:[294]

1. First, never compete with the group members. When you contribute and favour your own ideas, your group members will be less committed to the process. You may contribute ideas during the task explanation phase and build on a team member's idea but give precedence to the team ideas.
2. Listen to the group members. Understand the point of view of your team members, paraphrasing your understanding.
3. Don't permit anyone to be put on the defensive. Do not pressure anyone to provide or justify an analogy or a wild and seemingly irrelevant idea.
4. Use every member of the group. Try to give equal airtime to the quiet member and compulsive talker. Talk to the talkative member privately if possible about the importance of hearing from everyone.
5. Keep the energy level high. Introduce challenging questions, humour and interesting topics that involve everyone. Use body language and quicken the pace or surprise the group if you notice boredom.
6. Keep the members informed about where they are and what is expected of them. Use easel pads on the stages and steps. Restate where you are in the process and what you want the group to do as you move the meeting along.
7. Keep an eye on the expert. This is the task owner, so observe this person's reactions to ideas or possible solutions. Involve this expert task owner to build on or reshape ideas.
8. Remember that you are not permanent. Rotate the role of chair of the meeting. This rotation motivates a potential chairperson to participate actively and cooperatively.
9. Do not manipulate the group. While you manage the process, do not lead the group down your own preferred way of thinking.
10. Work hard at the technique of being chairperson. Learn meeting procedures, listening skills and appropriate responses to situations until these become natural to you.

The discount/revenge dynamics

When you 'discount' a group participant by relegating their importance in any way, the discounted person could withdraw or flee from further contribution to the process by self-censoring any other idea that may crop up in their mind.

This self-censoring is analogous to the individual production blocking of ideas mentioned in the brainstorming chapter. Often, the 'discounted' person will wait for an opportunity to seek revenge by attacking your idea. This flight or fight phenomenon is unhealthy in a creativity session. Fight the problem but not the person!

Wishing

This technique gives freedom to participants to wish for anything during the problem-solving process. Prince cited the example of Edwin Land's three-year-old daughter expressing a simple wish to see her photographs immediately, leading to Land pondering the matter before developing the Polaroid instant camera a few years later. When I was attached to Lintas Advertising in Sydney for management training, I saw the researchers getting children to wish for new flavours of ice cream.

Approximate thinking

Prince advocated approximate, imprecise and ambiguous thinking during the speculative wishing stage and the connection-making step. Precise thinking can be saved for the convergence stage. Also allow approximate or mistaken hearing. For example, in one of my sessions a participant voiced 'line dancing' but I had written 'blind dancing', to much laughter among the group. While participants initially struggled to connect 'blind dancing' to the task of building teamwork, approximate connection-making eventually led to a precise idea for the task owner!

Excursions

These are a form of 'safe' chaos, where you take participants mentally and behaviourally into another, disconnected dimension to relax and have fun before continuing with the creativity process—where they can connect seemingly irrelevant images to the task. Prince referred to an excursion as a 'metaphoric vacation'. This is a powerful tool and I have had participants do excursion exercises such as doodling and personification of objects. In one training session that I facilitated in Asia, participants talked about what they did for fun (play ping-pong, watch action movies, watch X-rated movies, etc) and when they continued with wishing for ideas for a selected task, one participant wished for 'XXX-rated food'. This generated laugher and intrigue and became one of the shortlisted wishes for further idea development. Finding analogies of 'ratings' in different industries, such as credit ratings and cinema ratings, provided concrete concepts for the client!

If you wish to learn more about the work of Prince, visit the website http://georgemprince.com. Kimberly Hooks set up this website in 2003 with Prince (who died in 2009), and it features his published and unpublished works, his doodles and his favourite authors.

GORDON

Gordon was an inventor and psychologist who believed in the power of metaphor for learning and innovative problem solving. In 1944 he started analysing thought processes of participants during invention sessions.[295] Gordon concluded that a person could consciously and actively unlock the unconscious mind through the use of analogies.[296] Although Parnes had strengthened the Creative Problem Solving process with Synectics' metaphorical approaches,[297] Gordon critiqued brainstorming for trying to arrive at a solution too quickly, preferring a longer multiple-perspective process (which has also been criticised as being fatiguing).[298]

Gordon left Synectics in the 1960s to focus on developing the process for education, and there have been numerous research studies in this sector. He died in 2003.

Gordon was known for his use of direct analogies, personal analogies and symbolic analogies. Gordon's friend Al Capp, creator of the cartoon strip 'Li'l Abner', captured Gordon's approach for designing a stair-climbing wheelchair in the June 1965 issue of *Fortune Magazine*:[299]

1. Direct analogies of 'climbing' from nature, such as a mountain goat and a snake.
2. Personal analogies of a selected direct analogy; for example, how participants would feel as a mountain goat. Participants felt nervous, confident and like the lightened muscle of a hind leg.
3. Symbolic analogy (paradox or compressed conflict as described in other literature) of a selected personal analogy image. Participants looked at the essence of the goat's leg muscle in an abstract and seemingly contradictory statement, such as 'blind direction'.
4. Direct analogy of the symbolic analogy or paradox statement. Direct analogies of 'blind direction' were a snake pit and how a snake 'screws' itself to a tree. The final solution was a self-propelling wheelchair with long rotating screws.

Another example of how Gordon's analogical thinking has been applied was by journalism professor Mitchell Land in his 1995 article in *Journalism & Mass Communication Educator* called 'Awakening the right brain in feature writing'.

Land used Gordon's analogical process over six steps: topic description, direct analogies, personal analogy, paradoxes, new direct analogies and rewriting the original topic.

Topic description

Assign any topic, such as a character, celebrity, concept, object, process or sport. Encourage students to write freely whatever comes to mind on the topic in ten minutes, with a one-page minimum. Then get each student to read out one key word they wrote on the topic (for example, descriptors for a baseball topic might include America, ball, boring and hot dogs); the professor will write these in red on the board.

Direct analogies

Ask students to review the words on the board and draw mental images when they hear or see the words. Ask students to choose a word category *unrelated* to the topic. If the topic is baseball, choose a category such as animals, chemicals, machines, minerals, plants and technologies. If a category emerges from the descriptors, such as machines, ask students for machine examples that come to mind. By consensus, focus on a machine that best reflects the descriptors, such as a popcorn machine.

Personal analogy or personification

This technique taps into the emotion and imagination of the students, enabling an excursion into the creative right brain. Ask students to imagine themselves as the selected machine and express their feelings. Write the personified words in green on the board.

Paradoxes or compressed conflict

This process requires students to select the green words that seem to conflict with each other, such as 'mournful optimist', and write these paradoxes in orange on the board. Circle the paradoxes that the class feels best reflect the conflict, for example, 'angry joy', 'energetic exhaustion' and 'independent bondage'.

New direct analogies

Encourage students to create new direct analogies of the paradoxes, with examples from categories unrelated to machines, such as animals. Write in black on the board when students describe the animal examples and their characteristics. Ask students to vote on one animal analogy and share their stories about their choice. You may end up with a top three animal analogies.

Rewrite the original topic

Give the class ten minutes to rewrite the original topic, associating freely with analogies, personification and paradoxes. At the next class, ask for volunteers to read out their original writing and the rewrite.

Land strongly believes in the analogical power of the right brain, hence he repeats the six-step process to help students internalise Gordon's methods. He has groups work on the six steps, with alternating leaders facilitating the process. He also has a printed guide to enable students to work on the Gordon process individually.

Many educators have also adapted Gordon's use of analogies in different ways. Some educators in gifted education start with identifying the paradox within a situation, provide some examples of direct analogies of the paradox and then challenge students to create their own analogical examples of paradoxes and, hence, internalise the process.[300]

Some other teachers use Gordon's analogies as quick stretching exercises, such as: 'How is a school like a salad?' Other teachers follow a systematic process for creative writing and design projects, beginning with direct analogies and empowering students to make the connections. Then the teachers explore many personal analogies, engaging students to feel like a tennis ball, a pencil or a mobile phone. The teachers then switch back to more direct analogies and personal analogies; give examples of paradoxes or compressed conflicts from the analogies generated; encourage students to form paradoxes of words that do not seem to fit together, such as 'happy hurt' and 'tired energy'; and then have students review the original topic from the new perspective of an intriguing paradox to provide much broader insights.

Hence, teachers can develop conceptual distance to make the familiar strange (help students see familiar issues in new ways). If students need to understand a new or difficult curriculum, teachers would use familiar analogies for analysis and comparison to make the strange concept more meaningful. Overall, the Synectics model for teaching has instructional effects (metaphoric thinking, problem-solving skills and group productivity) as well as nurturing outcomes (achieving curriculum content, adventuresome value and self-esteem).[301]

Analogy-driven inventions and other approaches

Gordon also conducted research on analogy-driven inventions and discoveries, and identified some associative inventions in his 1974 article 'Some source material in discovery-by-analogy'.[302]

George B. Bissell borrowed the idea for pumping oil from the ground from a brine derrick, thus replacing the inefficient method of using buckets and blankets to collect oil. Johann Gutenberg used the analogy of coin manufacturing to switch from wood-carved printing to reusable metal-produced letters in his printing press.

Sir Marc Isambard Brunel observed how a shipworm constructed a tube as it tunnelled through a timber beam and used this analogy for river tunnelling. Samuel Morse found that telegraphic signals became weak and ineffective with distances of a few miles. One day he observed fresh horses replacing tired horses at relay post stations—hence, he set up stations along his telegraphic line to boost the signals.

Eli Whitney observed a cat stretching its claw through a fence to snatch a chicken and used this analogy to invent the cotton gin machine to pick cotton efficiently, separating the fibres from the seeds.

Gordon's analogical thinking approach is also featured in creativity textbooks. According to creativity professor Gary Davis, 'Analogical/metaphorical thinking is the ability to borrow ideas from one context and use them in another, borrow a solution from a related problem, or otherwise see a connection between one situation and another'.[303] In his book *Creativity is Forever* Davis provided an example of finding ideas to protect older people from mugging.

Focusing on the word 'protect', Davis provided analogies of protection in different categories, such as birds, plants and wind, as possible solutions. Birds travel in groups, so one idea is to have the elderly travel in groups. The howling wind suggests an idea of an electronic yelling device that older people could easily carry with them. Plants suggest a camouflage concept. Exploring the idea of protection among animals provided more associative ideas, such as a skunk type of spray can, a snake mask, glove claws and slip-on fangs.

NOLAN

Vincent Nolan, who passed away in August 2014, started the UK Synectics office in Hemel Hempstead in the 1970s and spread the training and consulting services of Synectics in Europe and other countries. His website is still running and features his articles and books on Synectics and innovation: www.vincentnolan.co.uk.

I learnt the Synectics process from Nolan in Bangkok and Hemel Hempstead in the 1980s. I learnt from his techniques of out-in listening for ideas and headlining wishes and working alone on the Synectics process.

Listening out-in

Listening 'out' occurs when you listen to a speaker. Listening 'in' is when you daydream or actively associate while listening to the speaker.

The principle behind the technique of listening out-in is that the mind thinks so much faster than a person's speaking speed. The authors of the book *The Einstein Factor* calculated that brain speed is 100,000 trillion flops (a flop is a measure of computing speed).[304] Hence, there is a tendency for a listener to 'daydream' because the speaker cannot speak quickly enough.

My own connection is that listening 'in' is like Googling your mind to search its rich resources—a mind has been estimated to have 280 quintillion bits of memory (280,000,000,000,000,000,000)[305]—and to tap into our multiple visual, intrapersonal, naturalistic, kinaesthetic, musical, interpersonal, linguistic and logical intelligences.[306]

I have taught out-in listening to workshop participants to use in non-problem-solving situations, such as listening to a speaker. Instead of wasting time writing everything the speaker says, it is more enriching to jot keywords from the speaker and then also note your connections. Participants were able to note their thoughts and use them to provide feedback on what the speaker had said.

You can practice out-in listening by drawing a line vertically down a page, with the left side reserved for what you hear outside your mind and the right side for what you connect inside your mind.

TABLE 7.1 Listening out-in

LISTENING OUT TO SPEAKER	LISTENING IN TO YOUR MIND
Jot keyword of speaker	Note images triggered by speaker's keyword

Headlining wishes

In a group problem-solving session, I have learnt that it is always good to offer a wish or idea as a news headline and then elaborate on it if necessary. This headline enables the listeners in the group to note the idea and use their thinking speed to jot down images triggered by the headline's words. An unproductive method is to ramble on with the background before headlining the main thought, possibly losing the attention of listeners.

For example, in a productive session, someone might suggest the headline: 'Drink recycled water', and your mind could quickly think of drinking, cycling, recycling, water or nature images in various forms. From these mental images, you can build on the headline idea and wish for natural, energy or chemical purification.

Work-alone exercise

While Synectics is a powerful group tool, I also learnt a useful work-alone exercise.

1. Task headline: write a one-sentence statement.
2. Task background: Write short answers to these questions:
   a. Why is this task a problem or opportunity?
   b. What is a brief history of this task?
   c. How is it a problem or opportunity for you personally? (You might be an influencer or decision maker.)
   d. What have you already tried for the task?
   e. What's the ideal solution you hope will come from this exercise? (The ideal solution could be several concepts and/or a detailed implementation plan of a selected concept.)
3. Springboards:
   a. Generate some wishes triggered by the task and task background.
   b. Excursion: Take a quick mental or physical excursion unconnected to the task.
   c. Generate more springboard wishes using excursion imagery as triggers.
4. Springboard selection: Don't overlook the intriguing and seemingly impossible springboards.
5. Ways and means:
   a. If there is already a suggested action, build on the action.
   b. If there is no specific action suggested in the springboard, think of an intriguingly feasible solution.
6. Emerging idea: Paraphrase the emerging beginning solution.

7   Itemised response on the emerging idea:
    a. Pluses of the idea
    b. Major concerns with the idea
8   Overcome concerns:
    a. Options to overcome first concern
    b. Options to overcome second concern if any
9   Possible action: Summarise the final solution to include options to overcome any concern/s and evaluate against newness, feasibility and personal commitment.

Of the skills I picked up from Nolan, listening out-in has been the most beneficial. I am constantly forming connections as I listen in different situations!

SYNECTICS CONSULTANTS

Working with various Synectics consultants over the years, I have also picked up skills in planning and facilitating team creativity sessions.

Planning

The planning meeting with the task owner covers the logistics for all stages of the team creativity meeting. It includes the process overview, roles, content, participant mix, task background, task analysis, excursion activities, resources and the next steps.

Process overview

It is important to brief the task owner on the process that you will use at the actual team creativity session, such as the interplay between process, people and place (climate) to produce a good creative product (content or outcome). Cover the dreamer, realist and critic stages of the process, and the specific steps of the process flow, such as task headline, task background, springboards (wishes) and so on.

Roles, process and climate, and content

The task owner also needs to be familiar with the three key roles in a team creativity session: facilitator, task owner and idea contributors.

In terms of process and climate, the facilitator manages the process and group dynamics. The facilitator in a small group is also often the scribe but sometimes there are two facilitators even for small groups, hence the second facilitator could serve as a scribe or they could take turns to facilitate and scribe.

The facilitator does not contribute to content but sometimes in training or consulting sessions I intentionally throw in a word or two during wishing, excursions or evaluation to model the type of thinking desired for that stage in the process. When asked for an opinion during the selection of wishes for further development, I respond by saying 'Which wish is so intriguing, weird and seemingly impossible to achieve for the task at hand?' We would then have subgroups developing feasible and unfeasible wishes, with each participant in a subgroup facilitating the breakout session.

The task owner is an active content contributor and active decision-maker at each stage of the process (task, background, ideas, selection and evaluation). The task owner should not take detailed notes except keywords for out-in listening. It is also important that the task owner models encouraging behaviour, such as headlining wishes, building on ideas and nodding or gesturing to show appreciation for creative ideas. The task owner should also accept the importance of equal airtime during the team creativity session.

All participants should be idea contributors, actively contributing headline wishes and ideas, listening out-in, and building on and appreciating ideas. Idea contributors could also help the task owner select wishes for expansion, develop action plans and so on.

Participant mix

The facilitator should discuss with the task owner the best participant mix for small or large groups.

A manageable group for one facilitator is six to eight participants, but the size of the group could be larger with an experienced facilitator or when participants are divided into subgroups of four working in different parts of the room or venue. The participant mix should ideally be cross-disciplinary, because it's more fruitful to net ideas from diverse minds.

When the group size is more than thirty participants, you would require a second facilitator to walk around, and work with, break-out groups. I have worked with Synectics consultants in sessions where we all started in one large room and then, divided, moved into several other rooms with our own groups. Again, a diverse participant mix is desired.

Task background

See the five task background questions to ask the client under the work-alone exercise, earlier in this chapter.

Task analysis

This method aims to help the task owner determine the real focus for the team because the original task headline may not be sufficiently clear. This is similar to the 'logic tree' in brainsteering and the fact-finding step in Creative Problem Solving.

The process involves a series of 'why' and 'how' questions flowing from the task headline. The process is also referred to as backward (why) and forward (how) task analysis. The steps in the process are listed below (see Figure 7.1 for a working example):

1. Start with the task headline in the middle of the page.
2. Ask why the client wishes to address the task.
3. Write the answer that the client offers.
4. Ask 'why' to probe the answer and continue the 'why' process.
5. Move to the 'how' question to extract a beginning idea to resolve the task.
6. Write the answer and ask a 'how' question on the answer, and so on.
7. Review the list of 'why' and 'how' answers to determine which is a better focus for the team to spend energy on. You may decide to choose the original task headline or a 'why' or 'how' statement.

FIGURE 7.1 Task analysis example

4 Why?	To free up resources
3 Why?	To make the customer less dependent on us
2 Why?	To facilitate implementation
1 Why?	To define the product we are selling
Task headline	**To devise a way of defining customer needs more precisely and more quickly**
1 How?	Establish a simpler structured procedure
2 How?	Reduce the number of consumer questions
3 How?	Eliminate duplication, establish norms and eliminate redundant questions
4 How?	Develop specific software tool for the job

Excursion activities

It is always good to be prepared with diverse excursions for different tasks and stages of the team creativity process, because these activities give participants the freedom to do irrelevant, irrational, chaotic and fun things as a break from routine thinking. A general guideline is to choose an activity that is the opposite of the task or situation. For example, if the task is a people problem, I would plan activities that focus on non-people dimensions, such as the weather, animals, objects, cartoons and mythology. People and non-people dimensions could also be used for a technical task. Such excursions align with the Synectics way of making the familiar strange; that is, the task is perhaps too familiar to the group, so the excursion would create a strange moment, after which participants could make the strange familiar by creatively connecting the excursion experience to the task.

Some of the excursion activities that task owners and I have used include fun videos; print images; word associations or analogies; funny stories; unusual careers, for example an 'ant census' or an 'armpit sniffer'; personification, for example feelings of a chair; childhood games; favourite cartoon characters; favourite celebrities; favourite music, movies, books, holidays, or cities; random doodling; and local food delights, for example durian.

Resources
There should also be a checklist of resources required for the team creativity session, such as venue, audio and video facilities, flipcharts and stands, sticky notes, marker pens, crayons, and physical examples for excursion activities.

Next steps
You could plan for a second meeting with the task owner before the team creativity session or in the post-session review meeting. There is also the question: 'What would you like to do with the flipcharts that have all the written and visual content from the team creativity session?' The task owner often collects the charts, with the help of participant colleagues, to get the content typed and reviewed. Hence, it is important to number every flipchart page and write big headlines for sections of the charts. Some clients have a non-participant scribe in the team creativity session to type idea contributions on a laptop and then print the output for different stages of the process.

Facilitating
Effective team creativity sessions flow from good planning. The facilitator has to manage the beginning of the session, provide a session overview, highlight ground rules, introduce energisers and manage the end of the session.

The beginning
I often introduce myself through the metaphor of a tree and ask participants to tell me why I am a tree. There can be associations of knowledge, age, strength, shade, lovers carving out messages, renewal and firewood. In small groups, I encourage individual introductions through metaphors, verbally and visually. In larger groups, participants share their metaphors in pairs or groups of three. This is one form of introducing excursion or 'metaphorical vacation' as described by George Prince.

Session overview
This serves as the agenda for the training or innovation workshop to give an idea of what is scheduled, when and approximate duration. Breakout rooms are included in the schedule for large groups.

Ground rules
A traditional way of introducing ground rules is to talk about them. I prefer to get participants' input into what makes a successful team creativity session. Input often covers the ground rules on brainstorming, such as quantity of ideas, wild ideas, building on ideas and deferred judgment. I then introduce the Synectics concepts of roles, process versus content, out-in listening and headlining.

Energisers
While excursions are effective to divert participants from the task and return with refreshed thinking, energisers are important to relax the body and mind at different times of the day. These energisers could be over a minute or two and longer, depending on the time of the day and group size. You would have to adjust your energisers to suit the abilities of the group, such as accommodating any less physically abled people. Some energisers that I have run, often with participant input, include Samson, Tiger and Delilah; the massage chain; doing the opposite; and guessing what's happening.

In Samson, Tiger and Delilah, I have two teams compete against each other. The two teams do not face each other at first but have their backs to the opposing team. The team members decide which action to demonstrate simultaneously when they turn around at the facilitator's count of 'three'. Samson would be strong arms, Tiger would display ferocity and Delilah a sexy pose. Samson would beat Tiger, Tiger would beat Delilah and Delilah would beat Samson. I run 'elimination' rounds if there are four or more teams until there is one winner.

In the massage chain, the group forms a circle and participants put their hands on the back of another participant. When everyone is ready, get the massage going. Then turn the participants around and start the massage chain again.

'Doing the opposite' is an ideal energiser for much larger groups. Every participant stands with some space around them. When the facilitator says 'small', everyone should expand their arms wide. When the facilitator calls out 'big', everyone should show a hand with fingers closed (or shrivel the body to look smaller). The fun starts when the facilitator quickens the pace with 'small' or 'big'!

For 'What's happening?', get everyone to stretch their legs and strain their necks to 'find out' what is happening in front of a 'crowd'. A few leg and neck stretches and straining often relax the participants. Getting participants to share what they 'see' could be material for the following team creativity activity.

End of session
It is important for the facilitator to summarise the next steps that the task owner would take, the support needed and the timing.

I have learnt a great deal about planning and implementing from various Synectics consultants. You may wish to visit the SynecticsWorld website for resources, including case studies of clients in consumer goods, energy, financial services, food and beverage, health care, hospitality, industry, services, science and technology, and transportation. Among the clients is Unilever, which Synectics has worked with for five decades across brands such as Lipton Ice Tea, Slim-Fast, Top Clean, Van den Bergh Foods and Wall's Ice Cream.[307]

You can also download the 2010 book *Imagine THAT! Celebrating 50 years of Synectics* (http://synecticsworld.com/imagine-that).

DREAM VARIATION
This section describes how I varied the Synectics process into the DREAM framework of dream, review, expand, assess and manage. This section covers the training background, my attempts to improve the process, my creative connections, reducing the training duration, and workshop design.

Training background
Synectics training initially had to be done in a small class of about six participants because of the need to videotape and review problem-solving sessions. The Synectics founders audio-taped and later video-taped team problem-solving sessions to determine specific interactions that helped or hindered the team creativity process between the facilitator, task owner and idea contributors.[308]

Participants at our team creativity workshops had concerns with the Synectics nine-step process. It was not easy to remember the nine steps and it was mentally taxing to learn the process over five days, with time spent on locating and reviewing video segments of team behaviour during practice sessions. Some participants also felt that the video review process reinforced the flaws in team creativity behaviours that had motivated them to sign up for the training workshops by anchoring participants on the flaws. Many participants also felt that it was not relevant in the Asian context to kick off the workshop with the task of finding a way to deter Canadian bears from attacking and destroying electrical boxes that seemed to resemble rival bears (the solution was to spray-paint the boxes with a pungent deterring smell that would be released when bears started to scratch the boxes).

Improving process

I explored ways to make the Synectics process more memorable, manageable and relevant by borrowing ideas from accelerated learning and neurolinguistic programming. Lozanov's accelerated learning methods involved play and music to help children learn,[309] while Bandler and Grinder's neurolinguistic programming had advocated a multidimensional process integrating the brain, language and behaviour.[310] Reading neurolinguistic programming practitioner Dilt's books on strategies of genius also led me to Walt Disney's thinking modes of dreamer, realist and critic.[311]

Creative connections

While thinking about simplifying the Synectics nine-step process and about Disney's thinking modes, I realised that the two methods were conveying the same messages in different frameworks. I first applied Disney's dream or divergence phase to the Synectics' springboard step, his realist or convergence phase to the selection—ways and means steps, and his critic phase to the itemised response step. See Figure 7.2 for the key Synectics steps illustrated through a diamond shape to show the divergence and convergence in the process.

FIGURE 7.2 Synectics steps and Disney's thinking modes

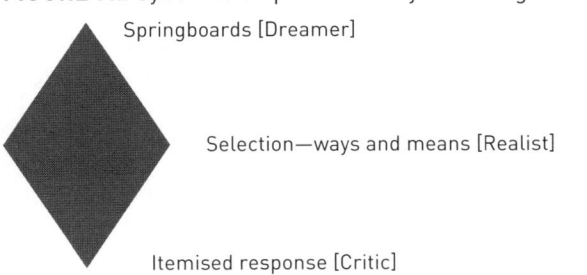

And voila! Thus was born the DREAM process of dream, review, expand, assess and manage. Dream wild wishes. Review wishes. Expand on seemingly undoable wishes. Assess the pluses and minuses of emerging concepts. Manage possible solutions.

FIGURE 7.3 Synectics steps and DREAM process

Task headline and task background
Springboards [Dream]
Selection [Review]
Ways and means + emerging idea [Expand]
Itemised response [Assess]
Possible solutions + next steps [Manage]

Within the DREAM framework, I adapted other techniques:

- Metaphors: I had participants introduce themselves metaphorically, personifying themselves as hamburgers and drawing composite metaphors to illustrate their workshop learning. Participants have introduced themselves as a bridge, 'mother hen', abstract painting, bush and river!
- Accelerated learning: I incorporated music and playful activities to relax and energise the learning process.
- Neurolinguistic programming: I modelled up front the DREAM steps and how to connect seemingly unconnected images from playful activities to the problem-solving task at hand. I anchored the DREAM process through charts that participants could refer to throughout each practice session.
- Buzan's mind mapping[312]: I used mind mapping for the DREAM process and associations around metaphors.
- Gardner's multiple intelligences[313]: I used an acronym of VINKMILL, with a drawing of a windmill, to illustrate that we all have visual, intrapersonal, naturalistic, kinaesthetic, musical, interpersonal, linguistic and logical abilities to draw upon for excursion activities, imagery and idea generation.
- Knowles' andragogy[314]: I designed the training workshops around facilitated learning, with me as facilitator in the beginning and with participants as facilitators in their problem-solving groups.

Training duration

I experimented with facilitating the training workshops with sixteen to twenty-four participants over two days. Participants who signed up for the DREAM workshops were advised to come to the training with some real tasks (problems or opportunities) that they would like to work on, plus prepare to introduce themselves metaphorically to the class.

The new training process had no video-taping and reviewing of video segments. With more participants than usual in a training space of about a hundred square metres, I grouped the learners into teams of four and rotated participants so that they could work with different people and play the roles of facilitator, task owner and idea contributor.

Since most participants prefer training of a shorter duration, I designed the workshop over two days. There was Mastery Modelling (benchmarking the DREAM process), Intensive Immersion (intensive hands-on practices), Group Germination (working with different groups) and Mind Netting (using different excursions and some of the creative thinking tools of participants, such as mind mapping). See Appendix F for the two-day workshop structure.

Workshop design

Adapting the Synectics process, with Disney-inspired thinking modes and accelerated learning tools, has made the DREAM process memorable and effective for participants. I have used the DREAM version of Synectics to train adults and to facilitate team creativity sessions for clients. One client, whose group doodled beautifully and saw a product possibility from an image that looked like dung in the drawing, commented that the DREAM version could complement the TRIZ inventive problem-solving method that they had been using (TRIZ is explained in Chapter 9). Developing the DREAM version of Synectics also led me to research the process and synthesise findings into team creativity catalysts for accelerating innovation.

Industry examples

Using direct, personal and symbolic analogies may be a Gordon approach to thinking creatively but many practitioners have used analogical thinking in more direct ways. Some of my favourite analogical thinking examples include Velcro, the Sydney Opera House, a Tourism Queensland campaign, the termite-inspired building in Zimbabwe, the desert refrigerator in Nigeria, the ZMET metaphor-based research process and marketing applications.

Velcro

Swiss engineer George de Mestral went for a walk with his dog in the Alps and found burrs (hook-bearing flowers) clinging to his pants. Removing the burrs gave Mestral the idea of creating the world's first hook-and-loop fastener, now known as Velcro and used in agriculture, apparel, industrial cleaning, medical and health care, personal care, packaging, transportation and turfing.[315]

Sydney Opera House
Danish architect Jørn Utzon designed the 'sails' of Australia's Sydney Opera House based on his exposure to shipbuilding. Utzon's design was one of 200 crowdsourced entries that were submitted in 1956 in the international competition to design an opera house in Sydney. The Sydney Opera House website indicates that Utzon's entry was in a rejected pile until a late-arrival judge from the USA saw it and declared it outstanding![316]

Tourism Queensland
Tourism Queensland used a job recruitment analogy to create awareness of and tourism in the Australian state. The 2009 advertisement was for 'the best job in the world': an island caretaker with a six-month contract worth A$150,000 to look after the islands of the Great Barrier Reef.[317] The campaign ran in social and traditional mass media, attracting global news coverage worth about US$400 million from media channels such as BBC, CNN, Oprah and *Time* magazine. The job ad website got more than eight million visits and 34,000 video applications from youthful educated travellers across nearly 200 countries. Englishman Ben Southall was the winner.[318]

Termite-inspired building
Architect Mick Pearce used a termite mound analogy to design the Eastgate Centre office-and-shopping complex in Zimbabwe. Termites construct their mound to draw in cool air at the base and expel hot air through a duct at the top. Using this natural means of cooling and heating the building means that the ventilation cost is only ten per cent of a similar air-conditioned complex.[319]

Desert refrigerator
Nigerian teacher Mohammed Bah Abba, Rolex Laureate in 2000, also used a natural cooling system to create a desert refrigerator. His challenge was to preserve perishable food in desert conditions. The problem then was that homes lacked electricity, young girls were enslaved to sell food fast or face food wastage and low income, and decayed food was a health hazard. Borrowing his knowledge of earthen pot usage in ancient Egypt, Abba devised his pot-in-pot cooling and preservation system in 1995, with wet sand used in between the pots as a cooling agent and a damp cloth to cover the inner pot containing fruit and vegetables. The pots could be produced at low cost, which started a pot production industry. The invention created employment, preserved food for longer, enabled girls to have their schooling and provided home sales and income. Abba financed production of 5000 pots in his first batch. After receiving the Rolex Laureate, Abba produced

and distributed more than 90,000 pots in eleven Nigerian states and neighbouring countries including Cameroon, Chad, Democratic Republic of Congo and Niger. Abba died in 2010 aged forty-six.[320]

ZMET

Olson Zaltman Associates, a research firm in the USA, has a proprietary Zaltman Metaphor Elicitation Technique in which consumers bring pictures that represent their feelings about a particular research topic. ZMET consultants ask questions about the pictures to uncover the subconscious thoughts of the consumers. For example, Olson Zaltman found that consumers associated Cisco with connection and suggested that the company reposition itself as 'the human network' in 2006. The campaign helped Cisco increase brand value, stock price, corporate ranking and the perception of it as a technology leader. Another example is Cheetos snacks, for which targeted adult consumers brought pictures that reflected escape, playfulness and mischief, leading to a campaign about freeing the mischievous child inside and increasing sales by eleven per cent.[321]

Marketing applications

I see analogical thinking as the transfer of an image from an analogy to another item. This technique is commonly used in sales promotion, such as when Kellogg's transferred images of Shrek and his buddies onto its packaging and McDonald's tied in with the Shrek movie through special merchandising.[322] Look at advertising featuring celebrities and you will see companies trying to transfer positive images of celebrities onto their brands. Vegemite also depended on attribute transferring in 2009 when it chose the name iSnack 2.0 (associating with snacks and technology) from a crowdsourcing competition to name its cheese-Vegemite spread. After a public outcry on the inappropriateness of the name for such an Australian icon, Vegemite eventually changed the name to Vegemite Cheesybite.[323]

I have found analogical or metaphorical thinking extremely useful during corporate training and university classes as mental stretching exercises. At different slots in creativity or teaching sessions, I would ask participants how the mind is like a parachute; why creative thinking is like cycling; what are examples of indestructability, a small attraction or 'time is crucial'; how two different occupations could enrich one another, such as pastor-chef, footy coach–travel agent, postal worker–nurse; and what's it like to be a floor mop, TV dinner, racing bike, torch, piece of bubble gum, bit of tissue paper, etc.

SUMMARY

This chapter focused on the Synectics process of leveraging diverse elements such as separating process from content, group dynamics, wishing, approximate thinking, excursions, energisers, various forms of analogies, out-in listening, headlining ideas, and planning and facilitating team creativity workshops. A Synectics facilitator has to look into various elements such as roles, task analysis, participant mix, resources and group energy. Prince, Gordon, Nolan and Synectics consultants have contributed to my Synectics learning directly and indirectly. This led to my DREAM variation of Synectics, modelled on Disney's dreamer-realist-critic thinking modes and various accelerated learning concepts. While Gordon is associated with direct, personal and symbolic analogies, the technique of analogical thinking is practised in all industries to achieve innovative solutions. The next chapter reviews creative thinking tools that share the same analogical and associative thinking as Synectics—lateral thinking and multidimensional thinking.

CHAPTER 8
MIND NETTING: LATERAL AND MULTIDIMENSIONAL THINKING

> Everyone knows that creativity has to be fun, lively, and crazy—so how can we have serious creativity?
>
> It is precisely this misconception about creativity that has done so much damage and has held back the development of creativity for at least two decades. There are far too many practitioners out there who believe that creativity is just brainstorming and being free to suggest crazy ideas ... In my courses, I find that people who have a brainstorming background tend to perform rather poorly. This is because they are always looking for the way out, exotic idea and often miss the simple, practical idea which is at hand. It is as if during a brainstorming session each participant is trying to make the other participant laugh at the craziness of an idea.[324]
>
> Edward de Bono, *The Journal for Quality and Participation*, Vol. 11–3.
> © The Association for Quality and Participation

INTRODUCTION

Dr Edward de Bono, the lateral thinking guru, is a staunch advocate for serious creativity and a critic of brainstorming. In turn, creativity researchers have criticised de Bono for lack of research on the theoretical coherence of lateral thinking.[325] Despite this, de Bono's lateral thinking process and the structured Six Thinking Hats are popular creative thinking tools among students and adults. This chapter explores de Bono's lateral thinking and Six Thinking Hats as well as Tony Buzan's complementary mind mapping method and my multidimensional thinking perspective to provide a contrast. Unlike the US-originated brainstorming, Creative Problem Solving and Synectics tools, the methods of de Bono and Buzan are European exports to the world.

LATERAL THINKING

De Bono, from Malta, coined the term 'lateral thinking' in 1967 to advocate thinking unusually and creatively. De Bono analogises lateral thinking as looking in a different direction and digging a different hole rather than digging the same hole deeper.[326] De Bono's lateral thinking techniques include the following:[327]

1. Alternatives: Look at concepts as springboards for alternative ideas.
2. Challenge: Challenge traditional vertical thinking.
3. Concept extraction: Extract the essence of an idea to develop an alternative idea; for example, the essence of an idea for a four-day work week is having a flexible work schedule, so an alternative idea could be having longer shifts over three days.
4. Focus: Define the focus of your thinking.
5. Harvesting: Capture practical and useful ideas.
6. Provocation: Generate provocative statements to develop new ideas. De Bono also coined the term 'PO', or 'provocative operation'—throw in a silly idea to disrupt the thinking pattern.[328] De Bono illustrated PO as a statement that is exaggerated, illogical, mad and unreasonable, such as, 'The police have six eyes'. The concept behind this was to have extra resources and the emerging idea was neighbourhood watch.[329]
7. Random entry: Re-channel thinking by introducing an unconnected input, such as a picture, sound, word or any stimulus.[330]
8. Treatment of ideas: Shape ideas to fit a situation or company.

De Bono's famous story about lateral thinking is the tale of the black and white pebbles in a small Indian village. A farmer owed money to an old village moneylender, who was willing to forego the debt in exchange for marriage to the farmer's beautiful daughter. Pretending to be fair, the moneylender said he would put a black pebble and a white pebble into a bag. If the girl picked the white pebble, she would not have to marry the moneylender and her father's debt would be waived. If she picked the black pebble, she would have to marry him to save her father from the debt. If she refused to pick a pebble, her father would go to jail. Standing on a path with black and white pebbles, the dishonest moneylender quickly picked up two black pebbles and put them into the bag, an act noticed by the girl. Not wanting to expose the moneylender as a cheat, the girl picked a pebble from the bag and purposely fumbled to drop it onto the pebble-strewn path. Apologising for her clumsiness, the girl told the moneylender to look in the bag. If he saw a black pebble, she must have picked and dropped the white pebble! Unwilling to reveal his dishonesty, the moneylender had to forgo the marriage and the debt.[331]

Companies that use lateral thinking methods include EDB Singapore, Mars, Merrill Lynch, Microsoft, Nestlé, Oracle, Procter & Gamble and Siemens.[332]

SIX THINKING HATS

De Bono introduced a parallel thinking process in 1985 called Six Thinking Hats, in which team members all focus on one mode at the same time:[333]

1. Blue hat thinking: Managing the process, focus, steps and actions.
2. White hat thinking: Information mode.
3. Green hat thinking: Creativity mode for alternatives, ideas and possibilities.
4. Red hat thinking: Mode for feelings, hunches, instinct and intuition.
5. Yellow hat thinking: Optimism mode on benefits of an idea.
6. Black hat thinking: Caution mode on potential difficulties with an idea.

Some of the lateral thinking techniques could be incorporated into the Six Thinking Hats process; for example, introducing a random entry as an excursion into the green hat mode. I saw this in practice when I attended a Six Thinking Hats training course in Singapore:

Blue hat: How to increase revenue on public phones.

Green hat: Random word on 'pipe'. 'Pipe' associations of 'smoke' led to the idea of selling products in the phone booth; 'tobacco' association led to the idea of aromatherapy coin-operated machines in phone booths; and 'dream' association led to the idea of a reward program for using public phones.

The Six Thinking Hats can be flexibly used, with some hats used more often:

Blue hat: Focus on a task such as how to be famous for something.

White hat: What information is known, for example, personal skills and interests, plus what information is needed, for example, knowledge of famous people by categories.

Green hat: Ideas to be famous for.

Red hat: What is your gut feeling on some of the green hat ideas?

Yellow hat: What are the benefits of Idea 1, Idea 2, etc?

Black hat: What are your concerns with Idea 1, etc?

Green hat: What are new ideas to overcome black hat concerns?

Blue hat: What are your possible solutions to be famous for something?

As the process above shows, the Six Thinking Hats are not used sequentially but could be adapted to fit situations. I see similarities between the Six Thinking

Hats, the Creative Problem Solving process and Synectics. For example, the white hat is analogous to the fact-finding step in the Creative Problem Solving process and to Synectics' task background. The green hat is like the idea-finding step in the Creative Problem Solving process and like Synectics' springboard or wishing stage. The yellow hat and black hat are analogous to Synectics' itemised response of pluses, cons and improvements of ideas.

Some success stories of the Six Thinking Hats are J. Walter Thompson, Motorola, 3M and Sri Lanka.

J. Walter Thompson

The advertising agency J. Walter Thompson was searching for ideas to connect its car client Ford Focus with youths. JWT unsuccessfully tried brainstorming with groups of fifteen people and then with four to five people. Then the agency used Six Thinking Hats and developed ideas to sponsor a large tent at two events: a three-day Detroit electronic music festival and a music tour. JWT jazzed up the tents with two Ford Focus cars fitted with stereo equipment, had DJs play music, included 'Fashion in Focus' dancers and integrated an interactive game in a computer kiosk. The result was that youths lined up to enter the tents. Six Thinking Hats is now 'creative caffeine' at JWT.[334]

Motorola

Motorola's task in 2002 was to develop a high-tech hand-held device with a price tag of under US$800. It hired a master trainer to facilitate a three-day product development event using Six Thinking Hats and lateral thinking techniques. White hat mode enabled product managers to share information on consumer profiles, products and technological benefits and limitations. Green hat mode focused on 'product for the future' ideas, using techniques such as random object, reverse provocation and concept extraction. The outcome was 'Accompli', a virtual office mobile business tool with flexibility to add applications and play games. Motorola launched Accompli Personal Communicator in Asia, Europe and North America.[335]

3M

The company was looking for an innovative duct tape to broaden its market. Over three half-day sessions, a 3M staff member trained in Six Thinking Hats worked with concept ideation experts. The green hat focused on ideas for a new version of duct tape. Smaller groups then discussed the benefits and concerns of each idea through the yellow and black hats respectively. Then the team put on their red hat to voice their favourite ideas. 3M launched a colourful variation of duct tape marketed towards women.[336]

CHAPTER 8: MIND NETTING: LATERAL AND MULTIDIMENSIONAL THINKING

Sri Lanka

After the 2004 tsunami destruction in Sri Lanka, government officials learnt Six Thinking Hats and lateral thinking techniques from master trainers and developed a reconstruction blueprint to house thousands of families within a year.[337]

You may have your own stories on thinking laterally or the use of Six Thinking Hats. Lateral thinking is analogously like digging for ideas in a different place, and its PO technique is analogous to a wacky wish. The Six Thinking Hats process is a flexible structure for parallel thinking by team problem solvers, with all energy focused simultaneously on one thinking mode.

MIND MAPPING

> Your brain is like a sleeping giant.
>
> Whatever your discipline, become a student of excellence in all things. Take every opportunity to observe people who manifest the qualities of mastery. These models of excellence will inspire you and guide you toward the fulfillment of your highest potential.
>
> Associate new and unique ideas with 'old' ideas that already exist to become exceptionally creative.
>
> Through using our memory to its fullest, we can unlock the vast reservoir of human potential.
>
> Normal linear note taking and writing will put you into a semi-hypnotic trance, while Mind Mapping will greatly enhance your left and right brain cognitive skills.[338]
>
> Tony Buzan

Britain's Tony Buzan introduced mind mapping in the late 1960s to harness the brain's cortical skills through observation, benchmarking mastery and associative thinking. This section discusses mind mapping 'laws', applications and research, before describing my concept of multidimensional thinking.

Laws of mind mapping

A mind map starts with a central idea and radiates to main branches and sub-branches of single keywords related to the idea illustrated visually with images, numbers and colours. Buzan's 'How to Mind Map' covers seven steps to better thinking:

1 Set your purpose or focus.
2 Start in the centre of a horizontal blank paper.

3 Sketch an image of your purpose in the centre.
4 Use at least three colours for creativity, emphasis, structure and texture.
5 Draw curved, thick to thin lines at each level from the centre.
6 Use one keyword or image on each line for more flexible thinking.
7 Use images throughout.

See Figure 8.1 from Buzan's website, which shows the main branches and their sub-branches emanating from the central focus.[339]

FIGURE 8.1 How to mind map

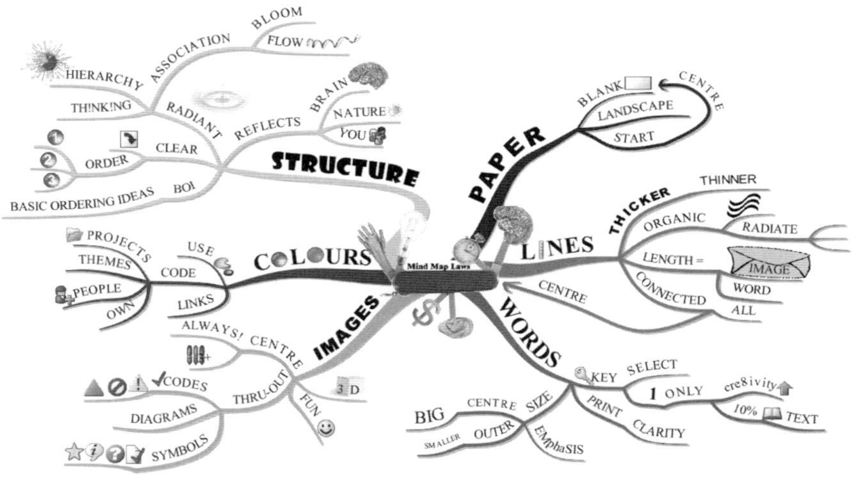

Bill Jarrard and Jennifer Goddart, Mindwerx International
www.mindwerx.com, reproduced with permission

Applications

Mind mapping can be applied in various ways; for example, for creative thinking, a ten-minute brainstorming session on challenges facing a small business, team success elements, exercises for relaxation and de-stressing, learning a language, an overview of statistics, remembering songs, reviewing science and chemical formulas, learning about William Shakespeare, planning Singapore's National Day, planning a sausage sizzle to raise money for charity, or getting the best from Google AdWords.

Visit the following websites to see various examples of mind maps: www.buzan.com.au/learning/mindmapgallery.html and www.mindwerx.com/mindexchange/browse-grid/mind-map.

More than 250 million people use mind mapping,[340] including individuals using the iMindMap software in organisations such as Apple, BBC, Disney, HP, IBM, Intel, Microsoft, NASA, PepsiCo, Procter & Gamble, Sony, Toyota and the United Nations.[341] While there are various software packages for mind mapping, Buzan endorses only iMindMap, which is positioned as the 'first dual brainstorming and mind mapping software'.[342]

Research

Several research studies have illustrated that mind mapping works: the process improves memory by ten to thirty-two per cent more than rote learning and traditional note taking; it helps students to quickly master learning materials through fun learning, connecting thoughts and ideas; it helps presenters convey integrated information confidently, professionally and effectively; it openly and synergistically harnesses the input of group members during project planning and implementation; it helps problem solvers visually see relevant issues and related ideas through a combination of left brain elements of words and numbers, plus right brain cues of colours, images and space; and mind mapping software has helped teachers present lessons pictorially, and enabled students to generate, organise and discuss ideas faster.[343]

MULTIDIMENSIONAL THINKING

Related to de Bono's random entry technique (to introduce an unconnected element for associations) and Buzan's radiant thinking through mind mapping, I have taught students and industry practitioners about multidimensional thinking by drawing on my knowledge of Synectics, brain memory, Gardner's multiple intelligences and traits of geniuses.

We have the ability to move beyond one-dimensional or single-minded thinking. In 1964, Koestler described single-minded associative thinking as habitual, routine, confined, repetitive thinking, and coined the alternative 'bisociative thinking' to signify double-minded thinking, where new connections are made by comparing two unrelated thoughts.[344]

Hence, connecting the unconnected or finding associations between seemingly unrelated elements has underpinned breakthrough thinking over the years. A six-year study of twenty-five entrepreneurs, 1000 executives and 500 individuals who had invented new products or started innovative companies discovered five skills in the DNA of innovators: associating, questioning, observing, experimenting and networking. Associating is the most powerful skill. An identical twin who creates ideas individually would have less chance of breakthrough thinking compared to the other twin who makes associations while interacting with diverse people such as a designer, an engineer and a musician; who visits innovative start-up companies to observe and benchmark; who samples new products; who shows their product prototype to obtain people's feedback; and who asks 'what if' and 'why' questions during interactions with people.[345]

Imagine if you could add diverse dimensions to your associative thinking. How would Amazon, Apple, Disney, Google, Southwest Airlines, Starwood Hotels and Zara solve your problems on costs, data, design, consumer loyalty and supply chain?[346] Imagine drawing on the thinking patterns of geniuses by using metaphors, analogies, multiple perspectives and sensory synthesis! Imagine tapping into some of the 280 quintillion bits of memory stored in your brain!

I remember being in a mind mapping training workshop where the class was creating a group map around the theme of love. Initially the associations were on the same track or single dimension explicitly connected with romance, sex, breakup and heartbreak.

Knowing that the mind has stored diverse 'love' data in our brain, I mentioned tennis. Everyone was taken aback until someone then associated with the tennis scores of 'love, fifteen, etc'. Then I moved into other love associations, such as Courtney Love the musician and actor, Davis Love III the golfer, puppy love and the movie *To Sir with Love*. During the break, some participants came up to me and said that they appreciated my input into multidimensional thinking because they had always been associating in the same dimension or in the same box. Thus, multidimensional thinking helps you to think outside the box and expand your solution space. See my rendition of the 'love' mind mapping in Figure 8.2.

FIGURE 8.2 Multidimensional mind mapping around 'love'

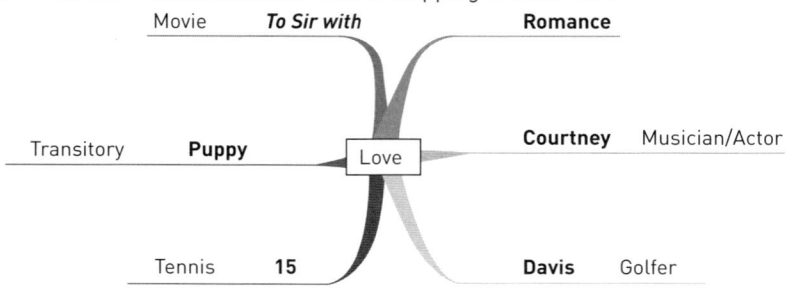

Consider another association around the word 'strip'. The one-track or one-dimensional thinking is often around clothes or to strip-search a person. Based on your group's diverse experiences, you could have a multidimensional mind map such as Figure 8.3.

FIGURE 8.3 Multidimensional mind mapping around 'strip'

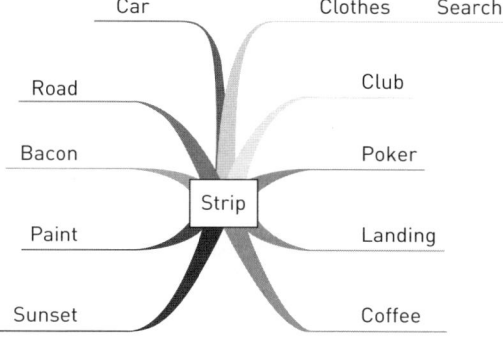

I once teased participants by asking how stripping was connected with creative thinking. Participants mentioned stripping inhibitions, stripping one's self-concept, stripping a negative attitude and stripping a hidden idea!

Although Buzan advocates using one word in each line of mind mapping, some of the examples shown in the Buzan mind mapping galleries use more words for the central theme, such as 'Challenges facing small business'. So I have used more than one word in the central theme of my last example of mind mapping in this chapter, 'sources of ideas' (Figure 8.4).

FIGURE 8.4 Mind mapping 'sources of ideas'

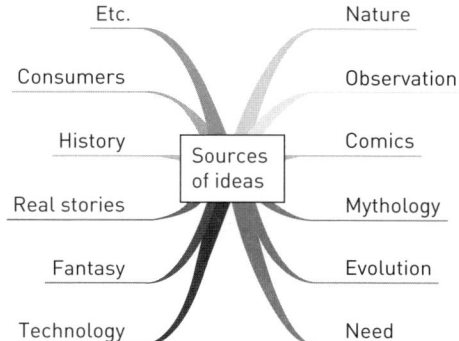

SUMMARY

This chapter discussed de Bono's lateral thinking and Six Thinking Hats, Buzan's mind mapping as a tool to harness the brain's cortical skills, and my variation of multidimensional thinking as a way to think outside the box to tap into diverse stored images in the brain's memory (just like geniuses do). I have seen participants use mind mapping when using lateral thinking techniques such as random entry or engaging with the Six Thinking Hats (and even with the Synectics techniques such as excursions and wishing). Mind mapping multidimensionally is fun in a group, because you are able to tap into diverse experiences, sources and analogies for the task to be solved. The next chapter looks at another analogical approach to creative thinking—TRIZ inventive problem solving.

MIND NETTING: TRIZ INVENTIVE PROBLEM SOLVING

CHAPTER 9

Somebody has already solved your problem somewhere! This analogical thinking method is the philosophy of the Russian TRIZ inventive problem-solving process. For example, the beer industry provided the pharmaceutical industry with a solution for managing foam during production; the banking industry had privacy protection answers for the medical industry; the nuclear waste disposal industry had ideas for preventing sludge build-up in the paint industry; the concentrated orange juice industry had a hydrophilic gas solution to separate liquid from solids for the dairy industry; and the diet food industry had customer response techniques for the patio-building industry.[347]

INTRODUCTION

Brainstorming, Creative Problem Solving and Synectics spread from the USA to other countries. This chapter looks at a Mind Netting tool that spread from Russia to Eastern and Western countries. TRIZ inventive problem solving is another form of analogical or associative thinking. The chapter explores the origin of TRIZ, its forty principles, its contradiction matrix to accelerate solution finding, its association with SCAMPER and other creative thinking tools, plus some industry examples.

ORIGIN

TRIZ is an acronym for Teoriya Resheniya Izobretatelskikh Zadach, or the Theory of Inventive Problem Solving. It is a systematic problem-solving process modelled on Russian inventors to solve technical problems by finding the ideal final result.

Genrich Altshuller is regarded as the 'father of TRIZ'. Altshuller received his first patent for an underwater breathing device in 1940, when he was only fourteen years old. After several more patents and an engineering degree, Altshuller worked in a naval patent office and analysed thousands of patents. He theorised that invention is about removing technical contradictions and concluded that there are forty invention principles that could be used in most engineering and technical situations. He published two books in the 1960s: *How to Learn to Invent* and *Algorithm of Inventing*.

According to the website of the Altshuller Institute for TRIZ Studies, which was established in the USA in 1998, TRIZ spread from the Soviet Union to the West and is now used by companies such as Boeing, Chrysler, Eastman Kodak, Exxon, Ford, General Motors, Hewlett Packard, Intel, LG Electronics, Motorola, Procter & Gamble, Samsung and Xerox. The website even has a quote from George Prince of Synectics: 'I know of no other approach to inventing that offers such a rich arsenal of both practical and imaginative thinking tools.'[348]

THE FORTY PRINCIPLES

The *TRIZ Journal* (www.triz-journal.com/archives) has published articles on the forty principles as analogical patterns of patents that can be applied across diverse domains such as architecture, biology, business, customer relations, design, education, finance, food, journalism, management, marketing, planning and retail. The forty TRIZ principles are used as checklists, hence there is no need to remember all of them.

Following are the forty principles, with illustrations of how they can be applied to the food business:[349]

1. *Segmentation*: Divide into parts, such as fruit and yoghurt portions in a container, variety packs, potato chips with a separate flavour sachet, individual coffee sachets or multiple doors in frozen-food cabinets.
2. *Taking out or detachment*: Single out an essential part, such as low-fat products or NutraSweet sweetness without the calories.
3. *Local quality*: Make parts perform a useful function, such as date stamping on eggs and sugar coating on cakes.
4. *Asymmetry*: Change from symmetrical to asymmetrical, such as a PET bottle that fits into a car's cup holder or a spout on a Ribena bottle.
5. *Merging*: Combine, such as multigrain products, alcohol with ice cream or vegetable mixes.
6. *Universality*: Standardise, such as a food container becoming a storage jar or a package of Nutella spreadable chocolate becoming a drinking glass.

7. *Nested doll*: Place one thing inside another, such as sauce sachets in pre-packed food products.
8. *Anti-weight*: Piggyback on something better, such as mix air into soufflé.
9. *Preliminary anti-action*: Control possible harmful effects, such as a widget or device to introduce nitrogen into beer to give it a creamy head.
10. *Preliminary action*: Pre-arrange, such as pre-cooked food, deseeded fruit and sliced vegetables.
11. *Beforehand cushioning*: Prepare emergency means, such as tamper-proof packaging and deboned fish.
12. *Equipotentiality*: Same potential at all points, such as offshore outlets.
13. *The other way round*: Invert or reverse, such as iced tea, a drive-through restaurant and home delivery shopping.
14. *Spheroidality*: Use curved rotary motion, such as a lettuce spinner, kebab spit and pasta spirals.
15. *Dynamics*: Provide adjustability, such as flexible drinking straw, fold-up spoon and re-foldable packaging.
16. *Partial or excessive actions*: Use slightly less or more, such as mini-packs or over-size containers.
17. *Another dimension*: Provide multi-dimensions, such as crinkle-cut potato chips and spaghetti twists.
18. *Mechanical vibration*: Oscillate or vibrate, such as multispeed blenders and shaking a bottle before opening.
19. *Periodic action*: Change the season, such as Easter eggs and Christmas cake.
20. *Continuous useful action*: Ensure full load, such as year-through production.
21. *Skipping or rushing*: Make haste, such as freeze-drying to retain freshness.
22. *Blessing in disguise*: Turn negative into positive, such as meat tenderising and beneficial yoghurt cultures.
23. *Feedback*: Cross-checking, such as sensors to change temperature and thermo-chromic containers that signal when the product is properly heated.
24. *Intermediary*: Provide a bridging process, such as a spice dispenser.
25. *Self-service*: Serve itself, such as self-heating tinned food and a coffee cup that self-regulates its temperature.
26. *Copying*: Use simpler, inexpensive copies, such as imitation fish cake and house-brand products.
27. *Cheap short-lived objects*: Replace expensive with inexpensive, such as disposable packaging.
28. *Mechanics substitution*: Use something else, such as intelligent microwaves.

29 *Pneumatics and hydraulics*: Use different forms, such as coffee concentrates and spreadable cheese.
30 *Flexible shells and thin films*: Use flexible forms, such as waterproof cardboard milk containers and egg boxes.
31 *Porous materials*: Add or use porosity, such as hollow Easter eggs and whipped cream.
32 *Colour changes*: Change colour, such as a thermo-chromic spoon that changes colour when temperature is too hot.
33 *Homogeneity*: Similar or uniform, such as using the same material for the content and container, for example edible Yorkshire pudding container.
34 *Discarding and recovering*: Discard and restore, such as dried desiccated fruit and dried milk in Kellogg's Cereal and Milk bars.
35 *Parameter changes*: Change the state, such as yoghurt on a stick or vacuum packaging.
36 *Phase transitions*: Different stages, such as frozen products.
37 *Thermal expansion*: Expand event or process, such as dough expansion in bread making.
38 *Strong oxidants*: Boosted interactions, such as carbonated drinks and 'exploding' chocolate bars.
39 *Inert atmosphere*: Replace normal environment with inert one, such as preservatives and nitrogen top-off in bottled products.
40 *Composite materials*: Combine system, such as cereal bars and multivitamins.

One scholar concluded that ten principles are most frequently used in management (see Table 9.1) but I think they could be equally popular in other disciplines.[350]

My observation is that TRIZ principles could be applied everywhere. Outdoor advertising sites that automatically change advertisement panels every few seconds would be under Principle 19 (Periodic action), Principle 35 (Parameter changes) and Principle 36 (Phase transitions). The waterless urinal could have been based on Principle 2 (Taking out or detachment). The vending machine would be based on Principle 25 (Self-service) but could also incorporate other principles such as Principle 1 (Segmentation), Principle 5 (Merging), Principle 7 (Nested doll), Principle 24 (Intermediary) and Principle 40 (Composite materials). The shopping mall, including the duty-free shop in the airport, would incorporate Principle 1 (Segmentation), Principle 5 (Merging) and Principle 7 (Nested doll).

TABLE 9.1 TRIZ principles frequently used in management

FREQUENCY OF USE	TRIZ PRINCIPLE	PRINCIPAL FOCUS
1st	35	Parameter changes
2nd	2	Taking out or detachment
3rd	25	Self-service
4th	10	Preliminary action
5th	13	The other way round
6th	3	Local quality
7th	1	Segmentation
8th	15	Dynamics
9th	5	Merging
10th	24	Intermediary

CONTRADICTION MATRIX

The contradiction matrix works on the philosophy that obstacles always arise when looking for a possible solution, and that proven TRIZ principles are required to overcome these obstacles. There can be technical contradictions (such as requiring more power when increasing bandwidth) or physical contradictions (for example, serving hot coffee without burning drinkers).[351] TRIZ identifies thirty-nine features for contradictions spanning weight, length, area, volume, speed, force, pressure, shape, stability, strength, duration, temperature, illumination, energy, power, harm, quantity, precision, measurement, automation, reliability, productivity, ease and adaptability.[352]

In TRIZ, the ideal solution is to eliminate contradictions, compromises or obstacles when you improve a feature while preserving another feature, such as improving the strength of a product while preserving its speed. This contradiction is analogous to Gordon's use of paradox or compressed conflict in Synectics.

The TRIZ website www.triz40.com/TRIZ_GB.php provides suggestions for which principles are relevant for overcoming certain contradictions; some examples are presented in Table 9.2.

TABLE 9.2 TRIZ principles to resolve contradictions

CONTRADICTION	SUGGESTED PRINCIPLES
Improve productivity, preserve adaptability or versatility	P1 Segmentation P35 Parameter changes P28 Mechanics substitution P37 Thermal expansion
Improve reliability, preserve ease of operation	P27 Cheap short-lived objects P17 Another dimension P40 Composite materials
Improve ease of operation, preserve adaptability or versatility	P15 Dynamics P34 Discarding and recovering P1 Segmentation P16 Partial or excessive actions
Improve strength, preserve speed	P8 Anti-weight P13 The other way round P26 Copying P14 Spheroidality
Improve adaptability or versatility, preserve productivity	P35 Parameter changes P28 Mechanics substitution P6 Universality P37 Thermal expansion

TRIZ AND OTHER THINKING TOOLS

For teams that wish to diversify their array of creative thinking, there are ways to integrate TRIZ with the other tools in this book, such as SCAMPER, Creative Problem Solving, lateral thinking and Six Thinking Hats.[353]

TRIZ principles seem particularly related to SCAMPER (substitute, combine, adapt, magnify or minify, put to other uses, eliminate, reverse), which was described in Chapter 5. See Table 9.3 for my connections between TRIZ and SCAMPER—note that the biggest concentration of TRIZ principles falls under SCAMPER's adapt technique, followed by magnify/minify, reverse and combine.

TABLE 9.3 TRIZ principles and SCAMPER

TRIZ PRINCIPLES		SCAMPER
P27 Cheap short-lived objects P28 Mechanics substitution		Substitute
P5 Merging P7 Nested doll P8 Anti-weight	P24 Intermediary P31 Porous materials P40 Composite materials	Combine
P1 Segmentation P4 Asymmetry P12 Equipotentiality P14 Spheroidality P15 Dynamics P17 Another dimension P23 Feedback	P26 Copying P29 Pneumatics and hydraulics P30 Flexible shells and thin films P32 Colour changes P33 Homogeneity P34 Discarding and recovering P35 Parameter changes	Adapt
P16 Partial or excessive actions P18 Mechanical vibration P19 Periodic action P20 Continuous useful action	P21 Skipping or rushing P36 Phase transitions P37 Thermal expansion P38 Strong oxidants	Magnify/minify
P3 Local quality P6 Universality P25 Self-service		Put to other uses
P2 Taking out or detachment		Eliminate
P9 Preliminary anti-action P10 Preliminary action P11 Beforehand cushioning	P13 The other way round P22 Blessing in disguise P39 Inert atmosphere	Reverse

Since Creative Problem Solving and lateral thinking also use random stimulating words, some of the TRIZ principles could be used as stimuli in random order in those processes. The TRIZ contradiction matrix could be used during the evaluation phase in Creative Problem Solving and the Six Thinking Hats when there is an apparent contradiction or paradox.

The TRIZ principles could be used at random during green hat mode, and the 'reverse' principles could be used during black hat mode. During white hat mode, TRIZ questions could be asked about a system performance or design and which industries have dealt with a similar problem.

Industry examples

Samsung
Samsung began hiring TRIZ-trained Russian engineers from 2000, saved $100 million over several projects and had fifty new patents in 2003.[354]

Samsung embedded TRIZ by training all staff for twenty hours in fundamental TRIZ; its CEO for three to four days in classical TRIZ; and its 'creative elite' of twenty engineers in modern TRIZ and advanced TRIZ via boot camps and group project work. Samsung also holds a TRIZ festival where engineers present their projects and awards are given.[355]

Boeing
Boeing engineers attended a five-day TRIZ course in 2000 and developed ideal solutions for its 767 tanker transport development. Boeing's customer liked the TRIZ solution and placed eight orders worth $1.5 billion.[356]

Procter & Gamble
P&G's Herbal Essences brand faced a dilemma: sales declined and retailers did not want to stock the product. The brand needed revitalisation. The team explored the Generation Y women segment, positioning, packaging, design and colours, using TRIZ principles. Outcomes were that 'nested' shampoo and conditioner were to be packaged and sold together, in colours including green, orange, pink and purple, and with new product names that included Totally Twisted, Dangerously Straight and Drama Clean. Senior management bought the concept, the product was launched in a year and the brand became the number two in hair care in the USA.[357]

Singapore and SARS

When the 2003 global outbreak of the Severe Acute Respiratory Syndrome (SARS) hit a dozen countries in Asia, Europe, North America and South America, about 8000 people became sick and more than 700 died from the viral illness.[358] Singapore was benchmarked as having the most effective and innovative ideas to contain the disease.

Several TRIZ practitioners analysed diverse reports and concluded that the measures Singapore had taken reflected twenty-one TRIZ principles such as segmentation, detachment, merging, universality, nested doll, preliminary anti-action, preliminary action, beforehand cushioning, dynamics, partial or excessive solution, periodic action, continuous useful action, skipping or rushing, turning harm into benefit, feedback, intermediary, self-service, copying, cheap short-lived objects and colour changes.[359]

Here are some interesting highlights of the TRIZ principles in action during the SARS outbreak in Singapore. There was segmentation (Principle 1) of the infected, non-infected and possibly infected transient travellers; isolation wards in hospitals; and preventive measures at airports, land checkpoints and seaports.

SARS-infected patients were detached (Principle 2) from other patients, and families of the infected were quarantined at home to prevent the virus spreading. Infrared sensors were used for temperature tests at Changi Airport (Principle 6, Universality). About eighty markets and small shops were closed for a day of cleaning and disinfecting and people were encouraged to take medication to strengthen their immune system (Principle 9, Preliminary anti-action).

All companies, including Singapore Airlines, asked visitors to fill in a contact form for authorities to follow up in case of an outbreak (Principle 10, Preliminary action). Employees received thermometers; chalets were set aside as possible quarantine sites; Singapore Airlines provided health kits with masks, antiseptic wipes and thermometers; and the government provided a S$230 million relief package for services affected by SARS, such as tourism (Principle 11, Beforehand cushioning or expecting the worst).

A new dedicated television channel brought constant updates on the SARS situation (Principle 20, Continuous useful action) and hospitals used video and telephone conferences with patients rather than face-to-face visits (Principle 26, Copying). The government raised public awareness of environmental and personal hygiene (Principle 22, Blessing in disguise or turning harm into benefit). Singapore's credit rating increased from AA+ to AAA for its ability to cope with health and economic shocks.

Academia

According to the International TRIZ Association website, TRIZ is offered as a university course in RMIT University in Melbourne, Australia, and in Argentina, Belgium, Brazil, Czech Republic, Estonia, France, Germany, India, Iran, Ireland, Italy, Japan, Mexico, Romania, Russia, Singapore, South Korea, Taiwan, United Kingdom and United States.[360]

You may wish to read more about TRIZ through the following links:

- International TRIZ Association (MA TRIZ): http://matriz.org
- European TRIZ Association (ETRIA): http://etria.eu/portal
- TRIZ Canada: http://triz-canada.ca/home/index.php?option=com_content&view=article&id=51&Itemid=58
- The *TRIZ Journal*, which has archived articles from 1996 to 2012: www.triz-journal.com/archives

SUMMARY

This chapter introduced the Russian TRIZ inventive problem-solving tool with its forty principles, analogical patterns or associative thinking, and its contradiction matrix with suggested TRIZ principles as solutions. Some principles are used much more frequently than others and TRIZ principles can potentially be applied everywhere. The forty principles are related to some of the other innovation techniques covered in earlier chapters, such as SCAMPER, the Creative Problem Solving process and the Six Thinking Hats. This chapter then looked at how industries as well as academia are applying TRIZ to inventive problem solving. The next chapter discusses analogical as well as inside-the-box approaches to creative thinking—attribute listing and morphological synthesis.

MIND NETTING: ATTRIBUTE LISTING AND MORPHOLOGICAL SYNTHESIS

CHAPTER 10

I am a Subway fan. I love the idea of mixing different types of bread (multigrain, wheat, honey oat, flatbread or Italian herbs and cheese), salad (spinach, capsicum, carrot, cucumber, jalapenos, lettuce, olives, pickles, tomato or onion), cheese (cheddar, natural Swiss or mozzarella) and sauce (BBQ, chipotle, honey mustard, marinara, mayo, ranch, sweet chilli, sweet onion, Thousand Island, tomato or hot chilli). Subway has come a long way since seventeen-year-old Fred DeLuca set up a submarine sandwich shop in 1965 in Bridgeport, Connecticut, USA to help fund his university education. Subway now has about 44,000 stores in 110 countries, making it a leader in the quick service restaurant industry.[361]

INTRODUCTION

If lateral thinking and multidimensional thinking are ways to think outside the box, attribute listing and morphological synthesis may be considered as ways to think within the box. This chapter explains attribute listing, morphological synthesis (the mixing method) and synthesises the creative thinking tools covered under Mind Netting: brainstorming, Creative Problem Solving, Synectics, lateral thinking, Six Thinking Hats, mind mapping, multidimensional thinking, TRIZ, attribute listing and morphological synthesis.

ATTRIBUTE LISTING

Creativity professor Robert Crawford is credited with introducing the technique of attribute listing in his books *The Techniques of Creative Thinking* (1954)[362] and *Direct Creativity with Attribute Listing* (1979).[363]

The attribute listing process enables individuals or groups to start from an objective, to look at the main components of a product or service and then to list possible attributes of each component that need modification or improvement. In its simplest form, you look at the attributes of a product and brainstorm to improve those attributes. See Table 10.1 for an example of modifying sticks for toffee apples.[364]

TABLE 10.1 Attribute listing—toffee-apple sticks

ATTRIBUTES	IDEAS
Wood-made	Biodegradable material
Handheld	Free-standing
Disposable	Edible

Hence, attribute listing or modifying is a common problem-solving technique. Some examples of success in improving the attributes of products: modifying the conventional lithium-ion battery into a lightweight sheet-paper battery for consumer electronic devices[365]; modifying the traditional face-to-face Scrabble game into online Scrabble[366]; modifying the Sony PlayStation Portable gaming console by adding Skype and Global Positioning System (GPS)[367]; and modifying the thickness of a TV—the world's thinnest LCD TV panel is only 2.6 millimetres thick.[368]

I have also noticed changes on reality TV shows. *Dancing with the Stars* has changed some of its features over the years: changing the judges and co-host, having contestants swap dance coaches for a day. *The Bachelor Australia* has also changed an attribute by bringing in gatecrashers to add more spice to the show. Australia's long-running television drama *Home and Away* has also changed its location by bringing some episodes to the city or overseas, and has also modified its cast by bringing in short-term or long-term appearances by new actors. What attribute would you like to modify for your product or service?

MORPHOLOGICAL SYNTHESIS

In the more complex forms of attribute listing, you take the next step of mixing or synthesising the attributes. This section discusses the origin and applications of morphological synthesis.

Origin

In 1948 Fritz Zwicky described the process as morphological analysis,[369] while in 1962, Myron Allen used the term morphological creativity.[370] The mixing of attributes on two axes is also known as morphological synthesis or morphological combination.[371]

Applications: Two or three axes

Once you have determined your task, you could place two axes in a box; for example, sandwich favourites on one axis and ingredients to add zest on another axis (see Table 10.2). You then use symbols to create different variations of sandwiches![372]

TABLE 10.2 Morphological synthesis of sandwich favourites and food companions

SANDWICH FAVOURITES	FOOD COMPANIONS TO ADD ZEST					
	Raisin	Banana	Tomato	Apple sauce	Nuts	Dates
Jelly	✪					
Beef			✔			
Chicken	✪					
Peanut			✔			
Tuna				ʋ		
Egg			✔			

You could mix any combination to create diverse types of sandwiches. Based on the example in Table 10.2, your variations would be:

✪ Jelly + chicken + raisin
✔ Beef + peanut + egg + tomato
ʋ Tuna + apple sauce

You could also add another axis to create more sandwich variations.[373] See Table 10.3 with bread types included as the third dimension.

TABLE 10.3 Morphological synthesis of favourite sandwiches, food companions and bread types

SANDWICH FAVOURITES	FOOD COMPANIONS TO ADD ZEST					BREAD TYPES
	Raisin	Banana	Tomato	Apple sauce	Nuts	
Jelly	✪					White
Beef			✓			Wholemeal
Chicken						Rye
Peanut						Wrap
Tuna				ʋ		Bun
Egg						French

Based on the simple example above, your sandwich combinations would be:

✪ Jelly + raisin + white bread
✓ Beef + tomato + wholemeal bread
ʋ Tuna + apple sauce + bun

Applications: Dimensions as categories

A variation of morphological synthesis is to have dimensions as categories and then list attributes below each dimension. If you were to generate ideas for children's educational toys, for example, you might use dimensions of material, usage location and educational purpose. In Table 10.4 there are 9 x 8 x 9 attributes for each dimension respectively, creating 648 possible combinations of ideas.[374]

TABLE 10.4 Morphological synthesis for children's educational toys

MATERIAL	USAGE LOCATION	EDUCATION PURPOSE
Felt	Bath	Alphabet
Inflatable plastic	Beach	Colours
Luminescent	Car	Construction
Metal	Cot	Coordination
Plastic	Garden	Numbers

MATERIAL	USAGE LOCATION	EDUCATION PURPOSE
Rubber	Holidays	Shapes
Transparent perspex	Playpen	Smell
Wood	Pram	Sounds
Wool		Textures

There could be more dimensions for the 'Zwicky box' or 'morphological box', shown in Table 10.5's example of a morphological box for creating a new lamp.[375]

TABLE 10.5 Morphological box to create a new lamp

POWER SUPPLY	BULB TYPE	SIZE	STYLE	FINISH	MATERIAL
Battery	Bulb	Handheld	Antique	Black	Bone
Crank	Coloured	Large	Art	Enamel	Ceramic
Flame	Daylight	Medium	Ethnic	Fabric	Concrete
Gas	Halogen	Small	Industrial	Metallic	Glass
Generator		Very large	Modern	Natural	Metal
Mains			Roman	Terracotta	Plastic
Oil				White	Stone
Solar					Wood

If you do not wish to follow Zwicky's rigorous method of looking at optimal possible combinations of ideas, you could randomly mix the attributes. For example, I could look at the basic filling of a candy bar to think of different attributes, followed by attributes of additional filling, coating and shape. I could combine peanut filling with jelly as an additional filling plus add nuts coating the bar in a rocket shape (see Table 10.6).[376]

TABLE 10.6 Morphological synthesis of a candy bar

BASIC FILLING	ADDITIONAL FILLING	COATING	SHAPE
Butter	Candy	Chocolate peanut	Animal
Cherry	Dates	Cookie crumbs	Doughnut

(continued)

TABLE 10.6 Morphological synthesis of a candy bar (*continued*)

BASIC FILLING	ADDITIONAL FILLING	COATING	SHAPE
Orange	**Jelly**	Crème fruit	**Rocket**
Peanut	Marshmallow	**Nuts**	Triangle
White chocolate	Raisins	Pretzel crumbs	Truck

You could also play around with thinking inside the morphological box with creations for cereals and Vegemite. For example, you could have banana-flavoured cereal with added almonds in a cartoon character shape in an odd size (see Table 10.7) or a Vegemite variant with rainbow colour, nuts, a fruity taste and cube packaging (see Table 10.8).

TABLE 10.7 Morphological synthesis on cereals

FLAVOUR	INGREDIENT	SHAPE	SIZE
Milo	Wheat	Star	Miniature
Honey	**Almond**	**Cartoon character**	Giant
Banana	Fish oil	Alphabet	Single
Coffee	Meat	Pod	**Odd**

TABLE 10.8 Morphological synthesis on Vegemite variants

COLOUR	INGREDIENT	TASTE	PACKAGING
Rainbow	Chocolate	Mild	Tube
Pink	**Nuts**	Strong	Sachet
Bright	Veggies	Extra strong	**Cube**
Red	Honey	Spicy	Bottle
Yellow	Sugar	**Fruity**	Tub

I have also imagined how I would modify the *Home and Away* television series with different characters, objectives, obstacles and outcomes, followed by random combinations of an attribute from each dimension or several attributes from each dimension (see Table 10.9).

TABLE 10.9 Morphological synthesis for Home and Away

CHARACTERS	OBJECTIVES	OBSTACLES	OUTCOMES
Playboy	**Love**	Law	**Mental asylum**
Scientist	Wealth	Blind	Memory loss
Nurse	**Honour**	**Disloyal**	Migration
King	Escape	Tradition	Prison
Grave digger	Revenge	**Coward**	Murder

I used the attribute listing and morphological synthesis methods to create the Creative Services major when I was at Edith Cowan University. I listed the existing majors and their key courses, then I asked students to circle eight courses that they would like to take under a new creative services major. Based on students' submission of their choices, I was able to design the major with the most popular courses—see Table 10.10.

TABLE 10.10 Creating the Creative Services major

MAJORS	COURSES [MIX EIGHT COURSES FOR A CREATIVE SERVICES MAJOR]			
Advertising	Strategic branding	IMC	Creative strategy	International advertising
PR	Foundations of PR	PR techniques	PR events	International PR
Design	Identity	Publication	Desktop	Ad design
Film	Video production	Drama and documentary	Scriptwriting	Independent study
Journalism	Introduction to journalism	Specialist writing	Broadcasting skills	Broadcasting in digital age
Photomedia	Photo work	Studio work	Images and pleasures	Digital photomedia

I have also played around with the morphological box and multiple intelligences to see what book ideas I could generate—see Table 10.11.

TABLE 10.11 Morphological synthesis of multiple intelligences for book ideas

VISUAL	INTRAPERSONAL	NATURALISTIC	KINAESTHETIC
Crayons	Priest	Vet	Dancer
Paint	Teacher	Gardener	**Surfer**
Rainbow	**Nun**	**Explorer**	Skater
Maps	Spirit	Zookeeper	Golfer
MUSICAL	**INTERPERSONAL**	**LINGUISTIC**	**LOGICAL**
ABBA	Oprah	Poet	Math
Bee Gees	Waiter	**Speaker**	Scientist
Mozart	Kids	Radio	CSI
Cats	**Host**	Trainer	**Technology**

When MasterCard ran its 'Priceless' campaign a few years ago, I was also imagining how the creative people were developing various executions of the same theme. I looked at the agency's dimensions of location, products, cast and priceless moments—see Table 10.12.

TABLE 10.12 Analysis of three MasterCard commercials

AD	LOCATION	PRODUCTS	CAST	PRICELESS MOMENTS
1	Music store	Strap guitar	Dad and son	Rock 'n' roll memory
2	Movie set	Freshener, socks, paper clip	*MacGyver*	Things that get you through the day
3	Zoo	Soup, tissues, medicine, blanket	Zookeeper, elephant, money	Making it all happen

The creative thinking tool of morphological synthesis has its variations: two or three axes of product categories or different dimensions as categories to explore idea options and mix the ideas up rigorously or randomly for intriguing solutions. Implicit in these techniques is the need for action to review and implement the ideas.

SYNTHESISING CREATIVE THINKING TOOLS

Using the morphological box, I have also tried synthesising the various creative thinking tools described in this book—brainstorming, Creative Problem Solving, Synectics, lateral thinking, Six Thinking Hats, mind mapping, multidimensional thinking, TRIZ, attribute listing and morphological synthesis. I have tried to connect the various creative thinking tools under a central framework of CIA or Challenge-Ideas-Action, as this framework seems to underpin most, if not all, creative thinking tools. See Table 10.13 for the synthesis.

TABLE 10.13 Morphological box for creative thinking tools and techniques

CIA FRAMEWORK	BRAINSTORMING	CREATIVE PROBLEM SOLVING	SYNECTICS	LATERAL AND MULTIDIMENSIONAL THINKING	TRIZ	ATTRIBUTE LISTING AND MORPHOLOGICAL SYNTHESIS
Challenge	Objective Ground rules 1 Defer judgment 2 Freewheel 3 Quantity 4 Piggyback	1 Objective finding/ explore the vision 2 Fact finding/ gather data 3 Problem finding/ formulate challenges	Prince 1 Task 2 Wishes 3 Selection 4 Develop wish 5 +/- on idea 6 Action steps Synectics consultants Planning Facilitating	Blue hat White hat Mind mapping laws and applications	Task	Task
Ideas	Divergence variations: SCAMPER » Reverse brainstorming » Electronic brainstorming » Round-robin brainstorming » Brainswarming » Brainwriting	Idea finding/ explore ideas	Prince Wishing **Metaphorical** excursions Gordon Excursion **Direct analogies** Personification Paradox	Green hat Lateral thinking PO **Random word** **Associative thinking** Concept Extraction	**Analogies** of forty principles	Attribute listing and modifying

TABLE 10.13 Morphological box for creative thinking tools and technique (Continued)

CIA FRAMEWORK	BRAINSTORMING	CREATIVE PROBLEM SOLVING	SYNECTICS	LATERAL AND MULTIDIMENSIONAL THINKING	TRIZ	ATTRIBUTE LISTING AND MORPHOLOGICAL SYNTHESIS
	» Brainsketching » Rolestorming » Hybrid brainstorming » Brainsteering » Brainstorming boxes **Use of metaphors and associative thinking**		Nolan Out-in listening Headlining **wishes** **Analogical thinking** **DREAM** **Dream**-Review-Expand-Assess-Manage	<u>Multidimensional thinking</u> Multi-tracks	Frequently used principles SCAMPER-related principles	Morphological synthesis: mixing
Action	Convergence	Solution finding/ formulate solutions Action finding/ formulate a plan	Action steps in Synectics and 'manage' in DREAM process	Yellow hat Black hat Red hat	Contradiction matrix	Review and act

There are other creative thinking tools but the ones in Table 10.13 are ones that I have been trained in or have been using over the years. The synthesis shows the following common elements:

1 There is a structured facilitative process for creative thinking covering divergence and convergence, as manifested in the Creative Problem Solving process, Synectics, the DREAM process and Six Thinking Hats.
2 There is rational thinking and irrational or emotional thinking. Objective finding, fact finding, task analysis, white hat, solution finding and action finding are rational in nature, while excursions, PO and red hat are either emotional or irrational.
3 The 'challenge' stage in any form is to identify the task for the team to focus on, often through task analysis and asking probing questions.
4 Various creative thinking tools could be used for the idea generation process, such as brainstorming variations, analogies, TRIZ principles, random word, provocation, multidimensional thinking or mind mapping, attribute listing and modifying, and listening to connect the task with diverse sources.
5 Analogies and associative thinking seem to be commonly used, such as across brainstorming, Synectics, lateral thinking and TRIZ. This aligns with the use of analogies and metaphors by geniuses such as da Vinci.
6 There is an evaluation process, such as solution finding in the Creative Problem Solving process, itemised response in Synectics, 'assess' in DREAM, and yellow and black hats in Six Thinking Hats.
7 There is an overlap of the creative thinking tools; for example, with the Creative Problem Solving fact finding and de Bono's white hat; Osborn's freewheeling and Prince's wishing; Gordon's paradox and TRIZ's contradiction; and TRIZ's principles with SCAMPER, the Creative Problem Solving process and Six Thinking Hats.

Depending on your situation, interest, training and learning styles, you may have your favourite creative thinking tools or have a combination of tools to accelerate your company's innovation process. Examples in this book show that Procter & Gamble has people using brainstorming, Creative Problem Solving, metaphorical excursions, lateral thinking, mind mapping and TRIZ as well as mythology, neuroscience, theatre and Zen exercises.

SUMMARY

This chapter has explored the thinking-inside-the-box methods of attribute listing-modifying and morphological synthesis (also referred to as morphological analysis, morphological creativity, morphological box and Zwicky box). The morphological box can also be used to synthesise the various creative thinking tools under Mind Netting, such as brainstorming, Creative Problem Solving, Synectics, lateral thinking, Six Thinking Hats, mind mapping, multidimensional thinking and TRIZ as well as attribute listing and morphological synthesis. Many of the creative thinking tools can be used synergistically as 'baits' to net a spectrum of breakthrough ideas. The concluding chapter synthesises the team creativity catalysts that could accelerate team creativity and innovation in your organisation.

CHAPTER 11

CONCLUSION: ACCELERATING TEAM CREATIVITY AND INNOVATION

The advertisement opened on penguins swimming, waddling and flying. The BBC natural history presenter Terry Jones was in the Antarctic commenting on the yearly flight of the penguins to the rainforest of South America. Then the advertisement message came across: 'When amazing things happen on the BBC, you never have to miss them. Watch BBC programs on your computer. BBC iPlayer. Making the unmissable unmissable.' Astounded viewers later realised that it was an April fool hoax, something that the BBC had been doing since the 1950s. The fantasy idea of flying penguins was the result of the work of a whole production team, who sourced stock footage, created artificial snow, and carried out the filming, animation and post-production.[377]

INTRODUCTION

The BBC flying penguin hoax is just one example of how accelerated team creativity and innovation is practised. While some ideas come from individuals, it often takes a team to conceive, develop, evaluate and implement innovative ideas. This concluding chapter synthesises the preceding chapters on innovation and team creativity catalysts; Mastery Modelling and benchmarking innovation masters; Intensive Immersion and empowered exploration; Group Germination and collective growth; and Mind Netting through creativity 'baits' such as brainstorming, the Creative Problem Solving process, Synectics, lateral thinking and Six Thinking Hats, mind mapping and multidimensional thinking, TRIZ plus attribute listing and morphological synthesis. This chapter crystallises the key concepts through a question-and-answer format to help you reflect on how you could accelerate team creativity and innovation in your organisation.

INNOVATION AND TEAM CREATIVITY CATALYSTS

Q: What is the distinction between creativity and innovation, and what seems to be the innovation gap?

A: Creativity is about producing novel and useful ideas while innovation is the successful and creative implementation of these ideas. Only a small percentage of companies seem to be world-class innovators or innovation leaders, with barriers such as resources, leadership and culture.

Q: What are the four team creativity catalysts?

A: The team creativity catalysts are Mastery Modelling, Intensive Immersion, Group Germination and Mind Netting. These catalysts are analogous to the creativity 4Ps of product (Mastery Modelling benchmarks), place (Intensive Immersion), person (Group Germination) and process (Mind Netting). The creativity catalysts also align with solutions to overcome innovation barriers.

Q: How would the four team creativity catalysts facilitate the acceleration of team creativity and innovation in an organisation?

A: Mastery Modelling is about modelling your organisation against some highly desirable world-class best practices, benchmarks or vision—that everyone in your organisation can follow. Intensive Immersion is about an empowered innovation culture where mission-driven passionate employees intensively explore and turn your vision into reality. Group Germination is about strategically leveraging the talents, skills and experiences of diverse people internally and externally. Mind Netting is about netting the groups' spectrum of ideas through diverse creative thinking tools. The four catalysts work as an integrated whole to embody mental, emotional, physical and self-actualising dimensions to accelerate the creativity and innovation process.

MASTERY MODELLING

Q: Which geniuses, influential people, innovative people, innovative companies and/or innovative countries could you model against?

A: You could borrow from Leonardo da Vinci, Albert Einstein, Steve Jobs, Barack Obama, Oprah Winfrey, Lady Gaga, Larry Page, Sergey Brin, Jeff Bezos, Mark

Zuckerberg, Apple, Google, 3M, Amazon, Samsung, Tesla, Salesforce.com, Dropbox, Microsoft, IBM, Switzerland, Singapore, the USA, Sweden, Finland, South Korea, Hong Kong, Japan and Germany.

Q: How would it benefit team creativity and innovation to model against geniuses, influential people, innovative people, innovative companies and/or innovative countries?

A: These model people, companies and/or countries have skill patterns or best practices that we could learn from or benchmark against.

Q: What are the specific skill patterns that you could model on?

A: These model people have multiple ways of thinking. They are whole-brain thinkers using imagination–reality, macro–micro, abstract–concrete, back-and-forth, cognitive–emotional, visual–verbal or metaphorical–analogical thinking. They draw on multiple dimensions to innovate.

Q: What specific best practices could you learn from these model people?

A: These model people have attributes such as curiosity, pursuit of excellence and a vision to make a difference to society, if not the world. They ask questions, strive for continuous improvement and seek something larger than corporate achievements.

Q: What is the benefit of hiring people with passion rather than proficiency?

A: The late Steve Jobs hired people with diverse talents and interests rather than people with only specialist skills but no wide interests in the arts and sciences. Since creativity comes from connecting diverse knowledge, there is obviously a benefit in hiring people with broad interests in things such as culture, hobbies, volunteer work, travels etc.

Q: Why do famous people and companies allow mistakes?

A: Innovative people and companies such as Thomas Edison, Steve Jobs, Google, Amazon and 3M see failures as opportunities for success.

Q: Do you have to be a big company or country to be innovative?

A: Switzerland and Singapore are both small countries but have consistently been ranked as most innovative. Many companies started small and grew because they innovated in terms of research, products, services, processes and policies.

Q: How similar were the thinking patterns of Steve Jobs and Lee Kuan Yew?

A: Both Jobs and Lee were analogical thinkers who learned from the successes and failures of other people, companies and places. Jobs benchmarked against diverse sources such as Sony, Intel's Andy Grove, strategist Regis McKenna, Pixar, Xerox, Microsoft, Google, Nike, the Ritz-Carlton Hotel, New York's Central Park, Swiss watchmaking, calligraphy, department stores, inventor Edwin Land, Picasso and many geniuses. Lee benchmarked against Britain, Israel, the Vatican, Australia, New Zealand, Japan, Hong Kong, Shell, the Dutch economist Winsemius, First World countries and Confucian values.

INTENSIVE IMMERSION

Q: Why is it necessary to have clear visible statements on corporate mission, values and vision?

A: These mission-values-vision statements direct, empower and remind employees to explore innovation projects to achieve corporate goals. There is something to learn from the design firm IDEO, which displays giant Post-it Notes and charts on brainstorming rules to tap into spatial memory. IDEO also prints the brainstorming rules on their business cards. Why not check your mission, values and vision statements against companies such as Coca-Cola Company and PepsiCo?

Q: How could you grant your employees time and empowerment to immerse themselves in innovation projects?

A: You could have something similar to 3M's fifteen per cent Time to Think, Google's twenty per cent time for personal projects, Apple's time off for a few weeks to focus on a favourite engineering project, Procter & Gamble's Clay Street Project innovation centre where projects could take a few weeks to a few months, or LinkedIn's time off for three months to work on a funded project.

Q: How could you immerse your employees in innovation?

A: You could have corporate hackathons, skunk works, innovation labs, immersion centres or immersion programs for team creativity and innovation. Such collaborative immersion events could accelerate your computer programming or innovation outcomes. Such events also provide opportunities to learn about unfamiliar technology or presentation skills and work on a project unconnected to one's normal day work.

Q: Why do you think some companies allow their staff to work on a passion project that may not be work related?

A: Allowing this flexibility nourishes an innovation mindset that should eventually benefit the organisation and society. Microsoft's Garage idea factory allowed an employee to work on a metal volcano—this could have inspired or triggered other related innovations. Salesforce.com gives its employees six days off for their pet volunteer project and even matches up to US$5000 when their employees donate to non-profit firms.

Q: Why is it essential to have technical or other innovation forums?

A: Forums such as 3M's technical forum enable peers to talk about their projects, ask for feedback and seek team members with various skills (such as technical and presentation) to join the project team.

Q: How could you reward empowered employees who are high achievers?

A: You could adopt the 3M approach: provide grants for projects, recognise achievers by inducting them into a special Hall of Fame network or pay for overachievers and their partners to go on a holiday.

Q: How much should you invest in research and development?

A: Companies such as Intel and Roche spend about twenty per cent of sales on R&D projects—but it is not how much you spend. It's about how you leverage your R&D dollars through wise use of your people and data to gain deeper insights, just like Steve Jobs used to do with his much smaller R&D budget compared with that of IBM.

GROUP GERMINATION

Q: Why would you collaborate with a competitor?

A: Competitive collaboration could help expand the market or innovate for social good. Coca-Cola, PepsiCo and the Dr Pepper Snapple Group collaborated to reduce sugary drink calories.

Q: Why would you form or join an industry cluster?

A: An industry cluster of like-minded companies in a region helps to develop and accelerate external economies. There are many examples of industries that have successful cooperative clusters: California wine, Italian leather fashion, China's Datang 'Socks City', Boston Life Sciences, Queensland tourism, Australia's Savannah Way and Tasmanian light shipbuilding.

Q: Why would you outsource some services?

A: Companies outsource services to save on costs, to access better business, research, design and engineering services and to focus more on collaborative innovation.

Q: What is outside-in open innovation?

A: Outside-in open innovation enables you to use external resources to accelerate creativity and innovation. Amazon, Apple, Facebook, GE, IBM, Johnson & Johnson, Procter & Gamble, Samsung, Unilever, Xerox and Zara seek ideas from academic institutions, developers, partners, research centres, suppliers and users.

Q: What is inside-out open innovation?

A: Inside-out open innovation allows other companies to access your under-utilised or unused internal resources. You could use your company's skills and resources to benefit external parties, just like Philips Research does through contract research.

Q: How could you form partnerships with academia as part of open innovation?

A: You could have research projects, student projects, research awards, faculty awards and/or visiting faculty programs just like those of Apple, Google and IBM.

Q: How could you have a structured supplier collaboration process?

A: Suppliers could contribute to ideas, service differentiation and cost reduction. You could have something similar to Toyota, where its suppliers help to improve designs, systems and quality; or BMW, which has a Supplier Innovation Award; or Tesco, which has an online forum for its 5000 global retailers.

Q: Why is it useful to identify innovative leading-edge lead users in your product category?

A: These innovative lead users are usually already innovating with product applications. For example, 3M discovered that vets and Hollywood makeup artists had been advanced users of infection-prevention materials.

Q: Why and how would you use crowdsourcing or the wisdom and creativity of internet crowds?

A: Companies use crowdsourcing to tap the creativity of the internet crowd for design, writing, translations, multimedia productions and inventions. Unilever has used the crowdsourcing service provider eYeka for forty creative consumer contests across various brands. Procter & Gamble, Pepsi and Nestlé are also big users of crowd wisdom through creative contests.

Q: What is crowdfunding?

A: Crowdfunding is a variation of crowdsourcing but focuses on tapping the crowd to raise funds for non-profit or for-profit projects. For example, the crowdfunding service provider Kickstarter can help you raise funds for the arts, design, gaming and technology industries.

Q: What is the difference between an incubator and accelerator as resources for intrapreneurial and entrepreneurial projects?

A: An incubator funds a 'child' start-up business while an accelerator invests in an 'adult' business. Commonwealth Bank has incubator and accelerator programs to collaborate with start-ups and customers. The Virgin Group helps new entrepreneurs learn from existing entrepreneurs and also has an entrepreneurial foundation working with entrepreneurs, leaders, philanthropists and Virgin's diverse community to create a better world.

CHAPTER 11: CONCLUSION: ACCELERATING TEAM CREATIVITY

MIND NETTING

Q: What seems to be the underpinning framework common to the various creative thinking tools?

A: Most, if not all, creative thinking tools seem to follow a Challenge-Ideas-Action (CIA) framework. The creative thinking process often starts with a challenge, problem, opportunity or task. Then there is the ideas stage followed by action on emerging creative solutions.

Q: How could you use brainstorming in your organisation?

A: You could vary your brainstorming practice by using traditional facilitator-led brainstorming, individual brainstorming before and after the team process, SCAMPER, reverse brainstorming, electronic brainstorming, round-robin brainstorming, brainswarming, brainwriting, brainsketching, rolestorming, hybrid brainstorming, brainsteering and brainstorming boxes. The award-winning design firm and brainstorming evangelist IDEO shares stories about best practices; makes use of actual products or elegant solutions from competitors and other fields; and uses sketching, diagrams, mind mapping, stick figures, materials for building concept models, and 'bodystorming', a form of role playing consumer behaviour as a catalyst to improve the user experience.

Q: What is the Creative Problem Solving process and how could you use the tool?

A: The CPS process is a structured creative problem-solving process covering divergent and convergent thinking. It started with Alex Osborn and evolved over the years with variations from Sidney Parnes and various researchers. Depending on the CPS model that you use, there are several cyclical stages and steps that allow you to move back and forth but the basic format of the CPS process is to identify the challenge, find ideas to address the challenge and act on solutions. Hence, my CIA variation of Challenge-Ideas-Action.

Q: What is Synectics and how could you use the tool?

A: Synectics means bringing diverse elements together. Prince and Gordon founded the company in 1960 to focus on a behavioural approach to team innovation. You could use the Synectics process in whole or parts as a team, or on your own; for example, you might use task analysis, wishing, excursions or metaphoric vacation, listening out-in, headlining, approximate thinking, connection making, analogical thinking, idea development, idea evaluation and action. My variation of Synectics was to connect the divergent-convergent structure to Walt Disney's dreamer-realist-critic thinking modes and create a DREAM process of dream-review-expand-assess-manage.

Q: *How could you use lateral thinking and Six Thinking Hats tools?*

A: Lateral thinking is analogically looking in a different direction, with techniques such as concept extraction and provocative operation (a process to throw in a silly idea to disrupt the thinking pattern). The Six Thinking Hats is a parallel thinking process where all team members focus on one thinking mode simultaneously. The blue hat is analogous to the facilitator in any brainstorming, Creative Problem Solving or Synectics process. The white hat is similar to the CPS fact finding and Synectics task analysis steps. The green hat is connected to brainstorming, CPS idea finding, Synectics wishing and analogical thinking, TRIZ analogical patterns of problem solving and lateral thinking. The red hat reminds me of the Synectics behavioural dynamics while the yellow hat and black hat are equivalent to the Synectics itemised response of pros, cons and improvements. As in the cyclical flexibility of the CPS and Synectics processes, the six hats are not used sequentially, with some hats being used more often.

Q: *How could you use mind mapping and multidimensional thinking?*

A: Mind mapping is similar to whole-brain and analogical or associative thinking, where words and pictures are drawn to show connections between the central topic and sub-branches of related associations. A mind map could be used for brainstorming ideas, summarising reading, remembering songs and planning projects. Multidimensional mind mapping is a way to think in different dimensions and to move away from the habit of single-minded associative thinking. The mind has stored diverse associations of keywords, so aim to think like a genius by tapping into your five senses as well as your visual, intrapersonal, naturalistic, kinaesthetic, musical, interpersonal, linguistic and logical intelligences.

Q: *What is TRIZ and how could you use this creative thinking tool?*

A: TRIZ inventive problem solving is a systematic Russian creative thinking tool that spread to the East and West. Founder Altshuller had analysed thousands of patent registrations and concluded that there are forty invention principles

CHAPTER 11: CONCLUSION: ACCELERATING TEAM CREATIVITY

to address problem-solving contradictions or obstacles and find the ideal final result. The simple philosophy is that someone somewhere has already thought of a solution for a problem similar to yours (the late Lee Kuan Yew had this practice), so use the TRIZ principles instead of re-inventing the wheel. I have connected the forty principles with the brainstorming SCAMPER variation, as the principles seem to fit under SCAMPER's substitute, combine, adapt, magnify/minify, put to other uses, eliminate and reverse. Some of the TRIZ principles are frequently used, such as parameter changes, taking out, self-service, preliminary action and the other way round. You could use some of the TRIZ principles with other creative thinking processes such as a lateral thinking random word exploration during green hat mode or reverse thinking during black hat mode.

Q: *How could you use attribute listing and morphological synthesis tools?*

A: Attribute listing is a way of listing attributes and modifying them. You could do this through a table or mind map. Morphological synthesis (also known as morphological analysis, morphological creativity, morphological combination, morphological box or Zwicky box) is a mixing method where you rigorously or randomly mix ideas under different axes/columns of core dimensions and specific attributes.

Q: *How do you see the various Mind Netting creative thinking tools being connected?*

A: Brainstorming, the Creative Problem Solving process, Synectics, lateral thinking, Six Thinking Hats, mind mapping, multidimensional thinking, TRIZ, attribute listing and morphological synthesis seem to be different thinking tools but they are approximately or precisely connected in many ways under the Challenge-Ideas-Action (CIA) framework. Some tools are structured with a facilitator (brainstorming, CPS, Synectics, Six Thinking Hats), some include random entries (excursions, random word, PO) and some overlap (analogies and TRIZ principles, TRIZ principles and SCAMPER). There is often logical thinking (CPS fact finding, Synectics task analysis and de Bono's white hat) and emotional or irrational behaviour (Synectics fun excursions and de Bono's lateral thinking PO and red hat).

Q: *How could you have a morphological combination of the various creative thinking tools?*

A: You do not individually have to be trained in all the creative thinking methods described in this book, although experience tells me that it is good to have a repertoire to draw upon in intensive and extended innovation processes. You could have a team trained in several of the creative thinking tools and leverage the combined skills and learning styles of the group. The portfolio of thinking tools is like the patterns of thinking described by Dilts when he modelled geniuses; like the kaleidoscopic thinking of Edison; like Steve Jobs borrowing ideas from various sources and experiences; like Google looking for ideas everywhere; like the Procter & Gamble Clay Street Project facilitators using brainstorming, excursions, mythology, neuroscience, theatre, Zen exercises and TRIZ principles; like open innovation companies tapping the ideas of academic researchers, competitors, crowd wisdom, entrepreneurs, governments, private labs, regional clusters, research institutions, retailers, suppliers, trade partners and venture capital firms; and like brainstorming practitioners who use analogies, success scenarios, comic storytelling, video footages, rolestorming of saint or sinner, visits to different industries and shopping for products that metaphorically symbolise the proposed solutions. In my talks to industries and students, I often speak on borrowing from diverse sources, multidimensional associations and mixing techniques and ideas.

FINAL WORDS

How can you be the innovator? Accelerate creativity and innovation in your team or organisation through the four integrated team creativity catalysts of Mastery Modelling, Intensive Immersion, Group Germination and Mind Netting. Model or benchmark against geniuses, innovative people, companies and countries. Immerse empowered employees in the innovation journey through clearly communicated corporate mission, values and vision plus time-to-think passionate projects. Germinate through collaboration with various internal and external groups. Net ideas from diverse minds trained in different creative thinking tools. Modelling, immersing, germinating and netting could be your framework to overcome innovation barriers of leadership, culture and resources, thus enabling you to be a world-class innovator and innovation leader.

APPENDIX A: RESEARCH ON ADULT TEAM CREATIVITY

Introduction
This appendix is an extracted summary of my research on adult team creativity. It covers creativity literature, the research gap, research design and research findings.

Creativity literature
There are many creativity theories and most can be said to belong to the mental, emotional, physical and spiritual or self-actualising dimensions. This section briefly reviews classic, contemporary, brain and interconnected theories of creativity.

Classic creativity theories
Classic creativity theories fall into cognitive, psychoanalytic, behaviouralistic and humanistic areas. Cognitivists advocate process creativity. Psychoanalysts subscribe to instinctive creativity. Behaviouralists are concerned with conditioned creativity. Humanists believe in self-actualising creativity.

Following are key concepts of the classic creativity theories.

Cognitivists
1. Poincaré: Four-stage process covering hard work, incubation, illumination and verification.[378]
2. Wallas: Preparation and verification at the conscious level while incubation and illumination occur at the subconscious level.[379]
3. Osborn: Brainstorming in free-flow and convergent stages.[380]
4. Gordon: Proactive use of metaphors and analogies for creative insights[381] to consciously unlock the subconscious, skipping the incubation phase.[382]
5. Guilford: Divergent and convergent thinking.[383]
6. Koestler: 'Bisociational' or diverse connections from unrelated sources; also theorised about three personalities for creativity—the artist, jester and sage.[384]
7. Torrance: Defined creativity as originality/uniqueness, fluency/quantity, flexibility/categories and elaboration/details.[385]

Psychoanalysts
1. Freud: Creativity emerges from dreams, fantasies and unfulfilled wishes in the unconscious mind.[386]
2. Jung: The collective unconscious stores shared instincts, culture and experience.[387]

3. Kubie[388] and Kris[389]: Theorised that there is a pre-conscious phase between the unconscious and the conscious stages.
4. Berne: Creativity is a transactional analysis between the child (dreamer), adult (realist) and parent (critical or nurturing mode).[390]

Behaviouralists
1. Skinner: Observable conditioned creative response.[391]
2. Mednick: Associative routine or response repertoire; for example the common word 'cheese' links attributes such as cottage, blue and mouse or the common word 'sweet' links cookies, sixteen and heart.[392]

Humanists
1. Maslow: Primary creativity as an attribute of every person comes from the subconscious while secondary creativity is a conscious process, with the ideal of integrating both primary and secondary creativity.[393]
2. Rogers: Primary creativity is one per cent inspiration and secondary creativity is ninety-nine per cent perspiration.[394]

Contemporary creativity theories

Contemporary creativity theories encompass the popular 4Ps of creativity (place, product, process and person, although some authors have added persuasion and potential[395]), interaction theory, three-facet theory, componential theory and systems theory. Here is a brief summary of the contemporary creativity theories:

1. 4Ps theory: The creative product is the outcome of interactions between process, person and place (also described as press or environment).[396]
2. Interaction theory: The creative product is the interaction of process, aptitude and environment.[397]
3. Three-facet theory: The creative product is the outcome of cognitive style, domain intelligence and personality-cum-motivation.[398]
4. Componential theory: The creative product is the interaction of creative skills, domain skills and task motivation.[399] Amabile, who theorised about componential creativity, also distinguished between the 'small C' creativity of everyday living, the 'middle C' creativity of professional or organisational creativity and the 'big C' creativity of eminent domain experts.[400]
5. Systems theory: Creativity occurs at the intersection of the person (genetic, talent, experience), cultural domain (knowledge, values, tools, practices), and social field (gatekeepers, practitioners).[401]

APPENDIX A: RESEARCH ON ADULT TEAM CREATIVITY

The contemporary creativity theories appear to be related when you connect them to the popular 4Ps theory. For example, aptitude, personality and motivation are attributes of a person. See Table A.1 to see how the components of various contemporary theories could be connected to the 4Ps theory of creativity.

TABLE A.1 Interconnected contemporary creativity theories

4PS THEORY	INTERACTION THEORY	THREE-FACET THEORY	COMPONENTIAL THEORY	SYSTEMS THEORY
Place [Climate, environment]	Environment	Intelligence [domain skill]	Domain skills	Social field
Product	Creativity [novel, useful]	Creativity [novel, useful]	Creativity [novel, useful]	Creativity [novel, useful]
Process [Tools]	Process	Cognitive style	Creative skills	Domain culture
Person	Aptitude	Personality and motivation	Task motivation	Person

Brain theories

Brain theories cover hemispheric differences, Triune brain, whole brain and the integrated brain. Following is a summary of brain theories related to creativity:

1. The left brain is analytical while the right brain is creative.[402]
2. The left brain is the academic brain while the right brain is the metaphoric brain.[403]
3. The metaphoric right brain speedily connects with the left brain for effective thinking.[404]
4. The metaphoric right brain or analogical thinking contributes to eighty-five per cent of 'ahas'.[405]
5. The right brain is divine and the left brain is the servant but it is paradoxical that we tend to worship the left brain.[406]
6. The Triune brain is like three connected computers comprising the neocortex thinking brain, the limbic emotional brain and the reptilian instinctive brain which is prone to feed, fight, flee or have sex.[407]

7   The whole brain is made up of four quadrants of left brain facts and form plus right brain feelings and fantasy.[408]
8   Whole brain thinkers instinctively switch between the linear left brain and the metaphoric right brain.[409]
9   The right brain is yin and feminine while the left brain is yang and masculine, with the pair working effectively as a dynamic duo.[410]
10 The left and right brains, the unlikely couple, have different strengths, can act independently but do communicate with one another.[411]
11 Right brain artists can still use left-brain logic and rules.[412]
12 The brain has a hundred billion neuron cells with the potential of making a quadrillion synaptic connections or 'ahas' and the little brain is the muscle-memory area that stores all your learned skills and responds automatically in situations.[413]
13 Creativity is a neuroscientific mystery with three types of creativity: exploratory creativity, which uses existing rules or conventions to generate novel ideas; transformational creativity, where altering a rule or convention leads to an impossible idea; and combinatorial creativity, where an unfamiliar idea arises from mixing familiar ideas.[414]

Interconnected creativity theories
While the contemporary creativity theories seem to be connected, there is also a common factor in the classic, contemporary and brain theories. These all share a 'triple' phenomenon, such as the three-facet theory, small-middle-big creativity, the unconscious-preconscious-conscious interactions, the child-adult-parent factors, the artist-jester-sage elements and the reptilian-limbic-neocortex dimensions.

I have also tried to link the classic theories and brain theories with the contemporary creativity theories. The theories may be described differently but I believe that they are all interconnected. For example, humanistic theories are connected to place because humanists believe in self-actualising creativity as a way of life; behaviouristic theories are connected with product or form because seeing is believing for the behaviourists; cognitive theories are naturally linked to process; and psychoanalytic theories are related to the person. Domain or factual discipline skills are related to place, environment or field. The domain culture in the systems theory of creativity, with tools and practices, could link with the process of cognitive style, creative skills and fantasy. Table A.2 shows my attempt to link various theories, where I have chosen the whole brain theory to connect to other creativity theories.

TABLE A.2 Interconnected creativity theories

4PS THEORY	WHOLE BRAIN THEORY	INTERACTION THEORY	THREE-FACET THEORY	COMPONENTIAL THEORY	SYSTEMS THEORY	CLASSIC THEORIES
Place [Climate, environment]	Facts	Environment	Intelligence [domain skill]	Domain skills	Social field	Humanistic
Product	Form	Creativity [novel, useful]	Creativity [novel, useful]	Creativity [novel, useful]	Creativity [novel, useful]	Behaviouralistic
Process [Tools]	Fantasy	Process	Cognitive style	Creative skills	Domain culture	Cognitive
Person	Feelings	Aptitude	Personality and motivation	Task and motivation	Person	Psychoanalytic

For my research, I adapted numerous definitions by describing creativity as a multifaceted interaction of person-process-place dimensions that produces the product of situational 'aha' solutions.

Research gap

There are 'hard' approaches to creativity research (biological, computational, experimental, historiometric and psychometric) and 'soft' approaches (biographical and contextual).[415] The DREAM method (dream, review, expand, assess and manage) fits into the 'soft' cultural contextual approach, builds on creativity training research conducted mostly on the Creative Problem Solving process and Synectics, and addresses the gap in understanding the narratives of adult workers in their attempt to accelerate their creativity via intensive creativity training.

Research design

The central research goal was to uncover significant learning insights and perspectives of participants as they learnt the Synectics-based DREAM process over two days. Specifically, I investigated key factors, strategies and actions that facilitated accelerated team creativity, which was defined as the ability to effectively use the DREAM process and achieve intriguing, feasible outcomes for real tasks within two days of training. I examined feelings and symbols used by learners to express their extent of accelerated team creativity. And I considered what learning expectations were met or not met through the DREAM training program.

My thesis methodology consisted of the following:

- A pilot study to test whether data collection process, procedures and timing would affect the training process.
- Three Singapore groups of thirty-three human resource management managers from the public and private sectors, who had been trained in various thinking techniques such as lateral thinking, Six Thinking Hats, mind mapping, Klepnoe Tregoe, Herrmann Whole Brain Thinking, and Creative Problem Solving process.
- Triangulated data from personal metaphors, charts demonstrating the DREAM process, observing participants during practice sessions, mind map exercises, team problem-solving outcomes, team discussions, individual discussions, participant learning journals, metaphorical drawings of learning, casual chats with participants and a logbook of role playing on tasks and workshop feedback.
- Grounded Theory techniques of qualitative data analysis through four stages: analysing line-by-line content to discover keyword concepts; comparing similar and different concepts to build thematic categories; linking related categories

to uncover core themes and finally identifying the central idea to explain the phenomenon.[416]
- Presentation of initial research findings at the 2004 American Creativity Association Think Tank Conference in Houston, USA, where delegates provided valuable feedback to search for a bigger storyline behind the initial findings of accelerated creative competency, team bonding, creative confidence and paradigm shifts.
- Using mind maps to link data analysis themes and the central idea. See Figure A.1 for a mind map of creativity catalysts.

FIGURE A.1 Mind map of creativity catalysts

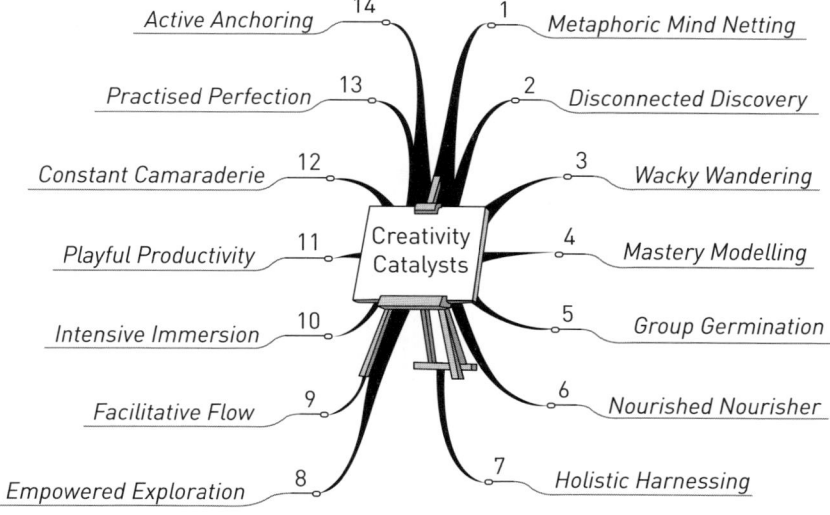

Research findings

From rigorous cross-checking data analysis, I found that two-thirds of the participants could use the DREAM process effectively within two days, either spontaneously or by referring to the visual cues. The remaining participants felt that they needed more practice. A majority of the learners found 'new confidence' in 'nurtured creativity' and a paradigm shift of 'disconnected discovery' in finding creative ideas from unconnected sources, such as life as a hamburger and a career as an armpit sniffer.

APPENDICES

Further synthesis of the various creativity catalysts led to four core themes of Mastery Modelling, Intensive Immersion, Group Germination and Mind Netting. Mastery Modelling is about modelling mastery or best practices; Intensive Immersion is about empowered immersion to achieve the benchmarked mastery; Group Germination is about achieving innovation through creative collaboration; and Mind Netting is about harvesting ideas of diverse groups through various creative thinking tools. All four creativity catalysts work synergistically, involving mental, emotional, physical and self-actualising dimensions.

APPENDIX B: OTHER AUTHORS MODELLING GENIUS

Besides neurolinguistic programming practitioners such as Bandler, Grinder and Dilts, several other authors have also explored the excellence of geniuses for us to emulate. This section looks at the work of Murray, Buzan, Keene, Gelb and Caldicott.

Murray

Scholar and author Charles Murray wrote *Human Accomplishment: The pursuit of excellence in the arts and sciences, 800 B.C. to 1950* (2003), covering 4000 eminent people including Leonardo da Vinci, Michelangelo, Beethoven, Bach, Rembrandt, Dante, Picasso, Goethe, Einstein, Marie Curie, Archimedes, Newton, Galileo, Pasteur, Descartes, the Wright brothers, Tesla, T. S. Eliot, Socrates, Plato and Aristotle.[417]

Buzan and Keene

Tony Buzan, developer of mind mapping, and Raymond Keene, international chess grand master, analysed the lives of a hundred geniuses and scored them on a 835-point scale covering field dominance, active longevity, ongoing influence, polymath, versatility, energy, prolificness, vision, originality and desire to leave a legacy. You may not agree with the scoring methodology but these are the top ten geniuses named by Buzan and Keene: Leonardo da Vinci, William Shakespeare, Goethe, Michelangelo, Sir Isaac Newton, Thomas Jefferson, Alexander the Great, Phidias, Albert Einstein and Thomas Edison.[418]

Gelb and Caldicott

Innovation trainer Michael Gelb analysed the following role models to uncover their genius traits:[419]

- Plato, Greek philosopher: love of wisdom
- Filippo Brunelleschi, Italian Renaissance architect: expanding perspectives
- Christopher Columbus, explorer: vision, courage, optimism
- Nicolaus Copernicus, astronomer: world vision
- Queen Elizabeth I, queen of England and Ireland: balance of power and effectiveness
- William Shakespeare, poet and playwright: emotional intelligence
- Thomas Jefferson, US president: happiness and freedom

- Charles Darwin, geologist and naturalist: open mind and observation
- Mahatma Gandhi, independence through non-violence: spiritual genius
- Albert Einstein, physicist: play and imagination.

Gelb also analysed the achievements of Leonardo da Vinci. Gelb describes da Vinci as 'history's greatest genius' because of his achievements in anatomy, architecture, botany, city planning, engineering, geology, invention, map making, mathematics, military science, music and painting. Gelb proposes a model of seven da Vinci principles:[420]

1. insatiable curiosity for continuous improvement
2. experiential learning and independent thinking
3. leveraging the senses
4. body–mind fitness
5. embracing ambiguity and change
6. whole brain thinking
7. systems thinking to look for new connections.

Gelb and Sarah Miller Caldicott, the great-grand-niece of Thomas Edison, also studied the works of 'history's greatest practical innovator', who is known for his inventions for lighting (including inventing the light bulb), motion pictures and the phonograph. Edison had more than 1000 patents in the USA and was known to fish without bait to get himself into the mode for fishing for breakthrough ideas. The authors concluded that Thomas Edison had five competencies of innovation:[421]

1. solution-centred mindset to learn from failures
2. kaleidoscopic thinking of possibilities and compelling ideas
3. full-spectrum engagement to find simplicity in complexity
4. master mind collaboration of leveraging diverse perspectives
5. super-value creation of profit with customer satisfaction.

APPENDIX C: NEWS MEDIA MODELLING MASTERY

This section explores leading news media outlets that have featured model creative and innovative people: *Time, Fast Company, Vanity Fair* and broadcaster CNBC.

Time magazine

Time's special issue in 1999 voted Einstein the 'person of the century' because he had an impact on the bomb, electronics and quantum physics. The magazine featured a hundred 'people of the century' by category. You may not agree with the selection, but you can view the list at ranker.com (search 'ranker time 100 people century').

After the popularity of its 1999 special edition, from 2004 *Time* began publishing annually a list of a hundred people influencing the world. The following people have appeared multiple times in the Time 100 between 2004 and 2014:[422]

- nine appearances: Barack Obama, president of the USA
- eight appearances: Oprah Winfrey, talk show personality, and Hilary Clinton, former US Secretary of State
- six appearances: Angela Merkel, Germany's transformational leader
- five appearances: Steve Jobs, Apple co-founder
- four appearances: Hu Jintao, China's ruler between 2002 and 2012; Bill Clinton, former US president; George W. Bush, former US president; Condoleezza Rice, former US Secretary of State; Aung San Suu Kyi, Burmese politician; George Clooney, actor and advocate against genocide and poverty; and Jamie Dimon, head of JP Morgan Chase, who helped to shape the financial services sector in the USA
- three appearances: Bill Gates, Microsoft founder; Warren Buffet, billionaire philanthropist; Larry Page, Google co-founder; Mark Zuckerberg, Facebook founder; Jeff Bezos, Amazon founder; and Rupert Murdoch, chairperson of News Corporation.

While politicians had the most multiple appearances, Oprah Winfrey was influential through her twenty-five-year talk show. Once this ended, Oprah did not appear in the Time 100 list (between 2012 and 2014). Steve Jobs featured in the Time 100 in 2004, 2005, 2007, 2008 and 2010 but was not featured when he died in 2011.

Fast Company

Fast Company has since 2009 featured the '100 Most Creative People in Business', who are accomplished, influential, creatively inspiring people with world-changing ideas. Each year's list is new, excluding previous honourees or people profiled.[423] Some of the featured people:

- 2009: Jonathan Ive, SVP of industrial design of Apple; Melinda Gates, co-chair and trustee of Bill & Melinda Gates Foundation; Shai Agassi, CEO of Better Place; Reed Hastings, CEO of Netflix; and Rich Ross, president of Disney Channels Worldwide[424]
- 2010: Lady Gaga, pop artist; Eddy Cue, VP of internet service at Apple; Elizabeth Warren, professor and consumer advocate, Harvard Law and Congressional Oversight Panel; Shiro Nakamura, chief creative officer, Nissan; and Ryan Murphy, creator and producer of *Glee*[425]
- 2011: Wadah Khanfar, director general, Al Jazeera Arabic; Scott Forstall, SVP of iPhone software, Apple; Yuri Milner, Russian venture capitalist, Digital Sky Technologies; Jack Dorsey, executive chairperson of Twitter and CEO of Square, where iPhone users can accept credit-card payments; and Sebastian Thrun, a Stanford professor now developing driverless robotic cars at Google[426]
- 2012: Ma Jun, director of Institute of Public and Environmental Affairs, China; Rebecca Van Dyck, head of consumer marketing, Facebook; Adam Brotman, chief digital officer, Starbucks; Ron Johnson, CEO, JC Penny; and Ceelo Green, entertainer[427]
- 2013: Nate Silver, author and principal, FiveThirtyEight baseball blog; Dong-Hoon Chang, EVP, head of design strategy, Samsung; Diana Balmori, Principal Associates, a landscape architect firm; Kirthiga Reddy, director of online operations, Facebook India; and Daniel Graf, director of Google Maps for Mobile[428]
- 2014: Princess Reema Bint Bandar Al-Saud, CEO, Alfa International, a Saudi Arabian luxury retailer; Gur Kimchi and Daniel Buchmueller, VP and software development engineer of Prime Air Amazon; Jill Wilfert, VP for global licensing and entertainment, Lego; Mario Queiroz, VP of product management, Google; and Raj Talluri, SVP of product management, Qualcomm[429]
- 2015: Charles Arntzen, professor, Arizona State University's Center for Infectious Diseases and Vaccinology; Rajan Anandan, managing director (India and Southeast Asia), Google; Dao Nguyen, publisher, Buzzfeed, who converted 'LOLs' into a media giant; Maria Claudia Lacouture, president, ProColombia, who repositioned the country as a popular and safe destination; and Jens Bergensten, lead creative designer at Minecraft.[430]

Vanity Fair

Some of the influential people in the *Fast Company* listings also appeared in *Vanity Fair*'s 'New Establishment' top five rankings between 2011 and 2014; for example, Apple's Jonathan Ive and Jack Dorsey of Twitter. The same entrepreneurs and visionaries tend to dominate the *Vanity Fair* listings, except for a couple of changes (see Table C.1).

TABLE C.1 Vanity Fair New Establishment entrepreneurs and visionaries

	2011[431]	2012[432]	2013[433]	2014[434]
1st	Mark Zuckerberg, Facebook founder	Tim Cook and Jonathan Ive	Jeff Bezos	Elon Musk, founder, Space Exploration Technologies (SpaceX spacecraft and Tesla electric car)
2nd	Larry Page and Sergey Brin, Google co-founders	Larry Page and Sergey Brin	Larry Page and Sergey Brin	Larry Page and Sergey Brin
3rd	Jeff Bezos, Amazon founder	Jeff Bezos	Tim Cook and Jonathan Ive	Tim Cook and Jonathan Ive
4th	Tim Cook (Steve Job's successor) and Jonathan Ive (SVP industrial design), Apple	Mark Zuckerberg	Mark Zuckerberg	Jeff Bezos
5th	Jack Dorsey, executive chairperson of Twitter, CEO of Square	Jack Dorsey	Elon Musk	Mark Zuckerberg

CNBC

Broadcaster CNBC voted Apple's Steve Jobs the number one person to have had an impact on business since its first live broadcast in 1989. The other top ten leaders in the 'first 25 rebels, icons and leaders' list are Bill Gates, Microsoft founder; Ben Bernanke and Alan Greenspan, former US Federation chairs; Sergey Brin and Larry Page, Google founders; Jeff Bezos, Amazon founder; Warren Buffett, US investor; Oprah Winfrey, billionaire media celebrity; Mark Zuckerberg, Facebook founder; Jack Bogle, Index mutual fund pioneer; and Larry Ellison, Oracle co-founder.[435]

APPENDIX D: MODELLING INNOVATIVE COMPANIES

Diverse sources publish different lists of innovative companies based on criteria such as perceptions of senior executives, research and development (R&D) spending, innovation management principles, innovation strides and invention patents. This section covers sources such as Boston Consulting Group (BCG), Strategy&, *Fast Company*, *Forbes*, *Fortune*, *MIT Technology Review*, Thomson Reuters and Innovation Leaders.org. Some companies appear in more lists, hence may be more worth emulating: Apple, Google, Amazon, Samsung and Tesla.

BCG

BCG has been surveying senior executives since 2004 to rank the most innovative companies. It found that Apple has been ranked number one since 2005 and Google ranked number two since 2006.[436] BCG indicated that innovative companies have leadership commitment, leverage intellectual property, manage portfolios, focus on the customer and have processes for strong performance.[437]

Strategy&

Strategy& has been studying the R&D spending of innovative companies. Its recent survey of 350 companies revealed that innovative companies spend about eight per cent of revenue on digital tools to accelerate innovation.[438] The Strategy& Global Innovation 1000 studies have ranked Apple as the number one most innovative company between 2010 and 2014, with Google at number two and Amazon and 3M changing places at number three.[439]

Fast Company

Fast Company looks at innovative leaps that transform consumer behaviour, where the culture of innovation includes dreaming big, expecting exceptional achievements, episodic innovation and unlocking global talent. It listed Google as the most innovative company in 2014; Apple was in the fourteenth spot.[440]

Forbes

Forbes looked at companies' innovation premium, which is the value that investors place on organisations based on expectations of new product launches, entering new markets with higher income streams and efficient use of existing resources. The *Forbes* list follows the 'innovator's method' of insight, problem, solution and business model. The *Forbes* list in 2014 had Salesforce.com, an application software corporation, at number one, with three biotechnology firms in the top ten.[441]

Fortune
Fortune looks at nine key attributes of innovation, people management, use of corporate assets, social responsibility, management quality, financial soundness, investment value, products/services quality and global competitiveness. The top three companies in the *Fortune* list are Apple, Amazon and Google.[442]

MIT
The *MIT Technology Review* list of smartest companies highlights impressive innovations of the previous year, not based on R&D spending or patents. Apple or Facebook were not in the 2014 list but Illumina appeared as number one because of its innovative price reduction for genome sequencing machines in medical practice.[443]

Thomson Reuters
The 2014 Thomson Reuters list of top global innovators analysed companies with at least a hundred unique inventions within a recent three-year period based on granted patents from authorities in China, Europe, Japan and the USA. Thomson Reuters claims its peer-reviewed methodology is unique because it quantifies and qualifies innovation, corporate commitment to innovation and protection of intellectual property by using global patent data, such as worldwide reach, volume, approval success rate and citations. Companies that have been highly ranked many times include 3M, Apple, Boeing, Brother Industries, Canon, Corning, Dow Chemical, DuPont, Emerson, Ericsson, Fujitsu, General Electric, Hewlett-Packard, Hitachi, Honda, Honeywell, IBM, Intel, LG Electronics, Microsoft, Mitsubishi, NEC, Olympus, Panasonic, Qualcomm, Roche, Samsung, SanDisk, Sharp, Siemens, Sony, Symantec, Toshiba, Toyota and Xerox.[444]

Innovation Leaders.org
The research done by this organisation since 2001 features an innovation leader in each of twenty-five sectors after analysing 1500 top companies against eight criteria: organisational and supporting culture; strategic innovation focus; new product launches and success ratios; revenue, profit and market capitalisation growth; average revenue and margin per customer or product; investment in innovation activities; growth in brand value and human capital; and industry

sector peer review. Unlike other sources, Innovation Leaders.org does not rank companies overall from one to ten and above. From available 2001–12 data, Starwood Hotels and Resorts is the only company that has been rated as the innovation leader each year in its category. Canon was the innovation leader in the office products category for ten out of twelve years.[445]

Synthesising the listings of most innovative companies and assigning weighted scores to the frequency of mentions, the highest-ranked companies are Apple, Google, Amazon, Samsung, Tesla, Salesforce.com, 3M, Dropbox, Microsoft and IBM (see Table D.1).

APPENDICES

TABLE D.1 2014's most innovative companies, synthesised from seven sources

	BCG	STRATEGY&	FAST COMPANY	FORBES	FORTUNE	MIT	THOMSON REUTERS
1st	Apple	Apple	Google	Salesforce.com	Apple	Illumina	3M
2nd	Google	Google	Bloomberg Philanthropies	Alexion Pharmaceuticals	Amazon	Tesla Motors	ABB
3rd	Samsung	Amazon	Xiaomi	ARM Holdings	Google	Google	Abbott Laboratories
4th	Microsoft	Samsung	Dropbox	Unilever Indonesia	Berkshire Hathaway	Samsung	Advanced Micro Devices
5th	IBM	Tesla Motors	Netflix	Regeneron Pharmaceuticals	Starbucks	Salesforce.com	Aisin Seiki
6th	Amazon	3M	Airbnb	Amazon	Coca-Cola	Dropbox	Alcatel-Lucent
7th	Tesla Motors	General Electric	Nike	BioMarin Pharmaceutical	Walt Disney	BMW	Altera
8th	Toyota Motor	Microsoft	Zipdial	CP All	FedEx	Third Rock Ventures	Apple
9th	Facebook	IBM	DonorsChoose	VMware	Southwest Airlines	Square	Arkema
10th	Sony	Procter & Gamble	Yelp	Aspen Pharmacare Holdings	General Electric	Amazon	Asahi Glass

APPENDIX E: MODELLING INNOVATIVE COUNTRIES

This section discusses six sources that highlight innovative countries: Boston Consulting Group (BCG) Innovation Friendly Countries, Bloomberg Innovation Quotient, Global Competitiveness Index, Global Innovation Index, Global Innovation Policy Index and IMD World Competitiveness Ranking.

Boston Consulting Group Innovation Friendly Countries

The BCG and the National Association of Manufacturer's Manufacturing Institute ranked countries by how government policies on education, infrastructure, trade and workforce quality influence innovation, research and development, employment and business performance. The 2013 results are listed below:[446]

1. Singapore
2. South Korea
3. Switzerland
4. Iceland
5. Ireland
6. Hong Kong
7. Finland
8. USA
9. Japan
10. Sweden.

Bloomberg Innovation Quotient

The Bloomberg Innovation Quotient (BIQ), modelled after innovation quotient scales, analyses countries by innovation ability across seven weighted factors: research and development intensity, productivity, high-tech density, researcher concentration, manufacturing capability, tertiary efficiency, and patent activity. The BIQ uses data from Bloomberg, International Monetary Fund, OECD, UNESCO, US Patent and Trademark Office, World Bank and World Intellectual Property Organization. The BIQ rankings for 2012–14 showed a different country each year but South Korea was consistently in the top three, and the USA was consistently highly ranked. For 2014, Bloomberg started with a list of 215 countries, shortlisted to 110 and then listed the top thirty. South Korea, Sweden and the USA were ranked the top three most innovative countries for 2014. See Table E.1 for the 2012–14 rankings.

TABLE E.1 Bloomberg Innovation Quotient 2012–14 rankings

	2014[447]	2013[448]	2012[449]
1st	South Korea	USA	Finland
2nd	Sweden	South Korea	Singapore
3rd	USA	Germany	South Korea
4th	Japan	Finland	Japan
5th	Germany	Sweden	Sweden
6th	Denmark	Japan	Germany
7th	Singapore	Singapore	USA
8th	Switzerland	Austria	Switzerland
9th	Finland	Denmark	France
10th	Taiwan	France	Austria

Global Competitiveness Index

The Global Competitiveness Index (GCI) from the World Economic Forum has since 1979 ranked countries by global competitiveness. Its thirty-fifth edition, for 2014–15, analyses twelve pillars of 144 economies under three sub-indices: basic requirements of private and public institutions, infrastructure, macroeconomic environment and health and primary education; efficiency enhancers of higher education and training, goods market efficiency, labour market efficiency, financial market development, technological readiness and market size; and innovation-driven factors such as business sophistication and innovation. Its weightings of the three sub-indices are twenty to sixty per cent for the basic requirements factors, thirty-five to fifty per cent for the efficiency enhancers and five to thirty per cent for the innovation drivers. Switzerland has been ranked number one over the past five years, with Singapore number two for four consecutive years.[450] See Table E.2.

TABLE E.2 Global Competitiveness Index

	2014–15	2013–14	2012–13	2011–12	2010–11
1st	Switzerland	Switzerland	Switzerland	Switzerland	Switzerland
2nd	Singapore	Singapore	Singapore	Singapore	Sweden
3rd	USA	Finland	Finland	Sweden	Singapore
4th	Finland	Germany	Sweden	Finland	USA
5th	Germany	USA	Netherlands	USA	Germany
6th	Japan	Sweden	Germany	Germany	Japan
7th	Hong Kong	Hong Kong	USA	Netherlands	Finland
8th	Netherlands	Netherlands	UK	Denmark	Netherlands
9th	UK	Japan	Hong Kong	Japan	Denmark
10th	Sweden	UK	Japan	UK	Canada

In terms of innovation drivers, the GCI analyses eighteen elements including supplier quality, value chain breadth, production process sophistication, extent of marketing, capacity for innovation, availability of engineers and scientists, quality of scientific research institutions, research and development spending, industry–university collaboration, patent applications, and intellectual property protection. Switzerland was ranked at either number one or two between 2010 and 2015 in this category but Singapore does not feature strongly compared to resource-rich countries such as Japan, Finland, Sweden, Germany and the USA. See Table E.3.

TABLE E.3 Global Competitiveness Index: Innovation top ten

	2014–15	2013–14	2012–13	2011–12	2010–11
1st	Finland	Switzerland	Switzerland	Switzerland	Japan
2nd	Switzerland	Finland	Japan	Sweden	Switzerland
3rd	Israel	Japan	Finland	Japan	Sweden
4th	Japan	Germany	Germany	Finland	USA
5th	USA	Sweden	Sweden	Germany	Germany
6th	Germany	USA	Netherlands	USA	Finland

(*continued*)

TABLE E.3 Global Competitiveness Index: Innovation top ten (*continued*)

	2014-15	2013-14	2012-13	2011-12	2010-11
7th	Sweden	Netherlands	USA	Israel	Taiwan
8th	Netherlands	Israel	Israel	Denmark	Netherlands
9th	Singapore	Taiwan	UK	Netherlands	Denmark
10th	Taiwan	UK	Austria	Taiwan	Singapore

Global Innovation Index

The Global Innovation Index, co-published by Cornell University, INSEAD and the United Nations' World Intellectual Property Organization, examines five pillars that influence innovation in more than 140 countries: institutions, human capital and research, infrastructure, market sophistication and business sophistication. Over seven editions since 2007, Switzerland has been ranked number one four times, the USA twice, and Sweden has been placed six times as number two or three.[451] See Table E.4.

Global Innovation Policy Index

The Information Technology & Innovation Foundation and the Ewing Marion Kauffman Foundation in the USA produce the Global Innovation Policy Index (GIPI). In 2012 the GIPI analysed fifty-five countries on eighty-four indicators across seven innovation-friendly policy areas: trade and foreign direct investment; science and research and development; domestic market competition; intellectual property rights; information and communications technology; government procurement; and high-skill immigration. Countries were ranked according to tiers: upper, upper-mid, lower-mid or lower on each of seven areas. Canada and Singapore were the only two countries that were ranked upper tier for all seven areas. Countries that were ranked in the upper tier for many areas were Australia, Austria, Chinese Taipei, Denmark, Finland, France, Germany, Hong Kong, Japan, Netherlands, New Zealand, Norway, Sweden, Switzerland, United Kingdom and the USA.[452]

TABLE E.4 Global Innovation Index 2008–14

	2013–14	2012–13	2011–12	2010–11	2009–10	2008–09	2007–08
1st	Switzerland	Switzerland	Switzerland	Switzerland	Iceland	USA	USA
2nd	UK	Sweden	Sweden	Sweden	Sweden	Germany	Germany
3rd	Sweden	UK	Singapore	Singapore	Hong Kong	Sweden	UK
4th	Finland	Netherlands	Finland	Hong Kong	Switzerland	UK	Japan
5th	Netherlands	USA	UK	Finland	Denmark	Singapore	France
6th	USA	Finland	Netherlands	Denmark	Finland	South Korea	Switzerland
7th	Singapore	Hong Kong	Denmark	USA	Singapore	Switzerland	Singapore
8th	Denmark	Singapore	Hong Kong	Canada	Netherlands	Denmark	Canada
9th	Luxembourg	Denmark	Ireland	Netherlands	New Zealand	Japan	Netherlands
10th	Hong Kong	Ireland	USA	UK	Norway	Netherlands	Hong Kong

APPENDICES

IMD World Competitiveness Ranking

The International Institute for Management Development, better known as IMD, was the successor of two business schools in Switzerland. Known for its MBA program, IMD published its first World Competitiveness Yearbook in 1989 through its World Competitiveness Center. Its yearbook analyses competitiveness of private and state-owned enterprises across four main factors (and twenty sub-factors): business efficiency, economic performance, government efficiency and infrastructure. It sources data from private institutions and international organisations. Its five-year reports show the USA as the most competitive nation, followed by Hong Kong, Singapore and Switzerland (see Table E.5).[453]

TABLE E.5 IMD World Competitiveness Ranking

	2014	2013	2012	2011	2010
1st	USA	USA	Hong Kong	USA	Singapore
2nd	Switzerland	Switzerland	USA	Hong Kong	Hong Kong
3rd	Singapore	Hong Kong	Switzerland	Singapore	USA
4th	Hong Kong	Sweden	Singapore	Sweden	Switzerland
5th	Sweden	Singapore	Sweden	Switzerland	Australia
6th	Germany	Norway	Canada	Taiwan	Sweden
7th	Canada	Canada	Taiwan	Canada	Canada
8th	UAE	UAE	Norway	Qatar	Taiwan
9th	Denmark	Germany	Germany	Australia	Norway
10th	Norway	Qatar	Qatar	Germany	Malaysia

Based on frequency of mentions of innovative countries from various sources, Switzerland, Singapore and the USA are the top three innovative countries, followed by Sweden, Finland, South Korea, Hong Kong, Japan and Germany (see Table E.6).

TABLE E.6 Most innovative countries, synthesised from five sources

	BCG 2013	BIQ 2014	GCI 2014–15	GII 2014	IMD 2014
1st	Singapore	South Korea	Switzerland	Switzerland	USA
2nd	South Korea	Sweden	Singapore	UK	Switzerland
3rd	Switzerland	USA	USA	Sweden	Singapore
4th	Iceland	Japan	Finland	Finland	Hong Kong
5th	Ireland	Germany	Germany	Netherlands	Sweden
6th	Hong Kong	Denmark	Japan	USA	Germany
7th	Finland	Singapore	Hong Kong	Singapore	Canada
8th	USA	Switzerland	Netherlands	Denmark	UAE
9th	Japan	Finland	UK	Luxembourg	Denmark
10th	Sweden	Taiwan	Sweden	Hong Kong	Norway

APPENDIX F: SYNECTICS-BASED DREAM TRAINING

This was how I designed the two-day training workshop for my DREAM (dream, review, expand, assess and manage) variation of Synectics innovative problem solving.

Day 1

1. During the first-day introductions, I introduced myself as a tree and asked participants to speculate why. Participants then introduced themselves through metaphors, either drawn or with computer-generated images (some personal metaphors were monkey, quilter, chilli, owl, gardener, lake, ant, sun, toolkit, turtle, candle and pathfinder).
2. Participants and I discussed their metaphors and the power of metaphors, including Walt Disney describing himself as a bee.
3. I introduced a connect-the-unconnected exercise by approximately connecting one of the individual metaphors to the topic of innovation. Participants in pairs then found connections between a selected individual metaphor and innovation. To close the exercise, I provided some examples of how innovators had connected the unconnected.
4. Before the break, I spoke about my mission of optimising individual potential and my vision of harvesting accelerated learning of team creativity with creative outcomes during the workshop. I asked participants what would facilitate or hinder a team creativity session and then introduced the Synectics concepts of process versus content.
5. During the first break, I quickly reviewed the tasks that participants had submitted on Post-it Notes stating what they would like to work on during practice sessions, and grouped them under themes.
6. After the break, I talked about Disneyland, Walt Disney, his dreamer-realist-critic modes, the connections I had made with the Synectics structure and how I had developed the DREAM framework. I then introduced the Synectics concepts of wishing, headlining and out-in listening.
7. I demonstrated the DREAM process using a submitted task, incorporating an excursion or seemingly irrelevant activities during the demonstration. Charts of the DREAM steps and ideas were pasted on the wall to provide a visual flow of the process.

APPENDIX F: SYNECTICS-BASED DREAM TRAINING

8   I then traced through the charts of the DREAM steps and asked the participants what's good about the process and which steps would be more challenging during the learning process.
9   In the afternoon of the first day, after an energiser, I selected another task and had small groups work through the DREAM process with me orchestrating each step (each group had its own scribe). For example, I would say:
    a. 'For this *dream* phase, please create imagery in your separate groups on an assigned activity such as "What questions would you ask an alien?", "What do birds chirp about daily" and "What do you see in this abstract painting?"'
    b. 'Use the generated imagery to connect wishes for the selected task.'
    c. '*Review* the wishes connected to select an intriguing idea that is seemingly unfeasible and needs the group to *expand* on.'
    d. 'Focus on the key word in your selected wish and think of different perspectives of the keyword; for example, different forms of "time".'
    e. 'Once a more doable idea has emerged during the expand phase, *assess* the pros and cons of the idea so that you could make a good idea better.'
    f. 'When you have an intriguing possible solution for your task, *manage* the next steps in terms of what needs to be done by whom and when.'
10 After the orchestrated session, each group reflected on the process in terms of what went well and what could be improved during the DREAM process, such as excursions, connection making and task outcomes.
11 Before closing Day 1, I asked participants about key learning for the day.

Day 2

12 On the morning of the second day, participants in their groups drew metaphors of their Day 1 learning and shared their composite metaphors with other groups. Metaphors have included mountain trekking, deep sea exploration, a holiday bus and a maze.
13 The rest of the second day morning was spent on planning and running problem-solving sessions on tasks with the designated task owner, facilitator and idea contributors. Each group implemented its own fun activities at different steps of the DREAM process whenever needed and finally reflected on the overall process at the end of the problem-solving session. I moved around each group, making notes and chipping in an image or wish to help participants focus on the process. After all groups had completed their problem-solving session within an hour in their own corner of the room or in adjoining rooms, the groups gathered as a class and the facilitator or task

APPENDICES

owner of each group presented the DREAM process and key outcomes. The planning, practices, reflections, presentations, my reinforcement, and further discussions helped to anchor the DREAM process into the memory of the participants.

14 The afternoon of the second day continued in the same format as the morning, except that groups were challenged to have two facilitators in each group, two dream excursions and two wishes to expand. I concluded the workshop by discussing applications of the DREAM process, the need for participants to continue experimenting with the process, and we considered how participants would describe themselves after the two days of training (many participants changed their introductory metaphors; for example, 'chilli' became 'an excited person on a first date' and 'owl' became a 'computer with lots of programmed knowledge').

NOTES

Chapter 1: Innovation and Team Creativity Catalysts

[1] HP-Aecus (2015) The innovation agenda: Mapping the new frontier in business—an HP and Aecus paper. Retrieved from www8.hp.com/h20195/V2/GetDocument.aspx?docname=4AA5-7346ENW

[2] Amabile, T. M. (1988) A model of creativity and innovation in organisations. *Research in Organisational Behavior*, 10: 123–67.

[3] Rickards T. (1996) The management of innovation: Recasting the role of creativity. *European Journal of Work and Organizational Psychology*, 5: 13–27.

[4] IBM (2010) IBM 2010 Global CEO Study: Creativity selected as most crucial factor for future success. Retrieved from www-03.com/press/us/en/pressrelease/31670.wss

[5] Miller, P., Klokieiters, K., Brankovic, A. & Duppen, F. (2012) Innovation leadership study. Managing innovation: an insider perspective. Retrieved from http://ebooks.capgemini-consulting.com/Innovation-Leadership-Study/index.html#/4

[6] HP-Aecus (2015) The innovation agenda: Mapping the new frontier in business—an HP and Aecus paper. Retrieved from www8.hp.com/h20195/V2/GetDocument.aspx?docname=4AA5-7346ENW

[7] Miller, P., Klokieiters, K., Brankovic, A. & Duppen, F. (2012) Innovation leadership study. Managing innovation: an insider perspective. Retrieved from http://ebooks.capgemini-consulting.com/Innovation-Leadership-Study/index.html#/4

[8] Andrews, P. (2006) Five barriers to innovation: Key questions and answers. Retrieved from www-935.ibm.com/services/uk/igs/pdf/g510-6342-00-5barriers-etr.pdf

[9] Hall, J. (2013) 10 barriers to employee innovation. *Forbes*. Retrieved from www.forbes.com/sites/johnhall/2013/04/29/10-barriers-to-employee-innovation

[10] Wall, M. (2014) Innovate or die: The stark message for big business. BBC. Retrieved from www.bbc.com/news/business-28865268

Chapter 2: Mastery Modelling: Benchmarking Innovation

[11] Bruce Lee Foundation (n.d.) Biography. Retrieved from www.bruceleefoundation.com/index.cfm/pid/10585

[12] Bandler, R. & Grinder, J. (1975) *The Structure of Magic I: A Book about Language and Therapy*. Science and Behavior Books Inc: 5–6.

[13] Dilts, R. (1994) *Strategies of Genius, Volume I*. New York: Meta Publications.

[14] Dilts, R. (1994) *Strategies of Genius, Volume II: Albert Einstein*. New York: Meta Publications.

[15] Dilts, R. (1995) *Strategies of Genius, Volume III: Sigmund Freud, Leonardo da Vinci, Nikola Tesla*. New York: Meta Publications.

[16] NLP University (2014). Retrieved from www.nlpu.com/NewDesign/NLPU_Archives.html

[17] Dilts, R. (1994) *Strategies of Genius, Volume I*. New York: Meta Publications.

[18] Dilts, R. (1996) Modeling the wisdom of Jesus. Retrieved from www.nlpu.com/Articles/article5.htm

[19] CBS (2013) What inspires Bill Gates? Retrieved from www.cbsnews.com/news/what-inspires-bill-gates

[20] Davies, A. (2013) Here's why Tesla Motors is named for a famous Serbian inventor. Retrieved from www.businessinsider.com.au/who-is-tesla-named-for-2013-8

[21] Haq, H. (2012) Amazon's Jeff Bezos as 'Businessperson of the year': Can the book world learn from him? *The Christian Science Monitor*. Retrieved from www.csmonitor.com/Books/chapter-and-verse/2012/1119/Amazon-s-Jeff-Bezos-as-Businessperson-of-the-Year-Can-the-book-world-learn-from-him

[22] Salesforce.com (2014) Salesforce.com named world's most innovative company by Forbes Magazine for a record fourth consecutive year. Retrieved from www.salesforce.com/company/news-press/press-releases/2014/08/140820.jsp

[23] Perez, S. & Ha, A. (2013) Marc Benioff says, 'There would be no Salesforce.com without Steve Jobs'. Retrieved from http://techcrunch.com/2013/09/10/marc-benioff-says-there-would-be-no-salesforce-com-without-steve-jobs

[24] Ostrow, A. (2011) Mark Zuckerberg pays tribute to Steve Jobs. *Mashable Australia*. Retrieved from http://mashable.com/2011/10/05/mark-zuckerberg-steve-jobs

[25] Parr, B. (2011) Google founders: Steve Jobs was an inspiration. *Mashable Australia*. Retrieved from http://mashable.com/2011/10/05/google-founders-steve-jobs

[26] Warren, C. (2011) Disney CEO: 'Jobs was an original'. *Mashable UK*. Retrieved from http://mashable.com/2011/10/05/disney-ceo-jobs

[27] Parr, B. (2011) Bill Gates: 'I will miss Steve immensely'. *Mashable Australia*. Retrieved from http://mashable.com/2011/10/05/bill-gates-steve-jobs

[28] Schlender, B. & Tetzeli, R. (2015) *Becoming Steve Jobs*. New York: Crown Business.

[29] Schlender, B. & Tetzeli, R. (2015) *Becoming Steve Jobs*. New York: Crown Business.

[30] Bonanos, C. (2011) The man who inspired Jobs. *The New York Times*. Retrieved from www.nytimes.com/2011/10/07/opinion/the-man-who-inspired-jobs.html?_r=0

[31] Isaacson, W. (2011) *Steve Jobs*. New York: Simon & Schuster.

[32] Chen, B. X. (2014) Simplifying the Bull: How Picasso helps to teach Apple's style. *The New York Times*. Retrieved from www.nytimes.com/2014/08/11/technology/-inside-apples-internal-training-program-.html?_r=0

[33] Colt, S. (2015) Here's what it's like to attend Apple's secret university. *Business Insider*. Retrieved from www.businessinsider.com.au/heres-what-its-like-to-attend-apples-secret-university-2015-2

[34] Apple Confidential (1997) Steve Jobs on 'Think Different'—internal meeting Sept 23, 1997. Retrieved from www.youtube.com/watch?v=9GMQhOm-Dqo

[35] Gallo, C. (2014) The 7 innovation secrets of Steve Jobs. *Forbes.* Retrieved from www.forbes.com/sites/carminegallo/2014/05/02/the-7-innovation-secrets-of-steve-jobs

[36] Jobs, S. (2005) Steve Jobs' 2005 Stanford commencement address. Retrieved from www.youtube.com/watch?v=UF8uR6Z6KLc

[37] Wojcicki, S. (2011) The eight pillars of innovation. Retrieved from www.thinkwithgoogle.com/articles/8-pillars-of-innovation.html

[38] Google (2014) Ten things we know to be true. Retrieved from www.google.com/about/company/philosophy

[39] Google (2014) A better world, faster. Retrieved from www.google.org/index.html

[40] Google (2014) Google Ideas. Retrieved from www.google.com/ideas

[41] Google (2014) Google Online Marketing Challenge. Retrieved from www.google.com.au/onlinechallenge

[42] Google (2014) Google Ad Grants—AdWords for nonprofits. Retrieved from www.google.com.au/grants

[43] Finn, H. (2011) Missions that matter. Retrieved from www.thinkwithgoogle.com/articles/missions-that-matter.html

[44] Swissworld.org (2014) Switzerland's official information portal. Retrieved from www.swissworld.org/en

[45] Swissworld (2014) Swiss watches. Retrieved from www.swissworld.org/en/switzerland/swiss_specials/swiss_watches/introduction

[46] Swissworld (2014) Switzerland and chocolate. Retrieved from www.swissworld.org/en/switzerland/swiss_specials/swiss_chocolate/switzerland_and_chocolate

[47] Swissworld (2014) Caviar—made in Switzerland. Retrieved from www.swissworld.org/en/know/innovation_switzerland/caviar_made_in_switzerland

[48] ReferNews (2015) Top 10 richest countries in the world by GDP [2015 IMF Report]. Retrieved from www.refernews.com/top-10-richest-countries-in-world-by-gdp-imf-report-902

[49] Ong, C. (2009) Albert Winsemius. Retrieved from www.nas.gov.sg/archivesonline/speeches/view-html?filename=20091112002.htm

[50] Economic Development Board (2014) Future Ready Singapore. Retrieved from www.edb.gov.sg/content/edb/en.html?

[51] OECD (2011) *Lessons from PISA for the United States, Strong Performers and Successful Reformers in Education*: 159–76, OECD Publishing.

[52] Ministry of Education, Singapore (2012) International studies affirm Singapore students' strengths in reading, mathematics & science. Retrieved from www.moe.gov.sg/media/press/2012/12/international-studies-affirm-s.php

[53] IEA (2014) Brief history of IEA: 55 years of educational research. Retrieved from www.iea.nl/brief_history.html

[54] SkillsConnect (2015) Singapore Workforce Development Agency. Retrieved from www.skillsconnect.gov.sg/web/guest/home

[55] Lee, K. Y. (1998) *The Singapore Story*. Singapore: Marshall Cavendish.
[56] Lee, K. Y. (2000) *From Third World to First*. Singapore: Marshall Cavendish.
[57] Goh, C. T. (2009) A distinctive city, a harmonious home. Retrieved from www.nas.gov.sg/archivesonline/speeches/view-html?filename=20091112002.htm
[58] IESingapore (2014) Venture overseas. Retrieved from www.iesingapore.gov.sg/Venture-Overseas/Overview
[59] PRNewswire (2010) Singapore teaches the world how to teach math, as success of 'Singapore math' curriculum spreads. Retrieved from www.prnewswire.com/news-releases/singapore-teaches-the-world-how-to-teach-math-as-success-of-singapore-math-curriculum-spreads-91587324.html
[60] S'pore held up as a model. (2015, June 3) *The Straits Times*.
[61] Purnell, N. (2014) Singapore aims to be Silicon Valley of the East. *The Australian*. Retrieved from www.theaustralian.com.au/business/wall-street-journal/singapore-aims-to-be-silicon-valley-of-the-east/story-fnay3ubk-1226839157155
[62] Singapore Economic Development Board (2015) Southeast Asia's innovative start-up boom. Retrieved from www.edb.gov.sg/content/edb/en/news-and-events/news/singapore-business-news/Feature/southeast-asias-innovative-start-up-boom.html

Chapter 3: Intensive Immersion: Empowered Exploration

[63] Johnson, W. (2014) To innovate in a big company, don't think 'us against them'. *Harvard Business Review*. Retrieved from https://hbr.org/2014/09/to-innovate-in-a-big-company-dont-think-us-against-them
[64] Catmull, E. (2008) How Pixar fosters collective creativity. *Harvard Business Review*, September. Retrieved from https://hbr.org/2008/09/how-pixar-fosters-collective-creativity
[65] Amazon (2015) About Amazon. Retrieved from www.amazon.com/Careers-Homepage/b?ie=UTF8&node=239364011
[66] Samsung (2015) Samsung Vision 2020: Inspire the world, create the future. Retrieved from www.samsung.com/au/aboutsamsung/samsungelectronics/vision2020.html
[67] Musk, E. (2013) The mission of Tesla. Retrieved from www.teslamotors.com/blog/mission-tesla
[68] 3M.com (2015) About us. Retrieved from http://solutions.3m.com/wps/portal/3M/en_US/Community-Giving/US-Home/about-us
[69] Microsoft (2015) A vision and strategy for the future. Retrieved from www.microsoft.com/about/en/xm/importedcontent/about/diversity/en/us/vision.aspx#Our%20Global%20Diversity%20&%20Inclusion%20Vision%20Statement
[70] IBM (2015) Our values at work. Retrieved from www.ibm.com/ibm/values/us
[71] Starwood Hotels and Resorts Worldwide, Inc. (2015). Online privacy statement. Retrieved from www.starwoodhotels.com/corporate/privacy_policy.html

[72] Guglielmo, C. (2013) Salesforce.com's Marc Benioff on innovation, acquisitions and reinvention. *Forbes*. Retrieved from www.forbes.com/sites/connieguglielmo/2013/08/15/salesforce-coms-marc-benioff-on-innovation-acquisitions-and-reinvention

[73] Dropbox (2011) Dropbox now open for business. Retrieved from www.dropbox.com/news/20111027

[74] Apple (2000) Media alert. Retrieved from www.apple.com/pr/library/2000/04/14Media-Alert.html

[75] Tyrangiel, J. (2012) Tim Cook's freshman year: The Apple CEO speaks. *Business Week*. Retrieved from www.businessweek.com/printer/articles/85214-tim-cooks-freshman-year-the-apple-ceo-speaks?src=longreads&utm_source=buffer&buffer_share=f156d

[76] Riddiford, M. (2012) The IBM CEO Study 2012. Retrieved from www.ceoforum.com.au/article-detail.cfm?cid=12411&t=/Mike-Riddiford-CEO-Forum/The-IBM-CEO-Study-2012

[77] Hemp, P. & Stewart, T. A. (2004) Leading change when business is good. *Harvard Business Review*, December, 82(12): 60–70.

[78] General Electric (2012) GE 2012 annual report. Retrieved from www.ge.com/ar2012/#!report=letter-to-shareowners

[79] Salesforce.com (2015) Salesforce. Retrieved from www.salesforce.com/au/company

[80] Canon (2015) Kyosei. Retrieved from www.canon.com/corporate/vision/philosophy.html

[81] Canon (2015) Business strategies. Retrieved from www.canon.com/corporate/vision/strategies.html

[82] Samsung (2015) Values & philosophy. Retrieved from www.samsung.com/us/aboutsamsung/samsung_group/values_and_philosophy

[83] BMW Group (2015) Company portrait. Strategy. Retrieved from www.bmwgroup.com/e/0_0_www_bmwgroup_com/unternehmen/unternehmensprofil/strategie/strategie.html

[84] Tesla (2011) Tesla Motors Company Overview. Retrieved from http://files.shareholder.com/downloads/ABEA-4CW8X0/0x0x494001/dd297293-ec2d-4dc5-8db4-63d491fb6bd0/Company_Overview_Q3_2011.pdf

[85] Microsoft (2015) A vision and strategy for the future. Retrieved from www.microsoft.com/about/en/xm/importedcontent/about/diversity/en/us/vision.aspx#Our%20Global%20Diversity%20&%20Inclusion%20Vision%20Statement

[86] Coca-Cola (2015) Our company: Mission, vision & values. Retrieved from www.coca-colacompany.com/our-company/mission-vision-values

[87] PepsiCo (2015) Our mission & values. Retrieved from http://pepsico.com/purpose/our-mission-and-values

[88] Singapore Economic Development Board (2015) Our vision, mission and core values. Retrieved from www.edb.gov.sg/content/edb/en/about-edb/our-strategy/mission-vision.html

89. Ministry of Education, Singapore (2015) About us. Retrieved from www.moe.gov.sg/about
90. Catmull, E. (2008) How Pixar fosters collective creativity. *Harvard Business Review*, September. Retrieved from https://hbr.org/2008/09/how-pixar-fosters-collective-creativity
91. 3M (2014) History. Retrieved from http://solutions.3m.com/wps/portal/3M/en_US/3M-Company/Information/Resources/History
92. 3M (2014) Time to think. Retrieved from http://solutions.3m.com/innovation/en_AU/stories/time-to-think
93. 3M (2014) A culture of innovation. Retrieved from http://solutions.3m.com/3MContentRetrievalAPI/BlobServlet?lmd=1349327166000&locale=en_WW&assetType=MMM_Image&assetId=1319209959040&blobAttribute=ImageFile
94. Arndt, M. (2006) 3M's seven pillars of innovation. *Business Week*. Retrieved from www.businessweek.com/stories/2006-05-09/3ms-seven-pillars-of-innovation
95. Gallo, C. (ed.) (2012) 7 courageous ways Apple became America's most valuable company. *Forbes*. Retrieved from www.forbes.com/sites/carminegallo/2012/08/21/7-courageous-ways-apple-became-americas-most-valuable-company
96. Apple (2014) Inclusion inspires innovation. Retrieved from www.apple.com/diversity
97. Merchant, N. (2010) Apple's startup culture. *Business Week*. Retrieved from www.businessweek.com/innovate/content/jun2010/id20100610_525759.htm
98. Tobak, S. (2011) 10 ways to think different—inside Apple's cult-like culture. Retrieved from www.cbsnews.com/news/10-ways-to-think-different-inside-apples-cult-like-culture
99. Morrison, C. (2009) How to innovate like Apple. Retrieved from www.cbsnews.com/news/how-to-innovate-like-apple
100. Lessin, J. E. (2012) Apple gives in to employee perks. *The Wall Street Journal*. Retrieved from www.wsj.com/articles/SB10001424127887324073504578115071154910456
101. He, L. (2013) Google's secrets of innovation: Empowering its employees. *Forbes*. Retrieved from www.forbes.com/sites/laurahe/2013/03/29/googles-secrets-of-innovation-empowering-its-employees
102. Google (2004) Founders' IPO letter. Retrieved from http://investor.google.com/corporate/2004/ipo-founders-letter.html
103. Carlson, N. (2015) The 'Dirty little secret' about Google's 20% time, according to Marissa Mayer. *Business Insider*. Retrieved from www.businessinsider.com.au/mayer-google-20-time-does-not-exist-2015-1
104. D'Onfro, J. (2015) The truth about Google's famous '20% time' policy. *Business Insider*. Retrieved from www.businessinsider.com.au/google-20-percent-time-policy-2015-4
105. Kirby, J. & Stewart, T. A. (2007) The institutional yes. *Harvard Business Review*, October. Retrieved from https://hbr.org/2007/10/the-institutional-yes

NOTES (CHAPTER 3)

[106] Kruse, K. (2013) How to be innovative: 6 secrets from Jeff Bezos. Retrieved from www.ceo.com/technology_and_innovation/how-to-be-innovative-6-secrets-from-jeff-bezos

[107] Twitchell, D. (2013) Skunks, pop-ups and hybrids: How to build a team of innovators. *Huffington Post*. Retrieved from www.huffingtonpost.com/daryl-twitchell/skunks-popups-and-hybrids_b_2815624.html

[108] Oxford Dictionaries (2014) Retrieved from www.oxforddictionaries.com/definition/english/hackathon

[109] Kuchinskas, S. (2014) How to run a winning hackathon. *Forbes*. Retrieved from www.forbes.com/sites/sungardas/2014/03/14/how-to-run-a-winning-hackathon

[110] Leckart, S. (2012) The hackathon is on: Pitching and programming the next killer app. *Wired*. Retrieved from www.wired.com/2012/02/ff_hackathons/all/1

[111] Scott, K. (2012) The LinkedIn [in]cubator. Retrieved from http://blog.linkedin.com/2012/12/07/linkedin-incubator

[112] Warnick, J. (2014) The Garage: Microsoft's 24-hour idea factory. Retrieved from http://news.microsoft.com/stories/garage/index.html

[113] Foley, M. J. (2014) Microsoft's Garage is now an incubator launching cross-platform consumer apps. Retrieved from www.zdnet.com/article/microsofts-garage-is-now-an-incubator-launching-cross-platform-consumer-apps

[114] Facebook (2004) Hackathon. Retrieved from www.facebook.com/hackathon/info?tab=page_info

[115] Keyani, P. (2008) The all-night hackathon is back! Retrieved from www.facebook.com/notes/facebook-engineering/the-all-night-hackathon-is-back/31942383919

[116] Zax, D. (2012) Secrets of Facebook's legendary hackathons revealed. Retrieved from www.fastcompany.com/3002845/secrets-facebooks-legendary-hackathons-revealed

[117] Keyani, P. (2012) Stay focused and keep hacking. Retrieved from www.facebook.com/notes/facebook-engineering/stay-focused-and-keep-hacking/10150842676418920

[118] Angelhack (2015) Global Hackathon Competition. Retrieved from www.angelhack.com/global-hackathon-competition

[119] Thompson, M. (2014) PayPal's job recruiting secret: Hackathons. Retrieved from www.cnbc.com/id/102160225#

[120] lockheedmartin.com (2015) Skunk Works. Retrieved from www.lockheedmartin.com/us/aeronautics/skunkworks.html

[121] Deutschman, A. (2005) Building a better skunk works. Fastcompany.com. Retrieved from www.fastcompany.com/55365/building-better-skunk-works

[122] Kennedy, J. (2013) Intel CEO Krzanich: driving the 'internet of things', Intel will embrace 'open'. Retrieved from www.siliconrepublic.com/enterprise/2013/10/03/intel-ceo-krzanich-driving-the-internet-of-things-intel-will-embrace-open

NOTES (CHAPTER 3)

[123] Anderson, P. S. (2014) NASA skunkworks team designs advanced new 'Dellingr' CubeSat. Retrieved from www.americaspace.com/?p=71570

[124] Carr, A. (2013) Apple's 'Skankphone' was the iPhone's ugly twin brother. Fastcompany.com. Retrieved from www.fastcodesign.com/3017083/apples-skankphone-was-the-iphones-ugly-twin-brother

[125] Blank, S. (2014) Why corporate skunk works need to die. *Forbes*. Retrieved from www.forbes.com/sites/steveblank/2014/11/10/why-corporate-skunk-works-need-to-die

[126] Nisen, M. (2013) 17 of the most mysterious corporate labs. *Business Insider*. Retrieved from www.businessinsider.com/coolest-skunk-works-2013-2?IR=T&op=1

[127] Johnson, L. (2014) Meet 7 brands that are building the future of digital retail through innovation labs. *AdWeek*. Retrieved from www.adweek.com/news/technology/meet-7-brands-are-building-future-digital-retail-through-innovation-labs-161470

[128] Commonwealth Bank (2014) Commonwealth Bank launches state-of-the-art innovation lab. Retrieved from www.commbank.com.au/about-us/news/media-releases/2014/commonwealth-bank-launches-state-of-the-art-innovation-lab.html

[129] BRW (2012) The 30 most innovative companies. Retrieved from www.brw.com.au/p/sections/features/the_most_innovative_companies_41oOvi59IKUTXAoKKtwk8I; BRW (2013) 50 most innovative companies 2013. Retrieved from www.brw.com.au/lists/50-most-innovative-companies/2013

[130] Starwood Hotels and Resorts Worldwide, Inc. (2012) Starwood Hotels & Resorts launches new design lab and brand immersion center in Stamford, Connecticut. Retrieved from http://development.starwoodhotels.com/news/4/484-starwood_hotels_resorts_launches_new_design_lab_and_brand_immersion_center_in_stamford_connecticut

[131] Peacock, P. (2012) Life at VMware: Take 3—innovation and rejuvenation among our technical community. Retrieved from http://blogs.vmware.com/careers/2012/12/life-at-vmware-take-3-innovation-and-rejuvenation-among-our-technical-community.html

[132] 650labs (2015) Pop Up Innovation Lab. Retrieved from www.650labs.com/pop-up-innovation-lab

[133] usfca.edu (2015) Silicon Valley Immersion Programs. Retrieved from www.usfca.edu/management/corporate/Silicon_Valley_Immersion_Programs

[134] Jaruzelski, B., Staack, V. & Goehle, B. (2014) Proven paths to innovation success. Retrieved from www.strategyand.pwc.com/media/file/Proven-Paths-to-Innovation-Success.pdf

[135] Kirkpatrick, D. & Maroney, T. (1998) The second coming of Apple through a magical fusion of man—Steve Jobs—and company, Apple is becoming itself again: The little anticompany that could. Retrieved from http://archive.fortune.com/magazines/fortune/fortune_archive/1998/11/09/250834/index.htm

[136] Branson, R. (2013) Richard Branson on embracing failure. *Entrepreneur*. Retrieved from www.entrepreneur.com/article/229876

137 MacBride, E. (2014) Kathryn Shaw: Entrepreneurship requires practice, practice, practice. Retrieved from www.gsb.stanford.edu/insights/kathryn-shaw-entrepreneurship-requires-practice-practice-practice

138 Neck, H. (2014) Five practices of entrepreneurs inside and out. Retrieved from www.babson.edu/executive-education/thought-leadership/education/Pages/five-practices-of-entrepreneurs-inside-and-out.aspx

139 Ucbasaran, D., Westhead, P. & Wright, M. (2011) Why serial entrepreneurs don't learn from failure. *Harvard Business Review*. Retrieved from https://hbr.org/2011/04/why-serial-entrepreneurs-dont-learn-from-failure/ar/1

Chapter 4: Group Germination: Collective Growth

140 Rio2016. (2015) Rio 2016. Retrieved from www.rio2016.com/en

141 Linder, J. C., Jarvenpaa, S. & Davenport, T. H. (2003) Toward an innovation sourcing strategy. *MIT Sloan Management Review*. Retrieved from http://sloanreview.mit.edu/article/toward-an-innovation-sourcing-strategy

142 KPMG (2014) Manufacturers look to improve profitable growth through innovation, collaboration and supply chain integration: KPMG outlook forecasts an 'era of disruptive complexity'. Retrieved from www.kpmg.com/global/en/issuesandinsights/articlespublications/press-releases/pages/manufacturers-improve-profitable-growth-innovation.aspx

143 Federal Trade Commission (2000 April) Antitrust guidelines for collaboration among competitors: Federal Trade Commission and the US Department of Justice. Retrieved from www.ftc.gov/sites/default/files/documents/public_events/joint-venture-hearings-antitrust-guidelines-collaboration-among-competitors/ftcdojguidelines-2.pdf

144 Hessman, T. (2013) Innovation: Collaborating with the competition. Retrieved from www.industryweek.com/innovation/innovation-collaborating-competition?page=3

145 Airbus (2012) Airbus, Boeing, Embraer collaborate on aviation biofuel commercialisation. Retrieved from www.airbus.com/presscentre/pressreleases/press-release-detail/detail/airbus-boeing-embraer-collaborate-on-aviation-biofuel-commercialisation

146 Strom, S. (2014) Soda makers Coca-Cola, PepsiCo and Dr Pepper join in effort to cut Americans' drink calories. *The New York Times*. Retrieved from www.nytimes.com/2014/09/24/business/big-soda-companies-agree-on-effort-to-cut-americans-drink-calories.html?_r=0

147 Elks, J. (2013) Nestle, Coke, Pepsi & Unilever join forces to combat waste in Chile. Retrieved from www.sustainablebrands.com/news_and_views/collaboration/jennifer-elks/nestle-coke-pepsi-unilever-join-forces-combat-waste-chile

148 Balch, O. (2014) Why rivals like PepsiCo, Coca Cola, Unilever and P&G are joining forces. *The Guardian*. Retrieved from www.theguardian.com/sustainable-business/2014/oct/23/pepsico-coca-cola-unilever-proctor-gamble-partner-business

NOTES (CHAPTER 4)

149. Hower, M. (2013) 8 major consumer brands and WWF form alliance to promote plant-based plastics. Retrieved from www.sustainablebrands.com/news_and_views/green_chemistry/mike-hower/8-major-consumer-brands-partner-wwf-form-organization-promote-pl

150. Strauss Group (2015) About us. Retrieved from www.strauss-group.com/partner/partnership_danone

151. Collectively.org (2015) Partners. Retrieved from http://collectively.org/en/partners

152. Clay, J. (2011) Precompetitive behaviour—defining the boundaries. *The Guardian*. Retrieved from www.theguardian.com/sustainable-business/precompetitive-behaviour-defining-boundaries?utm_source=twitterfeed&utm_medium=twitter

153. Porter, M. E. (1998) Clusters and the new economics of competition. *Harvard Business Review*, November–December: 78.

154. Porter, M. E. (2008) Clusters, innovation, and competitiveness: New findings and implications for policy. Retrieved from www.hbs.edu/faculty/Publication%20Files/20080122_EuropeanClusterPolicy_f93df2bb-7e8c-4bca-9147-61d4d4b4bd04.pdf

155. Rosenfeld, S. (2005) Beyond clusters: Current practices & future strategies. Retrieved from http://rtsinc.org/publications/pdf/beyond_clusters.pdf

156. Weiner, S. (2015) The absurdity of globalisation is exposed in these photos of Chinese manufacturing. Retrieved from www.fastcodesign.com/3041617/the-absurdity-of-globalization-is-exposed-in-these-photos-of-chinese-manufacturing

157. Wickham, M. & Hall, L. (2006) An examination of integrated marketing communications in the business-to-business environment: The case of the Tasmanian Light Shipbuilding Cluster. *Journal of Marketing Communications*, June, 12(2): 95–108.

158. SavannahWay (2015) Australia's adventure drive. Retrieved from www.savannahway.com.au/index.html

159. Oxford Dictionaries (2015) Retrieved from www.oxforddictionaries.com/definition/english/outsource

160. Hart-Smith, L. J. (2001) Out-sourced profits—The cornerstone of successful subcontracting. Retrieved from http://seattletimes.nwsource.com/ABPub/2011/02/04/2014130646.pdf

161. The Economist (2013) Coming home: Reshoring manufacturing. Retrieved from www.economist.com/news/special-report/21569570-growing-number-american-companies-are-moving-their-manufacturing-back-united

162. Bruce, M. (2014) Queensland jobs outsourced to Philippines by the hundreds of thousands. *The Courier Mail*. Retrieved from www.couriermail.com.au/business/queensland-jobs-outsourced-to-philippines-by-the-hundreds-of-thousands/story-fnihsps3-1226820940889?nk=c7687bd0604dd2e43841118b37166543

[163] Powell, R. (2013) Australian companies join the global rush to outsourcing. Retrieved from www.smartcompany.com.au/people/recruitment/33081-australian-companies-join-the-global-rush-to-outsourcing.html#

[164] IBM (2014) IBM's outsourcing services. Retrieved from www-935.ibm.com/services/au/en/it-services/ibm-outsourcing-services.html

[165] Lonsdale, C. & Cox, A. (2000) The historical development of outsourcing: the latest fad? *Industrial Management & Data Systems*, 100(9): 444–450.

[166] Caminiti, S. (2014) Outsourced R&D: The threat to American innovation. CNBC. Retrieved from www.cnbc.com/id/101888244#

[167] Salvino, M. J. (2012) Business process outsourcing: Partners in high performance. Retrieved from www.accenture.com/us-en/outlook/Pages/outlook-journal-2012-partners-in-high-performance-outsourcing-bpo.aspx

[168] IAOP (2015) Welcome to IAOP. Retrieved from www.iaop.org

[169] Pop, O. M. (2013) Open innovation past and present: an exclusive interview with Henry Chesbrough. Retrieved from www.innovationmanagement.se/2013/07/17/open-innovation-past-and-present-an-exclusive-interview-with-henry-chesbrough

[170] Chesbrough, H., Vanhaverbeke, W. & West, J. (eds) (2006) *Open innovation: Researching a new paradigm*. Oxford: Oxford University Press.

[171] Philips (2015) Open innovation. Retrieved from www.research.philips.com/open-innovation

[172] Richards, H. (2013) Interview: Talking #Open Innovation with Prof. Henry Chesbrough. Intelligent HQ. Retrieved from www.intelligenthq.com/innovation-management/interview-talking-open-innovation-with-prof-henry-chesbrough

[173] General Electric (2015) GE Open Innovation. Retrieved from www.ge.com/about-us/openinnovation

[174] Samsung (2015) Open innovation is a Samsung initiative to identify and grow the technologies and infrastructure of the future. Retrieved from www.samsung.com/global/business/semiconductor/aboutus/business/open-innovation/overview

[175] Johnson & Johnson (2015) Johnson & Johnson innovation. Retrieved from www.jnjinnovation.com

[176] Johnson & Johnson (2014) Idea portal. Retrieved from www.jnjinnovation.com/partner-with-us

[177] Unilever (2015) Open innovation. Retrieved from www.unilever.com/innovation/collaborating-with-unilever/open-innovation

[178] P&G (2014) Connect + develop. Retrieved from www.pgconnectdevelop.com

[179] Huston, L. & Sakkab, N. (2006) Connect and develop: Inside Procter & Gamble's new model for innovation. *Harvard Business Review*, March. Retrieved from https://hbr.org/2006/03/connect-and-develop-inside-procter-gambles-new-model-for-innovation

[180] PR Newswire (2004) Pringles announces first-of-its-kind technology that prints directly on individual crisps. Retrieved from www.prnewswire.com/news-releases/

pringles-announces-first-of-its-kind-technology-that-prints-directly-on-individual-crisps-74144137.html

181   Procter & Gamble (2012) P&G completes sale of Pringles to Kellogg. Retrieved from http://news.pg.com/press-release/pg-corporate-announcements/pg-completes-sale-pringles-kellogg

182   Apple (2015) Apple in education: Apple Distinguished Educators. Retrieved from www.apple.com/education/apple-distinguished-educator

183   Procter & Gamble (2013) University of Leeds and P&G join forces. Retrieved from www.pgconnectdevelop.com/home/stories/academia-partnerships/20131011-university-of-leeds-and-pg-join-forces.html

184   Procter & Gamble (2013) P&G goes back to school. Retrieved from www.pgconnectdevelop.com/home/stories/academia-partnerships/20130115-pg-goes-back-to-school.html

185   IBM (2015) University research and collaboration. Retrieved from www.research.ibm.com/university/index.shtml

186   Google (2015) Academic and external research support. Retrieved from http://research.google.com/university

187   Australian Government (2015) Local collaboration and innovation. Retrieved from www.business.gov.au/business-topics/business-planning/innovation/Pages/local-collaboration-and-innovation.aspx

188   ATKearney (2013) Innovation: A solid wager, in good times and in bad. Retrieved from www.atkearney.com/innovation/ideas-insights/article/-/asset_publisher/VHe1Q1yQRpCb/content/innovation-a-solid-wager-in-good-times-and-in-bad/10192

189   Tevelson, R., Zygelman, J., Farrell, P., Benett, S., Rosenfeld, P. & Alsen, A. (2013) Buyer-supplier collaboration. Retrieved from www.bcgperspectives.com/content/articles/sourcing_procurement_supply_chain_management_buyer_supplier_collaboration_roadmap_for_success

190   AW (2014) BMW Group recognises suppliers for best innovation. *Automotive World*. Retrieved from www.automotiveworld.com/news-releases/bmw-group-recognises-suppliers-best-innovation

191   Johnson & Johnson (2014) 2013 Johnson & Johnson Supplier Enabled Innovation Awards. Retrieved 29 January 2015 from www.blogjnj.com/2014/02/2013-johnson-and-johnson-supplier-enabled-innovation-awards

192   nab.com.au (2014) NAB Supplier Awards. Retrieved from http://cr.nab.com.au/what-we-do/nab-supplier-awards

193   Tindall, J. (2015) Tesco launches online supplier network. Retrieved from http://invezz.com/news/equities/15887-Tesco-launches-online-supplier-network

194   CrowdSource (2013) The long history of crowdsourcing and why you're just now hearing about it. Retrieved from www.crowdsource.com/blog/2013/08/the-long-history-of-crowdsourcing-and-why-youre-just-now-hearing-about-it

NOTES (CHAPTER 4)

[195] Von Hippel, E. (1986) Lead users: A source of novel product concepts. *Management Science*, 32(7): 791–805.

[196] Von Hippel, E., Thomke, S. & Sonnack, M. (1999) Creating breakthroughs at 3M. *Harvard Business Review*, September–October: 3–9.

[197] Surowiecki, J. (2004) *The Wisdom of Crowds: Why the many are smarter than the few and how collective wisdom shapes business, economies, societies, and nations.* New York: Doubleday.

[198] Howe, J. (2006) The rise of Crowdsourcing. Retrieved from http://archive.wired.com/wired/archive/14.06/crowds.html

[199] Innocentive (2015) Innocentive. Retrieved from www.innocentive.com

[200] Howe, J. (2008) *Crowdsourcing: Why the power of the crowd is driving the future of business.* New York: Crown Business.

[201] Crowdsourcing.org (2015) Crowdsourcing.org: The industry website. Retrieved from www.crowdsourcing.org

[202] Crowdsourcing.org (2012) Enterprise Crowdsourcing Research Report by Massolution: Market, provider and worker trends. Retrieved from www.crowdsourcing.org/document/enterprise-crowdsourcing-research-report-by-massolution-market-provider-and-worker-trends/13132

[203] Ngak, C. (2013) 'Tweet,' 'crowdsourcing,' 'mouseover' added to Oxford English Dictionary. *CBS News*. Retrieved from www.cbsnews.com/news/tweet-crowdsourcing-mouseover-added-to-oxford-english-dictionary

[204] Grier, D. A. (2013) *Crowdsourcing for Dummies*. New York: John Wiley & Sons.

[205] Petavy, F. (2014) My top 10 global crowdsourcing campaigns of 2014. *Advertising Age*. Retrieved from http://adage.com/article/digitalnext/top-10-global-crowdsourced-campaigns-2014/296224

[206] Gartner (2013) Gartner reveals top predictions for IT organisations and users for 2014 and beyond. Retrieved from www.gartner.com/newsroom/id/2603215

[207] Lynch, A. (2014) Why has Australia become a global crowdsourcing hub? Retrieved from www.startupdaily.net/2014/12/australia-become-global-crowdsourcing-hub

[208] eYeka (2014) eYeka connects brands and creatives through online challenges. Retrieved from https://en.eyeka.com

[209] eYeka (2014) Show a LUX woman the best way to express her beauty. Retrieved from https://en.eyeka.com/contests/7971-lux/brief

[210] eYeka (2013) Cornetto—Enjoy the ride, love the ending. Retrieved from https://en.eyeka.com/contests/7196-cornetto-enjoy-the-ride-love-the-ending/brief

[211] Kazmark, J. (2013) Kickstarter before Kickstarter. Retrieved from www.kickstarter.com/blog/kickstarter-before-kickstarter

[212] Silveira, G. (2014) How political crowdfunding killed traditional campaign financing. Retrieved from http://crowdexpert.com/articles/crowdfunding-in-politics

NOTES (CHAPTER 4)

213. Outlaw, S. (2013) Which type of crowdfunding is best for you? *Entrepreneur.* Retrieved from www.entrepreneur.com/article/228524
214. Crowdsourcing.org (2015) Crowdfunding directory. Retrieved from www.crowdsourcing.org/directory
215. GoFundMe (2015) Top 10 crowdfunding sites. Retrieved from www.crowdfunding.com
216. Outlaw, S. (2013) 10 top crowdfunding websites. *Entrepreneur.* Retrieved from www.entrepreneur.com/article/228534
217. Lindegaard, S. (2014) 15 examples of open innovation between big companies & startups. Retrieved from www.innovationexcellence.com/blog/2014/08/13/15-examples-of-open-innovation-between-big-companies-startups
218. Sepulveda, F. (2012) The difference between a business accelerator and a business incubator? *Inc.* Retrieved from www.inc.com/fernando-sepulveda/the-difference-between-a-business-accelerator-and-a-business-incubator.html
219. Brigl, M., Roos, A., Schmieg, F. & Watten, D. (2014) Incubators, accelerators, venturing, and more. *BCG Perspectives.* Retrieved from www.bcgperspectives.com/content/articles/mergers_acquisitions_growth_incubators_accelerators_venturing_more_leading_companies_search_next_big_thing/#chapter1
220. International Business Innovation Association (n.d.) About NBIA. Retrieved from www.nbia.org/about_nbia
221. theincubatormagazine.com (2015) Network partners. Retrieved from http://theincubatormagazine.com/network-partners
222. IdeaLab (2015) IdeaLab. Retrieved from www.idealab.com
223. IdeaLab (2015) All companies. Retrieved from www.idealab.com/our_companies/show/all
224. Global Accelerator Network (2015) Global Accelerator Network. Retrieved from http://gan.co
225. techstars.com (2015) Do more faster by joining forces with the #1 startup accelerator in the world. Retrieved from www.techstars.com
226. Cohen, D. (2014) Announcing Disney Accelerator, powered by Techstars. Retrieved from www.techstars.com/announcing-disney-accelerator-powered-by-techstars
227. Disney accelerator (2014) Disney Accelerator 2014. Retrieved from http://disneyaccelerator.com/companies
228. Nike (2013) Nike+ Accelerator companies announced. Retrieved from http://news.nike.com/news/nike-accelerator-companies-announced
229. Microsoft (2013) The Microsoft Accelerator, powered by Techstars. Retrieved from www.microsoft.com/bizspark/accelerator
230. Samsung (2013) Samsung Accelerator. Retrieved from http://samsungaccelerator.com
231. Coca-Cola (2015) A new model for creating startups. Retrieved from http://cocacolafounders.com
232. Branson, R. (2015) How to turn your idea into a reality. Retrieved from www.virgin.com/richard-branson/how-to-turn-your-idea-into-a-reality

Chapter 5: Mind Netting: Brainstorming

[233] Tew, A. (2005) The Million Dollar Homepage. Retrieved from www.milliondollarhomepage.com

[234] Creative Education Foundation (2014) Brainstorming. Retrieved from www.creativeeducationfoundation.org/our-process/brainstorming

[235] Osborn, A. F. (1953) *Applied Imagination: Principles and procedures of creative thinking.* New York: Charles Scribner's Sons.

[236] Wallas, G. (1926) *The art of thought.* London: Butler & Tanner Ltd.

[237] Isaksen, S. G. (1998) A review of brainstorming research: Six critical issues for inquiry. Retrieved from www.cpsb.com/resources/downloads/public/302-Brainstorm.pdf

[238] Sawyer, K. (2007) *Group genius: The creative power of collaboration.* New York: Basic Books.

[239] Girotra, K., Terwiesch, C. & Ulrich, K. T. (2010) Idea generation and the quality of the best idea. *Management Science,* 56(4): 591–605.

[240] Kohn, N. W. & Smith, S. M. (2010) Collaborative fixation: Effects of others' ideas on brainstorming. *Applied Cognitive Psychology,* 25(3): 359–71.

[241] Eberle, B. (1996) *SCAMPER: Let your imagination run wild.* Waco, TX: Prufrock Press.

[242] Painting, B. (2010) Using SCAMPER to generate article ideas. *Daily WritingTips.* Retrieved from www.dailywritingtips.com/using-scamper-to-generate-article-ideas

[243] Mind Tools.com (2015) Reverse brainstorming: A different approach to brainstorming. Retrieved from www.mindtools.com/pages/article/newCT_96.htm

[244] Gallupe, R. B. & Cooper, W. H. (1993) Brainstorming electronically. *MIT Sloan Management Review.* Retrieved from http://sloanreview.mit.edu/article/brainstorming-electronically

[245] News Medical (2004) Electronic brainstorming has been found to be an effective means of generating many good-quality ideas. Retrieved from www.news-medical.net/news/2004/08/09/3941.aspx

[246] ThinkTank.net (2015) Case studies. Retrieved from http://thinktank.net/case-studies

[247] Manktelow, J. (2010) Round-Robin brainstorming. Retrieved from www.mindtools.com/pages/Newsletters/30Nov10.htm#Article

[248] McCaffrey, T. (2014) Why you should stop brainstorming. *Harvard Business Review.* Retrieved from https://hbr.org/2014/03/why-you-should-stop-brainstorming

[249] Geschka, H. (1996) Creativity techniques in Germany. *Creativity and Innovation Management,* 5(2): 87–92.

[250] Geschka, H. (1983) *R&D Management,* 13(3): 169–82.

NOTES (CHAPTER 5)

[251] Thompson, L. (n.d.) Video: How brainwriting can neutralize the loudmouths. Retrieved from www.kellogg.northwestern.edu/news_articles/2014/06262014-video-thompson-brainwriting.aspx

[252] VanGundy, A. B. (2007) *Getting to Innovation: How asking the right questions generates the great ideas your company needs.* New York: AMACOM.

[253] Griggs, R. E. (1985) 'A Storm of Ideas', reported in *Training,* November, 22: 66.

[254] Girotra, K., Terwiesch, C. & Ulrich, K. T. (2010) Idea generation and the quality of the best idea. *Management Science,* 56(4): 591–605.

[255] Siler T. (1999) *Think Like a Genius: The ultimate user's manual for your brain.* New York: Bantam.

[256] Segal, D. (2010) In pursuit of the perfect brainstorm. *The New York Times.* Retrieved from www.nytimes.com/2010/12/19/magazine/19Industry-t.html?pagewanted=all&_r=1&

[257] Jump Associates (2015) Hybrid thinking. Retrieved from www.jumpassociates.com/hybrid-thinking

[258] Coyne, K. & Coyne, S. (2011) Seven steps to better brainstorming. Retrieved from www.mckinsey.com/insights/strategy/seven_steps_to_better_brainstorming

[259] Brainsteering.com (2014) A conversation with Kevin and Shawn Coyne, authors of Brainsteering. Retrieved from www.brainsteering.com/brainsteeringq&a.html

[260] De Brabandere, L. & Iny, A. (2013) Building new boxes: How to run brainstorming sessions that work. Retrieved from www.bcgperspectives.com/content/articles/growth_innovation_building_new_boxes_run_brainstorming_sessions_work

[261] Fredman, C. (2002) The Ideo difference. *Hemispheres*: 52–7.

[262] Siriwardane, V. (2010) How to run a brainstorming session. *Inc.* Retrieved from www.inc.com/guides/2010/11/how-to-run-a-brainstorming-session.html

[263] Scanlon, J. (2009) Brainstorming for better business. *Business Week.* Retrieved from www.businessweek.com/innovate/content/jun2009/id2009064_920852.htm

[264] Shell.com (2013) Shell & CNBC. Retrieved from www.shell.com/global/aboutshell/events/cnbc.html

[265] IBM (2006) IBM invests $100 million in collaborative innovation ideas. Retrieved from www-03.ibm.com/press/us/en/pressrelease/20605.wss

[266] IdeaConnection (n.d.) Tesco's successful open innovation experiment. Retrieved from www.ideaconnection.com/open-innovation-success/Tesco-s-Successful-Open-Innovation-Experiment-00251.html

[267] Wharton University (2011) Procter & Gamble: Mastering the art of the innovation tournament. Retrieved from http://knowledge.wharton.upenn.edu/article/procter-gamble-mastering-the-art-of-the-innovation-tournament

[268] Branson, R. (2013) Richard Branson on building brand loyalty. *Entrepreneur.* Retrieved from www.entrepreneur.com/article/228511

[269] Virgin (n.d.) Richard Branson Twitter Q&A. Retrieved from www.virgin.com/news/richard-branson-twitter-qa

[270] Branson, R. (2011) *Screw Business as Usual.* London: Virgin Books.

[271] Branson, R. (2012) Richard Branson on the art of brainstorming. *Entrepreneur.* Retrieved from www.entrepreneur.com/article/228511

Chapter 6: Mind Netting: Creative Problem Solving Process

[272] The Buffalo News (2013) Sidney J. Parnes, leader in creativity, creative studies. Retrieved from www.buffalonews.com/city-region/obituaries/sidney-j-parnes-leader-in-creativity-creative-studies-20130828

[273] CPSB (2003) Versions of CPS. Retrieved from www.cpsb.com/resources/downloads/public/Versions_of_CPS.pdf

[274] Osborn, A. F. (1952) *Wake Up Your Mind: 101 ways to develop creativeness.* New York: Scribner's.

[275] Osborn, A. F. (1953) *Applied Imagination: Principles and procedures of creative thinking.* New York: Charles Scribner's Sons.

[276] Parnes, S. J. (1967) *Creative behaviour guidebook.* New York: Scribner's.

[277] Treffinger, D. J. & Isaksen, S. G. (2000) *Creative Problem Solving: An introduction* (3rd edn). Buffalo: Prufrock Press.

[278] Basadur (2015) An 8-step process that asks "How might we" from problem finding to action. Retrieved from www.basadur.com/howwedoit/An8StepProcess/tabid/82/Default.aspx

[279] Creative Education Foundation (2015) The CPS Process. Retrieved from www.creativeeducationfoundation.org/creative-problem-solving/the-cps-process

[280] Schmincke, D. & Miller, E. (2011) What Apple learned about creativity. *Smart CEO.* Retrieved from www.smartceo.com/schmincke-miller-apple-learned-creativity

[281] CreativeIQ (2015) CreativeIQ: The program Apple uses to think differently. Retrieved from www.creativeiq.org/index.html

[282] The Creative Problem Solving Group, Inc. (2013) The Creative Problem Solving Group: Helping you meet the innovation challenge. Retrieved from www.cpsb.com/success

[283] Basadur (2013) Frito Lay's creative approach to cost improvement. Retrieved from http://web.basadur.com/media/default/downloads/case-studies/case-frito-lay.pdf

[284] Thompson, G. (2001) The reduction in plant maintenance costs using creative problem-solving principles. *Journal of Process Mechanical Engineering,* 215: 185–95.

[285] Businesswire.com (2009) Does Creative Problem Solving make a difference? You bet! *Business Wire.* Retrieved from www.businesswire.com/news/home/20090526005217/en/Creative-Problem-Solving-Difference-Bet!#.VY4FjEtDKIx

[286] udemy (2014) Creative Problem Solving: Out-of-the-box solutions to everyday problems. Retrieved from https://blog.udemy.com/creative-problem-solving

287 Gronstedt A. (2000) *The Customer Century: Lessons from world class companies in integrated communications,* New York: Routledge.
288 Creative Education Foundation (2015) Youth education (K–12) Retrieved from www.creativeeducationfoundation.org/programs-workshops/youth-education-k-12
289 FPSPI.org (2014) Future Problem Solving Program International. Retrieved from http://fpspi.org/index.html
290 Olysseyofthemind.com (2014) Odyssey of the Mind. Retrieved from www.odysseyofthemind.com/default.php

Chapter 7: Mind Netting: Synectics Innovative Problem Solving

291 Stein, M. I. (1992) Creativity programs in sociohistorical context. In Parnes, S. J. (ed.), *Source Book for Creative Problem Solving,* 85–8, New York: Creative Education Foundation Press.
292 George Prince (2014) George M. Prince: Thoughts on creativity. Retrieved from http://georgemprince.com
293 Ling, P. & Quek, G. C. (2001) *Dream to Innovate.* Singapore: Singapore Institute of Management.
294 Prince, G. M. (1969) How to be a better meeting chairman. *Harvard Business Review,* January/February, 47: 98–108.
295 Gordon, W. J. J. (1961) *Synectics—The development of creative capacity.* New York: Collier Books.
296 Gordon, W. J. J. (1972) On being explicit about creative process. *The Journal of Creative Behavior,* 6(1): 295–300.
297 Parnes, S. J. (1992) Creative Problem Solving and visionizing. In Parnes, S. J. (ed.), *Source Book for Creative Problem Solving: A fifty year digest of proven innovation processes,* 133–53. New York: Creative Education Foundation Press.
298 Arnold, J. E. (1992) Useful creative techniques. In Parnes, S. J. & Harding, H. F. (eds), *A Source Book for Creative Thinking,* 251–68. New York: Charles Scribner's Sons.
299 Capp, A. (1965) Bill Gordon. New York: *Fortune Magazine,* June.
300 Gordon, W. J. J. (1980) SES Synectics and gifted education today. *Gifted Child Quarterly,* 24(4): 147–51.
301 Joyce, B., Weil, M. & Calhoun, E. (2015) *Models of Teaching* (9th edn). Upper Saddle River, NJ: Pearson.
302 Gordon, W. J. J. (1974) Some source material in discovery-by-analogy. *Journal of Creative Behaviour,* 8(4): 239–57.
303 Davis, G. A. (2004) *Creativity Is Forever* (5th edn). Iowa: Kenhall/Hung Publishing: 10.
304 Wenger, W. & Poe, R. (1996) *The Einstein Factor: A proven new method for increasing your intelligence.* California: Prima Publishing.
305 Wenger, W. & Poe, R. (1996) *The Einstein Factor: A proven new method for increasing your intelligence.* California: Prima Publishing.

[306] Gardner, H. (1993) *Multiple Intelligences: The theory in practice.* New York: Basic Books.

[307] Synecticsworld (2014) Case study. Retrieved from http://synecticsworld.com/category/case-study

[308] Prince, G. M. (1982) Synectics. In Olsen, S. A. (ed.), *Group Planning and Problem-Solving Methods in Engineering,* 317–64, New York: John Wiley & Sons.

[309] Lozanov, G. (1978) *Suggestology and Outlines of Suggestopedy.* New York: Gordon and Breach Science Publishers.

[310] Bandler, R. & Grinder, J. (1979) *Frogs into Princes: Neuro Linguistic Programming.* Utah: Real People Press.

[311] Dilts, R. (1994) *Strategies of Genius, Volume I.* New York: Meta Publications.

[312] Buzan, T. & Buzan, B. (1995) *The Mind Map Book.* London: BBC Books.

[313] Gardner, H. (1993) *Multiple Intelligences: The theory in practice.* New York: Basic Books.

[314] Knowles, M. S. (1984) *Andragogy in Action: Applying modern principles of adult learning.* New York: Jossey-Bass.

[315] Velcro.com (2014) Velcro Industries history and George de Mestral. Retrieved from www.velcro.com/about-us

[316] SydneyOperaHouse.com (n.d.) Sydney Opera House—The architect. Retrieved from www.sydneyoperahouse.com/About/The_Architect.aspx

[317] Ads of World (2009) The best job in the world. Retrieved from http://adsoftheworld.com/media/print/tourism_queensland_best_job_in_the_world

[318] Advertising Educational Foundation (2011) Case study 13: The best job in the world. Retrieved from www.aef.com/pdf/best_digital_mktg_casestudy.pdf

[319] Arch Environmental Equipment Inc. (2007) Eastgate Centre in Zimbabwe: Modelled after termite mounds. Retrieved from http://nat-envir-sun.blogspot.com.au/2007/12/eastgate-centre-in-zimbabwe-modeled.html

[320] Rolex Awards (2000) Mohammed Bah Abba: 2000 Laureate, Applied Technology. Retrieved from www.rolexawards.com/profiles/laureates/mohammed_bah_abba

[321] olsonzaltman.com (2014) Expressing thoughts through metaphor. Retrieved from www.olsonzaltman.com/process.htm

[322] Bailey, J. (2007) Monster fast food tie-ins land Shrek in hot water. *Sydney Morning Herald,* 29 April. Retrieved from www.smh.com.au/news/national/monster-fast-food-tieins-land-shrek-in-hot-water/2007/04/28/1177460042245.html

[323] News.com.au (2009) Kraft renames iSnack 2.0—Cheesybite. 7 October. Retrieved from www.news.com.au/finance/kraft-renames-isnack-20-cheesybite/story-e6frfm1i-1225783684238

NOTES (CHAPTER 8)

Chapter 8: Mind Netting: Lateral and Multidimensional Thinking

[324] de Bono, E. (1995) Serious creativity. Retrieved from www.debonogroup.com/serious_creativity.php

[325] Sternberg R. J. & Lubart T. I. (1999) The concept of creativity: Prospects and paradigms. In: Sternberg R. J. (ed.) *Handbook of Creativity*. London: Cambridge University Press: 3–16.

[326] de Bono, E. (2014) Lateral thinking. Retrieved from http://edwdebono.com/lateral-thinking

[327] de Bono Thinking Systems (2014) Lateral thinking. Retrieved from www.debonothinkingsystems.com/tools/lateral.htm

[328] De Bono, E. (1995) Serious creativity. *Journal for Quality & Participation*, 18(5): 12–18.

[329] de Bono, E. (2009) *Think! Before It's Too Late*. Australia: Vermilion.

[330] debonoconsulting.com (2014) Lateral thinking tool: Random entry. Retrieved from www.debonoconsulting.com/lateral-thinking-random-entry.asp

[331] de Bono Consultants (2015) Lesson in lateral thinking: The tale of two pebbles. Retrieved from www.debonoconsulting.com/Lateral-Thinking-Lesson-Pebbles.asp

[332] The de Bono Group (2015) Reading on lateral thinking. Retrieved from www.debonogroup.com/lateral_reading.php

[333] de Bono Thinking Systems (2014) Six Thinking Hats. Retrieved from www.debonothinkingsystems.com/tools/6hats.htm

[334] de Bono for Schools (n.d.) J. Walter Thompson hits the mark with creative campaign. Retrieved from www.debonoforschools.com/pdfs/JWalter-Thompson-Ford-Focus-Six-Hats-Case-Study.pdf

[335] de Bono for Schools (n.d.) Motorola used Six Thinking Hats and Lateral Thinking to develop a high-tech, hand-held communications device. Retrieved from www.debonoforschools.com/pdfs/Motorola-Lateral-Thinking-Six-Hats-Case-Study.pdf

[336] de Bono for Schools (n.d.) 3M used Six Thinking Hats to create products for new markets. Retrieved from www.debonoforschools.com/pdfs/3M-Six-Hats-Case-Study.pdf

[337] Edward de Bono Training (2004) Thinking well through a crisis. Retrieved from www.debonotraining.com/clients2.html

[338] ThinkBuzan (n.d.) Top 10 Tony Buzan quotes. Retrieved from http://blog.thinkbuzan.com/training/top-10-tony-buzan-quotes

[339] Buzan.com.au (2012) Mind map gallery. Retrieved from www.buzan.com.au/learning/mindmapgallery.html

[340] Tony Buzan (2014) Mind mapping. Retrieved from www.tonybuzan.com/about/mind-mapping

341 thinkbuzan.com (2014) iMindMap mind mapping software. Retrieved from http://thinkbuzan.com/imindmap-software/?gclid=CLvsmqSbmcICFQEDvAodBH0AnQ

342 thinkbuzan.com (2015) iMindMap8. Retrieved from http://thinkbuzan.com

343 thinkbuzan.com (2014) Why mind mapping works. Retrieved from http://thinkbuzan.com/articles/mindmappingworks

344 Koestler, A. (1964) *The Act of Creation*. London: Hutchinson & Co Ltd.

345 Dyer, J. & Gregersen, H. (2014) About 'the innovator's method' research. *Forbes*. Retrieved from www.forbes.com/sites/innovatorsdna/2014/08/20/about-the-innovators-method-research

346 Capozzi, M. M., Dye, R. & Howe, A. (2011) Cultivating creative thinking at work. *Fortune*. Retrieved from http://fortune.com/2011/09/27/cultivating-creative-thinking-at-work

Chapter 9: Mind Netting: TRIZ Inventive Problem Solving

347 Domb, E. (2006) Think TRIZ for creative problem solving. *Quality Digest*. Retrieved from www.qualitydigest.com/aug05/articles/03_article.shtml

348 Altshuller Institute (2014) What is TRIZ? Retrieved from www.aitriz.org/triz

349 Mann, D. & Winkless, B. (2001) 40 inventive (food) principles with examples. *The TRIZ Journal*. Retrieved from www.triz-journal.com/archives/2001/10/b/index.htm

350 Mann, D. (2004) Some principles are more common than others – 40 management principles in frequency order. *The TRIZ Journal*. Retrieved from www.triz-journal.com/archives/2004/08/01.pdf

351 Domb, E. (2006) Think TRIZ for creative problem solving. *Quality Digest*. Retrieved from www.qualitydigest.com/aug05/articles/03_article.shtml

352 Domb, E., Miller, J., MacGran, E. & Slocum, M. (1998) The 39 features of Altshuller's contradiction matrix. *The TRIZ Journal*, 21 November. Retrieved from www.triz-journal.com/39-features-altshullers-contradiction-matrix

353 Hipple, J. (2003) The integration of TRIZ problem solving techniques with other problem solving and assessment tools. *The TRIZ Journal*. Retrieved from www.triz-journal.com/the-integration-of-triz-problem-solving-techniques-with-other-problem-solving-and-assessment-tools

354 Shaughnessy, H. (2013) What makes Samsung such an innovative company? *Forbes*, 3 July. Retrieved from www.forbes.com/sites/haydnshaughnessy/2013/03/07/why-is-samsung-such-an-innovative-company/2

355 Cheong, S. (2010) TRIZ at SMD: Unique situations, unique goals, unique approaches. Retrieved from www.osaka-gu.ac.jp/php/nakagawa/TRIZ/eTRIZ/epapers/e2011Papers/eSHCheongTRIZSymp2010/E01eS-Cheong(Korea)-TRIZ_at_SMD-100726.pdf

356 TRIZ Consulting, Inc. (2014) Solving participants' problems as a part of TRIZ training. Retrieved from www.trizconsulting.com/consulting_more.htm

NOTES (CHAPTER 10)

357 claystreet.pg.com (2014) The Clay Street Project. Retrieved from https://claystreet.pg.com/claystreet/default.aspx
358 cdc.gov (2012) SARS basics fact sheet. Retrieved from www.cdc.gov/sars/about/fs-SARS.html
359 Belski, I., Kaplan, L., Shapiro, V., Vaner, L. & Wong, P. W. (2003) SARS and 40 principles for eliminating technical contradictions: Creative Singapore. *The TRIZ Journal,* 21 June. Retrieved from www.triz-journal.com/sars-40-principles-eliminating-technical-contradictions-creative-singapore
360 TRIZ Consulting, Inc. (2014) Solving participants' problems as a part of TRIZ training. Retrieved from www.trizconsulting.com/consulting_more.htm

Chapter 10: Mind Netting: Attribute Listing and Morphological Synthesis

361 Subway (2015) Retrieved from www.subway.com/subwayroot/default.aspx
362 Crawford, R. P. (1954) *The Techniques of Creative Thinking: How to use your ideas to achieve success.* New York: Hawthorn Books.
363 Crawford, R. P. (1979) *Direct Creativity with Attribute Listing.* New York: Fraser Pub Co.
364 Proctor, T. (2010) *Creative Problem Solving for Managers.* New York: Routledge.
365 Paper-thin battery may revolutionise electronics. (2007). *Sydney Morning Herald,* 14 August. Retrieved from www.smh.com.au/news/technology/paperthin-battery-may-revolutionise-electronics/2007/08/14/1186857468350.html
366 Ramachandran, A. (2007) Scrabbling to play online. *Sydney Morning Herald,* 23 August. Retrieved from www.smh.com.au/news/technology/online-scrabble-breathes-news-life-into-old-game/2007/08/23/1187462408882.html
367 iTnews (2008) Sony brings PSP GPS add-on to Europe. 14 January. Retrieved from www.itnews.com.au/News/100867,sony-brings-psp-gps-add-on-to-europe.aspx
368 LGDnewsroom.com (2013) 42-inch LCD TV panel. Retrieved from http://lgdnewsroom.com/products-solutions/tv/710
369 Zwicky, F. (1948) *Discovery, Invention, Research through the Morphological Approach.* New York: Macmillan.
370 Allen, M. S. (1962) *Morphological Creativity: The miracle of your hidden brain power—a practical guide to the utilisation of your creative potential.* Madison: Prentice-Hall.
371 Starko, A. (2014) Jimmy Fallon does morphological synthesis. Retrieved from http://creativiteach.me/2014/09/07/jimmy-fallon-does-morphological-synthesis
372 Davis, G. A. (2004) *Creativity Is Forever* (5th edn). Iowa: Kendall/Hunt Publishing.
373 Davis, G. A. (2004) *Creativity Is Forever* (5th edn). Iowa: Kendall/Hunt Publishing.
374 Proctor, T. (2005) *Creative Problem Solving for Managers* (2nd edn). New York: Routledge.

[375] MindTools (2014) Attribute listing, morphological analysis and matrix analysis. Retrieved from www.mindtools.com/pages/article/newCT_03.htm

[376] Starko, A. (2004) Attribute listing/morphological synthesis. Retrieved from http://creativiteach.me/creative-thinking-strategies/attribute-listingmorphological-synthesis

Chapter 11: Conclusion: Accelerating Team Creativity and Innovation

[377] BBC (Producer) (2008) Penguins – BBC. Retrieved from www.youtube.com/watch?v=9dfWzp7rYR4

Appendices

[378] Sawyer, R. K. (2012) *Explaining Creativity: The science of innovation* (2nd edn). New York: Oxford University Press.

[379] Wallas, G. (1926) *The Art of Thought.* London: Jonathan Cape.

[380] Osborn, A. F. (1953) *Applied Imagination.* New York: Scribner's.

[381] Gordon, W. J. J. (1961) *Synectics—The development of creative capacity.* New York: Collier Books.

[382] Gordon, W. J. J. (1972) On being explicit about creative process. *The Journal of Creative Behavior*, 6(1): 295–300.

[383] Guilford, J. P. (1962) Creativity: Its measurement and development. In Parnes, S. J. & Harding, H. F. (eds), *A Source Book for Creative Thinking*: 151–68, New York: Charles Scribner's Sons.

[384] Koestler, A. (1964) *The Art of Creation.* New York: Dell Publishing.

[385] Torrance, E. P. (1974) *Torrance Tests of Creative Thinking.* Lexington, Massachusetts: Personnel Press.

[386] Freud, S. (1961) *The Ego and the Id, vol 19.* London: Hogarth.

[387] Jung, C. G. (1966) *The Spirit in Man, Art and Literature.* London: Routledge.

[388] Kubie, L. S. (1958) *Neurotic Distortions of the Creative Process.* New York: University of Kansas Press.

[389] Kris, E. (1952) *Psychoanalytic Explorations in Art.* New York: International University Press.

[390] Berne, E. (1961) *Transactional Analysis in Psychotherapy: A Systematic Individual and Social Psychiatry.* New York: Grove Press.

[391] Skinner, B. F. (1972) *Cumulative Record: A selection of papers.* New York: Meredith Corporation.

[392] Mednick, S. A. (1962) The associative basis of the creative process. *Psychological Review*, 69(3): 220–32.

[393] Maslow, A. H. (1962) Emotional blocks to creativity. Parnes, S. J & Harding, H. F. (eds), *A Source Book for Creative Thinking*: 93–103, New York: Charles Scribner's Sons.

NOTES (APPENDICES)

[394] Rogers, C. R. (1962) Toward a theory of creativity. In Parnes, S. J. & Harding, H. F. (eds), *A Source Book for Creative Thinking*: 63–72, New York: Charles Scribner's Sons.

[395] Kozbelt, A., Beghetto R. A. & Runco, M. A. (2010) Theories of creativity. In: Kaufman, J. C. & Sternberg, R. J. (eds) *The Cambridge Handbook of Creativity*. New York: Cambridge University Press: 20–47.

[396] Rhodes, M. (1961) *An Analysis of Creativity*. Phi Delta Kappan, 42: 305–10; Tardiff, T. Z. & Sternberg, R. J. (1988) What do we know about creativity? In Sternberg, R. J. (ed.), *The Nature of Creativity: Contemporary psychological perspectives*: 429–40, Cambridge: Cambridge University Press.

[397] Plucker, J. A., Beghetto, R. A. & Dow, G. T. (2004) Why isn't creativity more important to educational psychologists? Potentials, pitfalls and future directions in creativity research. *Educational Psychologist*, 39(2): 83–96.

[398] Sternberg, R. J. (1988) A three-facet model of creativity. In Sternberg, R. J. (ed.), *The Nature of Creativity: Contemporary psychological perspectives*, 125–47, Cambridge: Cambridge University Press.

[399] Amabile, T. M. (1983) *The Social Psychology of Creativity*. New York: Springer-Verlag.

[400] Amabile, T. M. (2012) Big C, little C, Howard and me: Approaches to understanding creativity. Working paper. Harvard Business School. Retrieved from www.hbs.edu/faculty/Publication%20Files/12-085_eb9ecda0-ec0a-4a32-8747-884303f8b4dd.pdf

[401] Csikszentmihalyi, M. (1988) Society, culture and person: A systems view of creativity. In Sternberg, R. J. (ed.), *The Nature of Creativity: Contemporary psychological perspectives*, 325–39, Cambridge: Cambridge University Press.

[402] Sperry, R. W. (1981) Nobel lecture: Some effects of disconnecting the cerebral hemisphere. Retrieved from www.nobel.se/medicine/laureates/1981/sperry-lecture.html

[403] Rose, C. & Nicholl, M. J. (1997) *Accelerated Learning for the 21st Century: The six-step plan to unlock your master-mind*. New York: Delacorte Press.

[404] Sanders, D. A. & Sanders, J. A. (1984) *Teaching Creativity through Metaphor*. New York: Longman Inc.

[405] Davis, G. (1998) Letters from the field. *Roeper Review*, 21(1): 81–2.

[406] Samples, B. (1976) *The Metaphoric Mind: A celebration of creative consciousness*. Reading, Massachusetts: Addison-Wesley Publishing.

[407] Maclean, P. D. (1990) *The Triune Brain in Evolution: Role in paleocerebral functions*. New York: Plenum Publishing Corporation.

[408] Herrmann, N. (1996) *The Whole Brain Business Book*. New York: McGraw-Hill.

[409] Buzan, T. (1988) *Make the Most of Your Mind*. London: Pan Books.

[410] Legati, J. J. (1981) Zen and creativity. *Journal of Creative Behavior*, 15(1): 23–35.

[411] Gazzaniga, M. S. (2014) *Tales from Both Sides of the Brain*. New York: Ecco (Harper-Collins).

[412] Jensen, E. (2000) *Brain-based learning* (revised edn). San Diego: The Brain Store.
[413] Sousa, D. A. (2001) *How the Brain Learns* (2nd edn). California: Corwin Press.
[414] Boden, M. A. (2013) Creativity as a neuroscientific mystery. In Vartanian, O., Bristol, A. S. & Kaufman, J. C. (eds), *Neuroscience of Creativity*, 3–18, Cambridge, Massachusetts: MIT Press.
[415] Mayer, R. E. (1999) Fifty years of creativity research. In Sternberg, R. J. (ed.), *Handbook of Creativity*: 449–60, Cambridge: Cambridge University Press.
[416] Corbin, J. (1986) Coding, writing memos and diagramming. In Chenitz, C. (ed.), *From Practice to Grounded Theory*: 102–20. Menlo Park, CA: Addison-Wesley.
[417] Murray, C. (2003) *Human Accomplishment: The pursuit of excellence in the arts and sciences, 800 B. C. to 1950*. New York: HarperCollins Publishers.
[418] Buzan, T. & Keene, R. (1994) *Buzan's Book of Genius and How to Unleash Your Own*. London: Stanley Paul and Company Limited.
[419] Gelb, M. J. (2003) *Discover Your Genius: How to think like history's ten most revolutionary minds*. New York: Harper Perennial.
[420] Gelb, M. J. (2000) *How to Think Like Leonardo da Vinci: Seven steps to genius every day*. New York: Dell.
[421] Gelb, M. & Caldicott, S. M. (2007) *Innovate Like Edison: The five step system for breakthrough business success*. New York: Plume.
[422] *Time* (2014) The 100 most influential people in the world. Retrieved from http://time.com/time100-2014
[423] FastCompany.com (2014) Introducing Fast Company's most creative people in business 1000. Retrieved from www.fastcompany.com/3025440/most-creative-people/introducing-fast-companys-most-creative-people-in-business-1000
[424] *Fast Company* (2009) Most creative people 2009. Retrieved from www.fastcompany.com/section/most-creative-people-2009
[425] *Fast Company* (2010) Most creative people 2010. Retrieved from www.fastcompany.com/section/most-creative-people-2010
[426] *Fast Company* (2011) Most creative people 2011. Retrieved from www.fastcompany.com/section/most-creative-people-2011
[427] *Fast Company* (2012) Most creative people 2012. Retrieved from www.fastcompany.com/section/most-creative-people-2012
[428] *Fast Company* (2013) Most creative people 2013. Retrieved from www.fastcompany.com/section/most-creative-people-2013
[429] *Fast Company* (2014) Most creative people 2014. Retrieved from www.fastcompany.com/section/most-creative-people-2014
[430] *Fast Company* (2015) The 100 most creative people in business. Retrieved from www.fastcompany.com/section/most-creative-people-2015
[431] Vanity Fair (2011) The new establishment list 2011. Retrieved from www.vanityfair.com/archive/the-new-establishment-list-2011

[432] Vanity Fair (2012) The new establishment list 2012. Retrieved from www.vanityfair.com/business/new-establishment/2012

[433] Vanity Fair (2013) The new establishment list 2013. Retrieved from www.vanityfair.com/business/2013/11/new-establishment-2013

[434] Vanity Fair (2014) The new establishment list 2014. Retrieved from www.vanityfair.com/news/new-establishment-2014

[435] CNBC (2014) The list: CNBC first 25 rebels, icons and leaders. Retrieved from www.cnbc.com/id/101577066

[436] Boston Consulting Group (2014) Innovation in 2014. Retrieved from www.bcgperspectives.com/content/articles/innovation_growth_digital_economy_innovation_in_2014

[437] Wagner, K., Foo, E., Zablit, H. & Taylor, A. (2013) The most innovative companies 2013: Lessons from leaders. Retrieved from www.bcgperspectives.com/content/articles/innovation_growth_most_innovative_companies_2013_lessons_from_leaders

[438] Jaruzelski, B., Loehr, J. & Holman, R. (2013) The global innovation 1000: Navigating the digital future. Retrieved from www.strategyand.pwc.com/media/file/Strategyand_2013-Global-Innovation-1000-Study-Navigating-the-Digital-Future.pdf

[439] Strategy& (2014) The top innovators and spenders. Retrieved from www.strategyand.pwc.com/global/home/what-we-think/global-innovation-1000/top-innovators-spenders#/tab-2014

[440] Safian, R. (2014) The world's most innovative companies 2014. *Fast Company*. Retrieved from www.fastcompany.com/section/most-innovative-companies-2014

[441] Forbes (2014) The world's most innovative companies. Retrieved from www.forbes.com/innovative-companies/list

[442] Fortune (2014) Most admired 2014. Retrieved from http://fortune.com/worlds-most-admired-companies

[443] MIT Technology Review (2014) 50 smartest companies. Retrieved from www2.technologyreview.com/tr50/2014

[444] Thomson Reuters (2014) Thomson Reuters Top 100 global innovators. Retrieved from http://top100innovators.com

[445] Innovation Leaders (2015) Innovation leaders. Retrieved from http://innovationleaders.org

[446] Einhorn, B. (2014) The 30 most innovation-friendly countries. *Business Week*. Retrieved from http://images.businessweek.com/ss/09/03/0312_innovative_countries/1.htm

[447] Lu, W. & Chan, M. (2014) 30 most innovative countries. Retrieved from www.bloomberg.com/slideshow/2014-01-22/30-most-innovative-countries.html#slide32

[448] Bloomberg Business (2013) 50 most innovative countries. Retrieved from www.bloomberg.com/slideshow/2013-02-01/50-most-innovative-countries.html

[449] Bloomberg Business (2012) The Bloomberg Innovation Quotient. Retrieved from www.bloomberg.com/slideshow/2012-06-12/the-bloomberg-innovation-quotient.html

[450] Schwab, K. (2014) The global competitiveness report 2014–2015. Retrieved from www3.weforum.org/docs/WEF_GlobalCompetitivenessReport_2014-15.pdf

[451] Cornell University, INSEAD & WIPO (2014) The Global Innovation Index past reports. Retrieved from www.globalinnovationindex.org/content.aspx?page=past-reports

[452] Atkinson, R. D., Ezell, S. J. & Stewart, L. A. (2012) The Global Innovation Policy Index. Retrieved from www.itif.org/publications/global-innovation-policy-index

[453] IMD (2014) IMD World Competitiveness Yearbook 2014 results. Retrieved from www.imd.org/wcc/news-wcy-ranking

INDEX

Abba, Mohammed Bah	102
academia	124
academic–industry partnerships	46–7
accelerators	55–8
Accompli	108
Airbus	37
Alcan	81
Allen, Myron	127
Altshuller, Genrich	115–16
Altshuller Institute for TRIZ Studies	116
Amazon	9, 22, 28
analogical thinking	
industry examples	101–3
processes	88–90
AngelHack	31
Apple	10, 43
allowing time for innovation	26–7
Apple Distinguished Educators	46
CreativeIQ	80
mission	22–3
products	11
skunk works	31
'Think Different' campaign	11
training program	11
approximate thinking	86
Aristotle	8
The Art of Innovation (Kelley)	70–1
AT Kearney	47
Atari	10
attribute listing	125–6, 133–6
Audi	32
Australia	
academic–industry partnerships with government	47
crowdsourcing in	52
Bandler, Richard	7
barriers to innovation	2
Basadur, Dr Min	76
BASF	45
BBC	138
BCG	163, 166, 173
behaviouralists	150

Benoiff, Marc	9
Bezos, Jeff	9, 28
BIC	69
Bioplastic Feedstock Alliance	37
Bissell, George B.	90
Bloomberg Innovation Quotient	167–8, 173
BMW Group	24, 48
Bock, Laszlo	28
Boeing	37, 48, 122
Boston Consulting Group	48, 55–6
Innovation Friendly Countries	167
Boston Life Sciences	39
bottom-up thinking	65
Brabandere, Luc de	69
brain speed	91
brain theories	151–2
brainsketching	67
brainsteering	68–9
Brainsteering (Coyne & Coyne)	68–9
brainstorming	60–74
choosing right method	70
electronic	63–5
group	61–2
hybrid	67
industry examples	70–3
'killers'	71
origin of	61
reverse	63
round-robin	65
SCAMPER	62–3
synthesising using morphological box	133–6
brainstorming boxes	69–70
brainswarming	65
brainwriting	65–7
brainwriting pool	66
Branson, Richard	35, 58, 73
Bridgestone Corporation	48
Brin, Sergey	9–10, 27
Brunel, Sir Marc Isambard	90
Buzan, Tony	109, 113, 157

INDEX

Cairns tourism cluster	39
Caldicott, Sarah Miller	158
Californian wine cluster	38–9
Canon	24
Capp, Al	87
card-circulatng technique	66–7
Catmull, Ed	10
caviar	16–17
Center for Creative Learning	76
Centre for European Economic Research	41
Challenge-Ideas-Action (CIA)	60, 79–80, 133–6
Chesbrough, Professor Henry	42–3
China	
Singapore and	19
Socks City	39
chocolate	16
Chrysler	48
Clay Street Project (Procter & Gamble)	28–9
cloud computing	9
cluster collaboration	38–41
CNBC	10, 72, 162
Coburn, James	7
Coca-Cola Company	24, 37, 58
cognitivist theorists	149
collaboration	
cluster	38–41
competitive	36–7
supplier	47–8
Collectively.org	37
Commonwealth Bank	32
competition law	37
competitive collaboration	36–7
componential theory	150–1
Conan Doyle, Sir Arthur	8
contradiction matrix	119–20
convergent thinking	61
Cook, Tim	22–3, 27
Cornetto	53–4
Corning Inc	48
corporate accelerators	55–8
corporate incubators	55–8
corporate labs	31–2
corporate–academic partnerships	46–7
Crawford, Robert	125
Creative Education Foundation	75, 77, 81
Creative Problem Solving (CPS) process	75–82
evolution of	76–7
industry examples	80–2
origin of	75–6
stages and steps in	77–80
synthesising using morphological box	133–6
Creative Problem Solving Group Inc	76
Creative Problem Solving Institute	75, 81
Creative Problem Solving Learner's Model	77
creativity	1–2
creativity literature	149
creativity research design	154–5
creativity research findings	155–6
creativity research gap	154
creativity theories	
brain theories	151–2
classic	149–50
contemporary	150–1
interconnected	152–3
crowd wisdom	49–52
crowdfunding	54–5
crowdsourcing	48–54
crowd wisdom	49–52
eYeka as provider	52–3
lead users	49
Crowdsourcing (Howe)	50
Crowdsourcing.org	50–1
da Vinci, Leonardo	8, 9
Danone	37
Darwin, Charles	8
Davis, Gary	90
de Bono, Dr Edward	105–6, 107
DeLuca, Fred	125
desert refrigerator	102
Dickens, Charles	9
Dilts, Robert	8
discount/revenge dynamics	85–6

INDEX

Disney, Walt	8
Disney Accelerator	57
divergent thinking	61
Dr Pepper	37
DREAM	98–101, 174–6
Dropbox	22
Eastman Chemical	41
Eberhard, Martin	9
Edison, Thomas	11
Edith Cowan University	131
education in Singapore	18, 19, 25
Einstein, Albert	8, 11, 69
electronic brainstorming	63–5
electronic brainstorming software	65
Eli Lilly	49–50
Embraer	37
energisers	97–8
Erickson, Milton	7
Esposti, Carl	50
European Commission	37
excursions	86–7
eYeka	52–3
Facebook	9, 30, 43
failure, learning from	35
Fast Company	2, 160, 163, 166
Federer, Roger	15
Forbes	163–4, 166
Ford	32, 37
Ford Focus	108
Fortune	164, 166
4Ps of creativity	4, 150–1
Foursquare	29
Fraunhofer	46
Freud, Sigmund	8
Frito Lay Corporation	81
Fry, Art	26
Future Problem Solving International	81–2
Gandhi, the Mahatma	11
Garner, James	7
Gates, Bill	9, 10
Gelb, Michael	157–8
General Electric	23, 43
General Motors	37

geniuses	8–12, 157–8
Geschka, Horst	66
Global Competitiveness Index	168–70, 173
Global Innovation 1000 Survey (2014)	34
Global Innovation Index	170, 171, 173
Global Innovation Policy Index	170
Google	11
academic–industry partnerships	47
allowing time for innovation	27–8
championing innovation	14–15
innovation commandments	14
as innovative company	12–15
pillars of innovation	13
Gordon, William	83, 87–90
Griggs, Rick	67
Grinder, John	7
group brainstorming	61–2
group germination	3, 36–59, 143–4
Grove, Andy	10
Gutenberg, Johann	90
hackathons	29–31
headlining wishes	92
Hewlett, Bill	10
Hewlett-Packard (HP)	
global survey	1, 2
HP Labs	32
Hingis, Martina	15
Hitchcock, Alfred	11
Homebrew Computer Club	10
Hong Kong	18
Hooks, Kimberly	87
Howe, Jeff	49, 50
humanists	150
hybrid brainstorming	67
IBM	23, 34
academic–industry partnerships	46–7
corporate lab	32
InnovationJam	72
mission	22
reports	2
skunk works	31

INDEX

Idealab	56–7
IDEO	70–1
IESE Business School (Spain)	2
Iger, Bob	10
IMD World Competitiveness Ranking	170, 172, 173
Immersion	21
incubators	55–8
Indiegogo	55
industry–academic partnerships	46–7
Innocentive	49–50
innovation	
allowing time for	25–33
barriers to	2
creativity versus	1–2
open innovation	42–8
team creativity catalysts and	1–6, 139
Innovation Leaders.org	164–5
innovative companies	12, 163–6
innovative countries	15, 167–73
innovative people *see* geniuses	
Intel	10, 31
intensive immersion	3, 21–35
accelerating team creativity	141–2
funding	33–4
interaction theory	150–1
International Association of Outsourcing Professionals	41
Iny, Alan	69
Israel	18
iStockphoto	49
Italian leather fashion cluster	39
J. Walter Thompson	108
Janssen	21
Jesus of Nazareth	8
Jobs, Steve	
2005 Stanford address	12
allowing time for innovation	26–7
innovation principles	11–12, 34
as inspiration	9–12
Johnson, Kelly	31
Johnson & Johnson	21, 43, 48
Jones, Terry	138
Jump Associates	67
Kaiser	71–2
Keene, Raymond	157
Kelley, Tom	70–1
Keyani, Pedram	30
Kickstarter	55
Koestler, Arthur	111
Land, Edwin	10, 86
Land, Mitchell	87–8, 89
Lasseter, John	10
lateral thinking	106–7, 133–6
lead users	49
leadership	85
learning from failure	35
Lee Jun Fan, Bruce	7
Lee Kuan Yew	17, 18–19
LinkedIn	29
listening out–in	91
Lockheed Aircraft Corporation	31
logic trees	68–9
Lowe's Home Improvement	32
Lucas, George	11
Lux	53
McKenna, Regis	10
McKinsey	68
McQueen, Steve	7
Magic Eraser	45
Marden, Carl	84
martial arts	7
Massolution	50–1
Master Card	132–3
mastery modelling	3, 7–20, 139–41
Mayer, Marissa	27–8
Mead Fine Papers	81
media	159–62
Mestral, George de	101
Method 635	66
Micklus, Dr Samuel	82
Microsoft	22, 24
the Garage	29–30
Microsoft Accelerator	58
Microsoft Windows	11
MIGN (Modelling, Immersion, Germination and Netting)	4–6
Million Dollar Homepage	60

INDEX

mind mapping	109–11, 133–6, 155
mind netting	3–4, 5
accelerating team creativity	145–8
attribute listing and morphological synthesis	125–37
brainstorming	60–74
Creative Problem Solving process	75–82
lateral and multidimensional thinking	105–14
Synectics innovative problem solving	83–104
TRIZ (Theory of Inventive Problem Solving)	115–24
mission	21–3
MIT Technology Review	164, 166
Monsanto	81
morphological box	129, 133–6
morphological synthesis	126–33
applications: dimensions as categories	128–33
applications: two or three axes	127–8
origin of	127
synthesising creative thinking tools	133–6
synthesising using morphological box	133–6
Morse, Samuel	90
Motorola	108
Mozart, Wolfgang Amadeus	8, 54
multidimensional thinking	111–13, 133–6
Murray, Charles	157
NASA	31
National Australia Bank	48
Nestlé	37
neurolinguistic programming	7
New York Central Park	11
news media	159–62
NeXT	11
Nike	11, 32
Nike+ Accelerator	57
Nolan, Vincent	83, 90–3
Nordam	48
Nordstrom Innovation Lab	32
Obama, Barack	19, 54
Odyssey of the Mind	82
Olson Zaltman Associates	103
Olympic Games	36
open innovation	42–8
open innovation challenges	52
organisational outcomes using MIGN	6
Osborn, Alex	61, 75–6
Osborn–Parnes Creative Problem Solving	75, 76
outsourcing	41–2
Page, Larry	9–10, 27
Palmisano, Sam	23
Parnes, Sidney	75, 76, 81
patterns of thinking	8
PayPal	31
Pearce, Mick	102
Peerbackers	55
PepsiCo	24–5, 37
Philips Research	42
Picasso	11
Pirelli	48
Pixar	10, 11, 22, 25
Polaroid	10, 86
police	78–9
Pop Up Innovation Lab	33
Pope, Alexander	54
Porter, Michael	38–9
Prince, George	83–7, 116
Pringles	45–6
Procter & Gamble	
brainstorming	72–3
Clay Street Project	28–9
collaboration	37
crowdsourcing	50
open innovation	44–6
TRIZ	122
psychoanalysts	149–50
Pulitzer, Joseph	54
Quaker Oats	81
random entry technique	111
Raytheon's Bike Shop	32
Refrigerants Naturally	37

research and development (R&D)	33–4	DREAM variation	98–101
reverse brainstorming	63	Gordon contribution to	83, 87–90
Rohrbach, Bernd	65–6	industry examples	101–3
rolestorming	67	nine-step framework	84
Romania	21	Nolan contribution to	83, 90–3
Rosenfeld, Stuart	39	Prince contribution to	83–7
round-robin brainstorming	65	synthesising using morphological box	133–6
Salesforce.com	9, 22, 23	team creativity sessions: facilitating	96–8
Samsung	22, 24, 32, 43, 58, 122	team creativity sessions: planning	93–6
SARS (Severe Acute Respiratory Syndrome)	123	SynecticsWorld	98
Satir, Virginia	7	systems theory	150–1
Savannah Way cluster	40		
SCAMPER	62–3, 120–1	Target	32
separating process from content	85	Tarpenning, Marc	9
Shell	18–19, 72	Tasmanian light shipbuilding cluster	39–40
Shrek	103	team bonding	5
Silicon Valley Immersion Program	33	team creativity acceleration	138–48
Silver, Dr Spencer	26	team creativity catalysts	
Singapore	17–19, 25	dimensions of	3–4
and SARS	123	innovation and	139
Singapore Airlines	123	MIGN (Modelling, Immersion, Germination and Netting)	4–6
Six Thinking Hats	107–9, 133–6	mind map of	155
650 Labs	33	typology of	4
skunk works	31	team creativity framework	5
Sony	10	Techstars	57
Southall, Ben	102	TED Open Translation Project	51
Sperry, Dick	84	termite-inspired building	102
Sri Lanka	109	Tesco	72
Staples Velocity Lab	32	Tesla, Nikola	8, 9
Starwood Hotels and Resorts	22, 32–3	Tesla Motors	9, 22, 24
Statue of Liberty	54	Tew, Alex	60
Stein, Moe	83	thinking patterns	8
Strategy&	34, 163, 166	Thomson Reuters	164, 166
Strauss Group	37	3M	22, 26, 49, 108
Subway	125	three-facet theory	150–1
supplier collaboration	47–8	time for innovation, allowing	25–33
Switzerland	15–17, 19	*Time* magazine	159
Sydney Opera House	102	top-down thinking	65
Synectics innovative problem solving	83–104	Torrance, Dr E. Paul	81–2
abbreviated framework	84	Tourism Queensland	102
DREAM training workshop	174–6		

INDEX

Toyota 48
TRIZ (Theory of Inventive Problem Solving) 115–24
    contradiction matrix 119–20
    forty principles 116–18
    frequently used principles 119
    industry examples 122–4
    origin of 115–16
    other thinking tools and 120–2
    synthesising using morphological box 133–6
TRIZ Journal 116

Unilever 37, 43–4
United Nations Development Program 17
Utzon, Jørn 102

values 23–4
Vanity Fair 161
the Vatican 18
Vegemite 103
Velcro 101
Vietnam 19
Virgin Group 37, 58, 73
vision 24–5

VMware 33
von Hippel, Eric 49

Walmart 37
Walmart Labs 32
watchmaking 16
Watson, Emma 37
Westfield Group 32
Whitney, Eli 90
Winsemius, Dr Albert 17
The Wisdom of Crowds (Surowiecki) 49
wishing 86
work-alone exercise 92–3
Wozniak, Stephen 10

Xerox 81
Xerox Corporation 10
Xerox PARC 32

Zappos 32
ZMET (Zaltman Metaphor Elicitation Technique) 103
Zuckerberg, Mark 9
Zwicky, Fritz 127
Zwicky box 129

UNIVERSITY OF ST THOMAS LIBRARIES